A - Z For a Healthy Pregnancy and Natural Childbirth

Jacky Bloemraad-de Boer

authorHOUSE®

AuthorHouse™
1663 Liberty Drive, Suite 200
Bloomington, IN 47403
www.authorhouse.com
Phone: 1-800-839-8640

First published by AuthorHouse 11/28/2007

ISBN: 978-1-4343-2832-8 (sc)

Printed in the United States of America
Bloomington, Indiana

This book is printed on acid-free paper.

How to use this book

This book is easy to use, just look up what you want to know according to the alphabet. As far as the self-help advice goes, there's a lot of it so what I have done with each pregnancy complaint is list the advice according to what I find works the best. You will most likely find that you'll need to use more than one piece of advice to achieve a good result, for instance with nausea you might find a combination of taking vitamin B6, wearing a sea band and visiting an acupuncturist works for you.

I have jotted down "my experience" each time I mention acupuncture as a possible therapy to give you an indication of how well, or not, I have found that acupuncture has worked for that particular complaint in my practice.

You will find my preferred brands of the products I advise under the 'PRODUCTS' chapter.

CONTENTS

Acknowledgements

This book would never have been written without the help, support and love of countless generous people. My thanks to: all the pregnant and birthing women who have passed through my practice over the years allowing me the opportunity to experience and learn; the wonderful midwives I work with especially Ruth Evers, Beatrijs Smulders and the amazing Red & Yellow teams at "Het Geboortecentrum, Amsterdam"; Dr. Gowri Motha for allowing me to use some information from her wonderful *Gentle Birth Method*; Diana Hemeon, Angela Ferin and Cathie Ellis for their proof-reading; Sharon Mombru for reading through the first draft and for some great editing; Jennifer Walker for her help and proofing; my sister-in-law, Lisa Martus, for her never-ending enthusiasm and belief in my ability to write this book; Ant, Sue and Ben you always make me feel loved and capable; Molly, my beautiful daughter for her undying support & endless ability to make me laugh; Tim and Marjolein for loving and accepting me; my wonderful mother and father who nurtured me and last but not least, Badger, without whose love, encouragement & endless patience I would never have reached this place.

PREFACE

By Yvon Jaspers, TV presenter, Amsterdam 2007

Dear reader,

It probably isn't too long ago that you did a pregnancy test, one on which a clear dot or stripe appeared. For a minute you couldn't breathe - either because you were pleased, shocked, in denial or just plain thrilled. It may have taken you a few weeks to let the realisation sink in that there is a tiny new life growing in your belly - a life that you will be caring for, for a long time, forever. And it begins now, with you, in you. You understand that you need to take good care of yourself. But how do you do that? Yes, information! You start by going into a bookshop to find books about pregnancy, something with a combination of natural, safe, healthy and practical. Congratulations, you have chosen perfectly! This is the book for you.

In the last year and a half I have given birth twice. Firstly to a beautiful little girl, Keesje and then a gorgeous little boy, Tijl. They are my wishes come true, my everything. I can't say the same about my pregnancies they were a nightmare. Plagued either by migraine or nausea, insomnia or pelvic pain, heartburn and Braxton Hicks - it sometimes felt as if I was just a walking symptom. Thank goodness that I had one hour a week to look forward to - my sessions with Jacky Bloemraad-de Boer. Although I had frequent visits to either my midwife or the hospital, I have to say that only my "acu-sessions" (this is what I called my acupuncture treatments) worked wonders. With her needles and herbs, her wise and experienced advice and especially her immense compassion, Jacky literally "hauls" women through difficult pregnancies. She helps you trust in your body and know that it is preparing in the right way for the coming birth. She teaches you to care for yourself so that you can care for your "little one" - exactly what a pregnant woman needs.

I wish you all the best for your exciting months ahead!

With loving regards,
Yvon Jaspers

FOREWORD

By Ruth Evers, Midwife, Amsterdam, May 2007

Ever since I've known her, she has been "over-booked".
Ever since I've known her, she has been full of ideas of what to do next.
And ever since I've known her, she has been the best professional in the field of Complementary Medicine and Midwifery I've ever met.

And now, at last, here it is! A book by her own hand, the answers to all the eternally asked questions by both pregnant women and their caregivers.

I met Jacky Bloemraad-de Boer years ago when she was the reflexology teacher on my course for "Complementary Medicine in Pregnancy and Childbirth". All the midwives on the course immediately identified her as the one professional we've all been looking for. We need Jacky desperately; we need her knowledge, her advice and her expertise.
Jacky was the first professional in complementary care to confirm our belief that there is more to midwifery than the basic assistance provided by most caregivers. It is very frustrating for us as regular caregivers to always have to say to pregnant women, 'Sorry, I know pregnancy can be a difficult time, but there's nothing we can do about it except wait for the baby to be born'. It is even worse for us to have to refer women through to gynaecologists during labour because we, as midwives, have run out of options. We knew there was more to it, but how could we get there? Who could we believe? How could we be sure that the advice was safe and evidence-based?

In her work, Jacky never finds herself at a dead end. She knows so much about nutrition, acupuncture, supplements, reflexology, herbs, homeopathy, massages and other disciplines that consulting her is like consulting a "multi-disciplinary team" and with her there will always be another option, something we haven't tried yet.

I have had the privilege of being close to Jacky and her way of working both as a midwife and as a pregnant mother-to-be. More than once, I have been so very grateful to have Jacky in my life both because of her knowledge and for the person she is. Thanks to this book, she can now follow her dreams to go to South Africa and we will still have a way to find the answers to all our daily questions. Hopefully, mothers-to-be and professionals will carry this book with them like they carry their car keys and their mobile phones. It will bring the peace of body and mind they have been looking for and, in addition, it will provide growth and development for those in great need in South Africa.

I feel certain that professionals, who invest the profits of their books for others in need, will be forever "over-booked".

INTRODUCTION

Jacky Bloemraad-de Boer

Pregnancy can be a notoriously joyful yet tricky time and what every woman needs at a time like this is a confidante. This book is that confidante.
Over the years I have been working intensively with pregnant and birthing women. In this time it has often amazed me how little couples know about the options and solutions available to help them achieve healthier pregnancies and to increase their possibilities for natural childbirth. Besides giving treatments I tend to spend an endless amount of time answering fundamental questions about pregnancy and childbirth. Just giving clear answers and some self-help tips helps to create happier, healthier and calmer mothers-to-be.

Both the information and the self-help advice in this book will also help mothers to make informed choices, removing the feeling that they play a passive role in their pregnancies and labours. This book is also an excellent quick-reference pocket for professionals working in the field of pregnancy and childbirth.

Having said all that I realise that this book has been written for and is aimed at a certain audience. My readers will probably be able to follow much of the advice I give and will - either due to their financial status or their good health insurance - be able to visit a complementary health practitioner. Of this I am well aware but also pleased, the more books I sell the more likely it becomes that I will be able to reach a less privileged minority because proceeds from this book will go towards financing a clinic for pregnant mothers in rural South Africa. These mothers cannot follow much (if any) of the advice that I give in this book and my clinic will create a place where these women can receive the kind of advice and support that will help them to achieve healthier pregnancies and safer childbirth.

A

ADRENALINE

Adrenaline is a hormone that has a profound effect, both negative and positive on labour.

The negative effect of adrenaline during labour

When the natural flow of your labour is disturbed, the body takes instinctive evasive action to ensure survival and protection of you and your baby. The survival mechanism produces adrenaline, the "flight or fight" hormone. Producing adrenaline is an automatic response in any frightening or threatening situation.

The release of adrenaline during birth may be initiated by any number of things: loud noises, strangers, unfamiliar or hostile birth environments, interruptions and distractions, lack of privacy, acute embarrassment and sometimes when you (as the birthing mother) need to make an important decision during labour.

The reason why the release of adrenaline has a negative effect on labour is that it inhibits the release of oxytocin (the hormone needed to stimulate contractions), which in turn can stop contractions.

A slowing in the birth process could be a sign that you are producing too much adrenaline.

What a birthing partner can do if an overproduction of adrenaline is slowing the birth process

Firstly your partner needs to identify the source of fear or disturbance and remove it.

Where possible one or more of the following panic control measures can be introduced:

- Re-assurance, massage, Bach Rescue Remedy, a warm shower, acupuncture and reflexology.

- Provide privacy.
- Avoid unnecessary discussions.
- Change the environment (ONLY if this is the threat because a move can also cause the release of adrenaline.)
- Dim the lights and try to provide warmth and quiet.
- Reduce attendants, beginning with unnecessary staff if you are in a hospital.
- Remove anyone who is showing signs of anxiety.
- Whisper and avoid asking the birthing mother too many questions thereby keeping conversation to a minimum.
- Allow at least an hour for the adrenaline levels to decrease and for endorphins and oxytocin to reappear once the situation has been addressed.

The positive effect of adrenaline during the second phase of labour

Adrenaline is essential in a normal birth during your final contractions just prior to the birth of your baby. The presence of adrenaline can be physically seen in the way you gain energy, become more focused and obtain new strength and alertness in this second stage. The baby also gets a burst of foetal adrenaline; this allows it to be born alert with wide-open eyes and dilated pupils. The reason for this is so that you and the baby are able to bond. The adrenaline gives you both the energy and alertness to begin your endless exploration of one another. The scene is set for a dependent baby who wants and needs love and protection, born to a mother who is primed to love strongly and protectively.

ALCOHOL

There is no known safe level of alcohol consumption during pregnancy; it is therefore recommended that if you are planning a pregnancy or are already pregnant not to drink alcohol.

Drinking excessive amounts of alcohol during pregnancy will cause physical and mental birth defects. Each year, many babies are born with some degree of alcohol related damage. Mothers who drink excessively or smoke in pregnancy are more likely to have a newborn diagnosed with an infection. A very occasional glass of wine is seen as acceptable but if you are able stop drinking all together you are giving your baby a better start in life.

ALLERGIES

An allergy is an over-reaction of your immune system to a substance, for example pollen or foods.

General food allergen list

- Eggs (mainly egg whites.)
- Peanuts or nuts.
- Cow's milk.
- Soy.
- Chocolate.
- Red wine.
- Bananas.
- Citrus fruits.
- Cheese.
- Pickled fish.
- Processed food.
- Shellfish.
- Strawberries.
- Tomatoes.

Possible symptoms of a food allergy

Itching (anywhere on the body.)

- Scratchy throat.
- Tightness in the throat.
- Redness.
- Headaches.
- Mild congestion.
- Tight chest.
- Wheezing.
- Sneezing.

- Stomach or abdominal pain.
- Diarrhoea, excessive wind or belching.
- Sudden tiredness after eating.
- Nausea.
- Urticaria (hives.)
- Rhinorrhea (nasal drip.)
- Oedema (swelling of areas of the skin.)
- In extreme cases, anaphylactic shock can occur.

A food allergy can be a trigger for **hay fever** or **asthma**.

Possible symptoms of hay fever

- Scratchy throat, sneezing.
- Inflamed nostrils, sore (raw feeling) on lining inside the nostrils.
- Itchy ears (deep inside), itchy nose, and itchy eyes.
- Mild congestion and a runny nose.
- Sensation of pressure behind the eyes.

Symptoms of asthma

- Tight chest, wheezing and whistling both when breathing in and when breathing out.
- Increased difficulty in breathing.

Allergens for Asthma

- Pollens, dust mites, moulds and pets.
- Foods, such as fish, eggs, peanuts, nuts, cow's milk and soy.
- Additives, such as sulphates.
- Work-related agents, such as latex.

Irritants that could cause asthma or make asthma worse

- Respiratory infections, such as those caused by viral "colds," bronchitis, and sinusitis.
- Drugs, such as aspirin, other NSAIDs (non-steroidal anti-inflammatory drugs), and Beta Blockers (used to treat blood pressure and other heart conditions.)

- Tobacco smoke.
- Outdoor factors: smog, weather changes and diesel fumes.
- Indoor factors: paint, detergents, deodorants, chemicals and perfumes.
- Work-related factors: chemicals, dusts, gases and metals.
- Emotional factors: excessive laughing, crying, yelling and distress.
- Hormonal factors: pregnancy.

Pregnancy And Allergies

Because of hormonal changes during pregnancy, allergies can become either better or worse. Most women notice a change for the better. If you happen to be one of the unfortunates and your symptoms are worse then you can try the following advice.

Food allergies and pregnancy

The important thing about food allergies is of course finding out which foods you are reacting to. To do this you eliminate all the foods from the general allergen list from your diet for at least forty-eight hours. If you experience no change then it is not one of the foods on the standard list and so you will need to find out which food it is by eliminating the foods you think you might be reacting to.

Asthma and pregnancy

Begin by identifying and then eliminating any triggers from your environment. Common allergens that can trigger asthma attacks include dust mites, mould and animal fur. Sometimes asthma is triggered by cold, dry air or exercise. Add protective covers to your pillows and mattresses. Exercise in humidified areas like swimming pools and avoid exposure to second hand cigarette smoke. Also avoid any foods that could trigger asthma (see general food allergen list.) Use air ionizers and/or humidifiers. Ionizers reduce house dust mite allergen levels and humidifiers increase the moisture content in the air improving the environment for the lungs.

If you still have asthma symptoms you can try complimentary therapy and also check with your doctor which inhaler you can safely use during pregnancy.

THERAPIES AND TIPS for allergies

Many women with asthma have found a variety of complimentary treatments beneficial both as prevention and as a support.

Golden Tip

Taking a digestive enzyme complex can dramatically reduce your allergic reaction to foods. Digestive enzymes help to break down your foods thereby reducing the amount of undigested foods entering your digestive system and blood stream. These undigested foods are seen as allergens by your immune system, which in turn results in an allergic reaction.

Nutrition & ☑ Supplements

Firstly check the food list of allergens that should be avoided. Then eat/take more of the following nutrients, which will help strengthen your body's resistance and possibly improve any symptoms.

Essential fatty acids (Omega-3)

Research shows that omega-3 fatty acid may decrease inflammation and improve lung function in adults with asthma. Take a 2000mg Omega-3 supplement (which must contain Vitamin E) per day and eat the following foods: cold-water fish such as salmon, mackerel, halibut, sardines and herring.

Vitamin C

Take 1000 mg anti-acid vitamin C three times a day if you are suffering from allergies and eat foods that contain vitamin C: Red peppers, pineapple, citrus fruits, strawberries, peas, broccoli, kiwi, potatoes, pawpaw, Brussels sprout, cauliflower, tomatoes, apples, dried apricots and asparagus.

Zinc

Zinc boosts the immune system and can helps fight allergies. The recommended intake for zinc increases during pregnancy. Zinc is necessary for the growth and development of your baby. Good sources of zinc containing foods that aren't allergens include: peas, beans, brown rice, pumpkin seeds, alfalfa and spinach. You can take 30 to 50mg of zinc a day when the allergies are very bad.

Homeopathy

Consult an experienced homeopath for a recommendation on which remedy may be effective for your allergy.

Acupuncture

Studies have found that in nine out of fifteen trials, improvements in lung function were seen in pregnant women visiting an acupuncturist for allergies.

☛My experience: I find allergies difficult to treat with acupuncture alone during pregnancy although women do notice a slight relief of their symptoms for three to four days after a treatment.

When to consult your caregiver

Always alert your caregiver if you have allergies or think you have an allergic reaction of any kind. Your caregiver should always be aware of the fact that you are an asthma sufferer.

Additional information

Allergies and your baby during pregnancy

If either you or your partner suffers from allergies it increases the risk of your baby developing allergies.

If this is the case you should try avoiding any allergens (see list) in the last three months of pregnancy.

Omega-3 and your baby during pregnancy

Omega-3 fatty acids have anti-inflammatory properties that affect the developing immune system in a way that makes your baby less prone to allergic reactions.

According to Reuters health report, preliminary research suggests that fish-oil supplements taken during pregnancy might help prevent allergies in babies at high risk.
A study in Australia published in the Journal of Allergy and Clinical Immunology, December 2003, found that babies whose mothers took fish oil were less likely to catch a common cold and in the first year of their lives showed signs of being less allergy-prone.
Omega-3 has well documented anti-inflammatory effects in vitro (in the womb) and has also been demonstrated to have health benefits in a range of chronic inflammatory diseases, including cardiovascular disease, rheumatoid arthritis and diabetes, supporting their role in modulating inflammation in vitro.

As a conclusion, supplementation of the maternal diet in pregnancy with Omega-3 may provide a non-invasive intervention with significant potential to prevent the development of allergic and possibly other immune-mediated diseases.

Nutrition and your baby during pregnancy
Don't eat any food allergens (see general food allergen list) in the last three months of your pregnancy if either you or the father of your baby has allergies. This will give your baby a better chance of being allergy free.

Breastfeeding and allergies
Breastfeeding is very important for infants where one or both parents have allergies. Breastfeeding protects against allergies in two ways. The first and most obvious reason breastfed babies have fewer allergies is that they are exposed to fewer food allergens in the first months of life. They aren't given formula based cow's milk or soy products. Less exposure to these foods means less chance of an allergy later on. The other reason breastfed babies have fewer allergies has to do with the development of their immune system. At birth, a baby's immune system is immature. Babies depend heavily on antibodies obtained from their mothers while in the womb. After birth a baby depends on mother's milk for protection. Fed from his/her mother's breast, a baby begins by receiving colostrum, the first milk, which is especially

rich in antibodies, including sIgA. The sIgA "paints" a protective coating on the inside of a baby's intestines to prevent penetration by potential allergens. Mature mothers' milk continues to provide protection to help the baby remain healthy and allergy-free. Human milk and colostrum also provide antibodies specifically designed to fight germs to which either the mother or baby are exposed.

AMNIOTIC FLUID

Amniotic fluid is the clear straw-coloured liquid contained in the membranes (amniotic sac) in which your baby grows. It cushions your baby against pressure and knocks and allows the baby to move around and grow without restriction. Your baby will drink amniotic fluid, it helps the lungs develop, it keeps your baby at a constant temperature and it provides a barrier against infection. The amount of fluid is controlled by a complex system of fluid exchange between you and your baby and new amniotic fluid is constantly being made.

The membranes (amniotic sac) that contain the amniotic fluid and your fetus may rupture naturally as labour begins, but they usually remain intact until the end of the first stage of labour. The membranes may also be broken by a caregiver to speed up a labour that is slow in progressing or as a way to induce labour when labour is delayed.

AMNIOTIC SAC

This is the sac or "bag" filled with amniotic fluid in which your developing baby grows. The amniotic sac is made up of a tough but thin transparent pair of membranes. The inner membrane, the amnion, contains the amniotic fluid and the fetus. The outer membrane, the chorion, contains the amnion and is part of the placenta.

ANAEMIA

Anaemia is an abnormally low level of red blood cells and haemoglobin in the blood. Haemoglobin and hematocrit tests show the ratio of red blood cells to volume of blood in your body. Anaemia is common during pregnancy because of an increased need for iron. You need more iron because your body is making more blood. A certain amount of anaemia is normal and even expected in pregnancy because as your blood volume increases, the number of red blood cells remains constant. The red blood cells are therefore spread thinner throughout the blood, resulting in a lower hematocrit reading. It is normal for the hematocrit reading to drop a little in the middle of pregnancy, an indication of increasing blood volume and stable red blood cell level.

Mothers carrying twins (or triplets), pregnancies close to one another and vegetarian or vegan mothers have a higher risk of becoming anaemic.

Your caregiver will generally check your blood twice during pregnancy for anaemia unless you have certain symptoms in which case they will check it again to be sure.

Keep an eye open for the symptoms listed below because severe anaemia may slow your baby's growth or result in a premature delivery. Also, because your body is weaker if you have anaemia, you may not recover as quickly from bleeding, infection, or other possible complications of childbirth.

Symptoms for anaemia can easily be confused with normal pregnancy symptoms but if you have any doubt and the following symptoms seem to be persistent you should suspect anaemia:

- Tiring easily.
- Weakness.
- Pale skin, gums, eyes, and nail beds.
- Fast or irregular heartbeat.
- Shortness of breath.
- Headache.
- Restless legs.

- Light-headedness.
- Cravings for starch, sand, chalk or ice (a symptom called pica.)

If you have anaemia due to a lack of iron your caregiver will most likely prescribe iron pills. Remember not to take these iron tablets with milk, milk products, tea or coffee because these prevent the iron from being absorbed.

Because iron is very difficult for the body to absorb from tablets, it will make your bowel movements very dark or even black in colour and will most likely cause constipation or upset your stomach.

If your iron is alarmingly low you will need to take iron tablets but if it is just on the low side check with your caregiver if it is possible to try alternatives to iron pills for a few weeks to see if you can improve your iron levels without the harshness of these pills.

THERAPIES AND TIPS for anaemia

Golden Tip

My favourite remedy to combat anaemia is liquid chlorophyll. Taking 1 tablespoon of liquid chlorophyll daily helps your body to manufacture more haemoglobin. If you can't find liquid chlorophyll then any "green food" supplement is also good. All green foods contain high amounts of chlorophyll so any powders made from young barley, wheat grass or spirulina are good. Always take the recommended dosage on the packaging.

Nutrition

- Eating foods that are high in Vitamin C to aid the absorption of iron is important.
- Foods that are high in iron include: Red meat, chicken, turkey, fish, beans, leafy green vegetables, dried fruits such as raisins, prunes and apricots, prune juice, bread, pasta, cereal and other foods made from fortified, enriched or whole grains.
- Foods that contain vitamin C include: Red peppers, pineapple, citrus fruits, strawberries, peas, broccoli, kiwi, potatoes,

pawpaw, brussel sprouts, cauliflower, tomatoes, apples, dried apricots and asparagus.
- If you are taking iron pills and they are causing constipation make sure you drink more fluids, eat more high-fibre foods such as fruits, vegetables, cereals and whole grains. Also remember to take your pills at mealtimes.

☑ Supplements

Taking a liquid iron tonic throughout pregnancy could prevent an iron deficiency and is preferable to a pill supplement.
Liquid chlorophyll – see Golden Tip.

♣ Phytotherapy/herbs

An excellent iron tonic for pregnant women is the humble herb, nettle. Not only is nettle rich in iron and other minerals, it also strengthens the blood vessels, the kidneys and the adrenal glands. You can take it daily throughout pregnancy. My own preference is for a very dark green and strong-tasting brew drunk as tea. Make it by steeping a large handful of the dried herb in one litre of boiling water until it is quite dark. If you prefer a milder brew, steep one tablespoon of the herb per litre of boiling water instead. Drink between one and four cups daily depending on your needs. I generally advise women to make one litre, strain out the leaves and poor it into a thermos to keep it warm. Drink it spread over the day. If you don't like the taste of nettle combine it with a tea that you do enjoy such as mint.

☯ Acupuncture and Shiatsu

Traditional Chinese Medicine will help treat the symptoms that are associated with anaemia: breathlessness, headaches, depression and exhaustion.

☛ My experience: anaemia as such is not easily addressed with acupuncture but the symptoms are good to treat with regular acupuncture sessions. I find that women suffer less from their anaemia symptoms while waiting for their supplement and or diet changes to kick in.

Homeopathy
The tissue salt, Calc Phos is a general nutritional tonic. As this tissue salt assists in digestion and assimilation it is excellent during pregnancy when the digestive system has slowed down and iron becomes difficult to digest. It is often used in conjunction with Ferrum Phos as a treatment for anaemia.

Bach Flower Remedies
Olive can help the extreme exhaustion you could feel with anaemia. It can help you to cope while you wait for iron tablets and nutritional changes to kick in.

When to consult your caregiver
If you suspect that you have anaemia you should always consult your caregiver. Anaemia lowers resistance to infection and can slow the growth of your baby.

Exceptions
Although an iron-deficiency is the most common form of anaemia sometimes anaemia during pregnancy can be caused by a lack of one of the B vitamins and folic acid. Your caregiver will determine this if your body does not respond to treatment for iron- deficiency anaemia.

ANXIETY

Although pregnancy can proceed without any debilitating physical symptoms, anxiety can sometimes play a negative role during pregnancy. The stress of impending motherhood, unstable family situations, guilt and fear can give rise to anxiety. Pregnancy is a notorious time for old emotions, problematic situations and long forgotten frustrations to bubble up.

THERAPIES AND TIPS for anxiety

Lifestyle

- Talking with a professional therapist or talking to family and friends is essential if you are feeling anxious. If there are specific influencing factors it is important that you discuss these with your caregiver.
- Stress can be a contributing factor to anxiety, so ensure that you take adequate time out.
- Adequate preparation for childbirth can sometimes alleviate unnecessary anxiety caused by lack of knowledge or clarity.

Bach Remedies

Bach remedies work subtly and gently to restore calm and emotional balance.

- Aspen: fear of unknown things.
- Elm: feeling overwhelmed by responsibility.
- Larch: lack of confidence.
- Gorse: hopelessness and despair.
- Mimulus: Fear of known things.
- Mustard: Deep gloom for no known reason.
- White Chestnut: mental argument, unwanted thoughts.
- Walnut: helps with adjusting to change.
- Rescue Remedy: for extreme or acute anxiety.

Nutrition

A lack of vitamins and minerals especially vitamin B, iron and zinc can cause anxiety. You should be eating a balanced diet to ensure you get enough of these nutrients. (See Vitamins and Minerals for food sources of the B vitamins, iron and zinc.)

☑ Supplements

- Omega-3 is used in treating depression and anxiety. A minimum of 1000mg should be taken per day.
- A pre-natal multivitamin containing B vitamins, iron and zinc could be adequate if you know that your anxiety is caused by a specific emotional situation.

☯ **Acupuncture**

Women with anxiety are known to respond very well to acupuncture treatments.

☛My experience: I find acupuncture is excellent for treating anxiety.

APGAR TEST

An APGAR test is used to assess your baby's health at the time of birth. It is named after Virginia Apgar and it is also an acronym for the things that are checked:

- Appearance (skin colour.)
- Pulse (heartbeat.)
- Grimace ("reflex irritability".)
- Activity (muscle tone.)
- Respiration (breathing.)

The score of the test ranges from 0 to 10. A baby who scores a 7 or above on the test at 1 minute after birth is generally considered to be in good health. However, a lower score doesn't necessarily mean that your baby is unhealthy or abnormal. For example, a score between 4 and 6 at one minute indicates that your baby simply needs more time to adjust or sometimes just needs his/her airway suctioned to aid breathing after which your baby will most likely improve.

At five minutes after birth the Apgar score is recalculated and if your baby's score hasn't improved to seven or greater, your caregiver may continue any necessary medical care and will closely monitor your baby.

B

BACKACHE (ALSO SEE PELVIC GIRDLE PAIN)

As your fetus grows, your abdominal wall stretches to accommodate your expanding womb. This causes the abdominal muscles to stretch far beyond their normal state and they lose their ability to perform their normal role in maintaining body posture. The hormone relaxin is the second explanation for low back pain. During pregnancy, the hormone relaxin is present in 10 times its normal concentration in the female body. Relaxin is good in the sense that its function, as you might guess from the name, is to relax the joints in your pelvis allowing your baby enough room to pass through the birth canal when it is time for the birth. Unfortunately relaxin also causes abnormal motion in these joints, making them feel unstable and possibly causing inflammation and pain.

THERAPIES AND TIPS for backache

Golden Tip

Visit a Chiropractor that specializes in pregnancy. Sometimes one trip is enough to relieve your backache!

Reflexology

Reflexology is an excellent way to relief backache for a few days at a time. Your reflexologist could show you where to massage your feet so you could continue helping to relieve your backache at home.

Lifestyle

- If possible, minimize certain activities that stress the back and pelvis. These activities include leaning more on one leg when standing, climbing stairs, sitting with your legs crossed, walking long distances and standing for long periods of time.
- When you are standing, put your weight on both feet and tilt your pelvis forward so that your bottom tucks in and under.
- Starting an exercise programme early in pregnancy can help strengthen the muscles in your back and legs. Swimming is an excellent exercise for women at all stages of pregnancy and helps strengthen the lower back. In addition the buoyancy of the water may help alleviate the strain on your back.
- If you find yourself sitting behind a computer or you need to be sitting for long periods of time, make an effort to keep your knees level to your hips so that your back is straight. Take frequent breaks to get up and walk around which will help stretch your muscles and ligaments.
- Wear comfortable shoes when walking distances.
- If you have to lift something, bend from your knees and not your waist.
- A firm mattress provides good back support rather than a very soft or very hard one. If your mattress is too soft, a board between the mattress and box spring will make it firmer. Sleep on your side instead of your back. Tuck a pillow between your legs when lying on your side. The pillow will help straighten your spine and give extra support to your back.
- Look for maternity pants that have a wide elastic band to be worn under the curve of your belly. This band will help support the extra weight. Special abdominal-support girdles can also provide this type of back support. They are available in maternity stores.
- A warm hot water bottle on your lower back can sometimes increase the blood flow, relax the muscles and so relieve some of the pain.

Yoga
Some yoga positions can help relieve backache. Find a pregnancy yoga class and ask your teacher to give you the right exercises for your type of back pain.

☯ **Acupuncture and Shiatsu**
Both acupuncture and shiatsu are very helpful for backache during pregnancy.
☛My experience: Acupuncture does help treat backache but it is best treated as soon as the symptoms start.

◐ **Osteopath**
An osteopath can help ease the strain on your muscular-skeletal system. An osteopath can also help prepare your pelvis for childbirth.

Swimming
Sometimes swimming can relieve backache. It can exercise and therefore strengthen your back and it also takes the pressure and weight off it. Check with your therapist if swimming is the right exercise for your particular backache.

✋ **Tennis ball massage**
Take a tennis ball and place it between you and a wall level with where your backache is. Now massage your back by applying a little pressure on the ball while moving your body in small circles over it.

⃠ **Exceptions**
If this is not your first pregnancy you might notice that your back pain starts much earlier in pregnancy, especially if you had backache in previous pregnancies.

💣 **When to consult your caregiver**
Severe back pain of any sort can be a sign of a problem, such as a kidney or bladder infection. Be sure to contact your caregiver if you

have severe back pain that doesn't seem to get better from the self-help advice, if you have any numbness, tingling, weakness in your legs, or radiating pain (radiating pain spreads out from a central point) or fever. Also contact your caregiver immediately if you are experiencing intermittent (at regular intervals) backache before 36 weeks you could have started premature labour.

BACTERIA AND TOXINS TO AVOID DURING PREGNANCY

Toxoplasmosis and Salmonella

Undercooked Meats

Though you may enjoy the occasional steak tartar, pregnancy is not a time to eat raw or even undercooked meats. Undercooked and raw meats can carry salmonella, e.coli and toxoplasmosis bacteria. These can cause symptoms like nausea and diarrhoea but more worryingly, they are also associated with miscarriage and preterm birth.

During pregnancy you should avoid:

- Undercooked chicken, pork or red meat.
- Pates (including chicken and veal.)
- Deli meats.
- Smoked meats.
- Raw seafood, especially shellfish.

Raw Eggs

During pregnancy it is important to be especially vigilant about raw eggs. Raw eggs can carry salmonella, which can cause food poisoning. The severe diarrhoea and vomiting caused by the salmonella bacteria could stress your baby and the bacteria could cause preterm labour. To prevent salmonella poisoning, avoid foods containing raw eggs including:

- Caesars salad dressing.
- Eggnog.

- Cookie or cake batter – no licking the batter spatula while baking!
- Homemade ice cream.
- Hollandaise sauce.
- Homemade mayonnaise.

Listeriosis – Non-pasteurized Food and Beverages

Most of our milk products are made from pasteurized milk. Pasteurized milk has gone through a special process to rid it of any bacteria, especially listeria. However, certain foods are now made with non-pasteurized milk and may contain listeria in small quantities. Listeria is a real problem, causing up to 2,500 illnesses every year. As many as 30% of listeria bacteria deaths involve pregnant women and their foetuses.

So to avoid listeria stay away from:

- Non-pasteurized soft cheeses, like goat's cheese, brie, and camembert.
- Mexican-style cheeses, including queso fresco and queso blanco.
- Raw milk - this means it hasn't been pasteurized.
- Coleslaw, pork tongue, hot dogs, processed meats and deli salads.

Mercury - found in some fish

Fish is an important part of a healthy pregnancy diet. Fish contains Omega-3, which can help build your baby's retinas, brain and nervous system. Omega-3 also reduces your chances for developing pre-eclampsia. However, you shouldn't eat shark, swordfish or marlin because of the high levels of methyl mercury they contain. You should also limit the amount of tuna you eat to no more than two tuna steaks (weighing about 140g when cooked, or 170g raw) or four medium-size cans of tuna a week (with a drained weight of about 140g per can). Methyl mercury can cause severe neurological damage and developmental problems in your baby.

Aspartame - artificial sweetener

Aspartame is a calorie-free sweetener used in a wide variety of soft drinks, candies, and food products. Long-term use of the chemical food aspartame has been linked with cancer and immuno-toxicity so regular use of aspartame during pregnancy is advised against.

GBS - B streptococcus

The group B streptococcus (GBS) bacteria are usually harmless in healthy adults, but they can cause, relatively rare but very serious infections in newborns. Group B is different from group A streptococcus, the bacteria that causes strep throat.

If you test positive for GBS, you'll need to have intravenous antibiotics as soon as your labour starts or your water breaks, whichever comes first. Ideally, you'll want to get started on the antibiotics at least four hours before you give birth, but if your labour is very rapid you may not have that much time. Take comfort that getting started even a couple of hours before delivery significantly lowers the risk to your baby.

If you don't get your first dose four hours before the birth, you'll need to stay in the hospital for at least 48 hours after delivery so your baby can be observed for any signs of an infection. Try not to worry, though, because the chance that your baby will get sick, especially if he's full term, you don't have a fever, and your membranes weren't ruptured for long, is small.

There is a fast and effective treatment for many situations. Medical research indicates that giving antibiotics through the vein to the mother during labour can greatly reduce the frequency of GBS infection in the baby immediately after birth or during the first week of life.

Treating the mother with oral antibiotics during the pregnancy may decrease the amount of GBS for a short time, but it will not eliminate the bacteria completely and will leave the baby largely unprotected at birth.

Screening for GBS

Some doctors routinely screen for GBS by doing cultures on their patients during pregnancy. These cultures must be taken from the lower vagina and rectum, not the cervix.

Because so many women carry GBS, and not all of their babies become ill, many physicians believe that antibiotics should not be given to all women who test positive for the bacteria. This would result in the unnecessary treatment of a large number of women. Instead, the focus is on the high-risk patients. If a woman is found to carry GBS and falls into one or more of the high-risk situations her doctor can immediately start antibiotic treatment during labour, which will help protect the baby and the mother.

High-risk situations for GBS

- When labour is premature - labour beginning prior to the 37th week of gestation.
- When there is premature rupture of the membranes - prior to the 37th week of gestation.
- When there is prolonged rupture of membranes (>12 hours) before the baby is born.
- If the mother has a fever (>100.4 F) before or during labour.
- Women who have a history of GBS in previous births.

Additional information

If you have to take an antibiotic cure then always take Probiotics directly after have taken antibiotics. See the information on Probiotics.

BAD METALLIC TASTE

During pregnancy, you may notice an increase in saliva and possibly a slight metallic taste in your mouth. You may find that this taste has a negative influence on how everything tastes. This makes it difficult for you to enjoy your food and it may even cause you to avoid eating many foods altogether.

THERAPIES AND TIPS for a bad metallic taste

☑ Supplements

A deficiency in zinc and iron is the most common reason for a metallic taste in the mouth. Most women find that if they suck on a zinc lozenge the taste goes away. You can take zinc in liquid form (take the dosage indicated on bottle) or in tablets. Take one tablet of 15mg per day.

Nutrition

Eating more foods that contain iron or zinc will help reduce the taste by reducing the deficiency of both these minerals.

Iron food sources: The best source of iron comes from red meat (such as beef, veal and lamb), with lesser amounts in chicken, fish, pork, ham and eggs. Shellfish are also quite high in iron content. These are known as 'haem' sources of iron and are readily absorbed by the body (up to 35%.)

Plant foods (or non-haem sources of iron) are not as readily absorbed into the body (up to 10%.) These include breads, grains, cereals, dark green leafy vegetables (spinach, broccoli and parsley), potatoes, dried fruits, beans (baked, green, kidney, black), nuts, sunflower seeds and tofu. However, their absorption can be increased by up to 4 times if they are eaten with foods or drinks rich in vitamin C.

When 'haem' and 'non-haem' foods are eaten together (especially with fruit and vegetables with vitamin C), they interact with each other to maximise the body's ability to absorb the iron they contain. For example, having baked beans with tomato and ham on toast will increase the iron you absorb from all these food when compared to eating them separately.

Zinc food sources: The richest sources of zinc are in meat, fish, oysters, shellfish, prawns (or shrimps), crab, turkey, chicken and ham. Zinc is also present in live yoghurt, ricotta, beans (green, kidney, baked), nuts, tofu, lentils, eggs, breads, cereals, pasta, rice, wheat germ, bran, onions, ginger and sunflower seeds.

Homeopathy:
Cocculus indicus 30c. and Catrum carbonicum 30c. are both remedies given to help reduce or get rid of a bad taste during pregnancy. Always take the dosage indicated on packaging.

Additional information
Some women find that chewing peppermint gum helps to get rid of the taste. Remember though that most chewing gum is sweetened with artificial sweeteners so try to limit the use of gum to once or twice a day.

BEST POSITION FOR THE BABY AT THE TIME OF BIRTH

Anterior Position
The best position for your baby to be in when you go into labour is head down with its back swivelled towards your front. This position is called an anterior position and labour is nearly always shorter and easier if the baby is anterior. In this position your baby fits snugly into the curve of your pelvis and it's easy for him/her to move downward during labour. When your baby moves down into the lower part of your pelvis during labour he/she will turn his/her head slightly so that the widest part of his/her head is in the widest part of your pelvis. The back of his/her head can then "slip" underneath your pubic bone.

Posterior Position
Some babies move down into the pelvis with the back of their head (and therefore their back) towards their mothers' spine. This is called a posterior position. When a baby is in a posterior position the waters are more likely to break at the beginning of labour. These labours will see mainly back contractions with a tendency to progress slower and an increased need for the use of forceps or ventouse (a suction device).

If your baby is in a posterior position at the onset of labour the close proximity between the baby's bony skull and your spine can be very uncomfortable and you might find that you will need to move around more, changing position, which will encourage your baby to change position.

It seems that western women are much more likely to have posterior babies than women who work in the fields, or those that spend time bent over their cooking pots. So lifestyle might be one cause of posterior babies. It's not difficult to understand why. When you are sitting in your car, or curled up on a comfortable armchair watching television, or working at a computer for many hours your lower back tends to curve and your pelvis tips creating a kind of hammock and because the heaviest part of your baby is the back of his/her head it will tend to swing around into your back. So he/she ends up in a posterior position, lying against your spine. If you have a lifestyle that involves very little sitting and a lot of upright activities your baby is far more likely to go down into your pelvis in an anterior position because your pelvis is often tipped more forwards.

Helping your baby into an anterior position

Helping your baby to move into an anterior rather than a posterior position is called "optimal foetal positioning". You can encourage your baby to take up this optimal position by making sure that you don't spend all day sitting and when you do sit make sure you don't slump into that "hammock shape" for your baby to lie in. Don't put your feet up; lying back with your feet up encourages posterior presentation. If you spend a long time watching television try to sit with a straight back and move onto hands and knees, rocking your pelvis from side to side for a at least five minutes every 20 minutes. If your baby is persistently posterior then you should crawl around on hands and knees for five minutes at a time a few times a day.

Getting ready for labour

If you are expecting your first baby you could try to adopt the lifestyle described in the previous section from around 34 weeks of pregnancy. This is when your baby starts to sink down into your pelvis. If you are expecting your second baby, the baby possibly won't engage into your pelvis until later but it is still wise to adopt the same lifestyle from about 34 weeks. Sometimes women have a lot of indistinct pains for several days before labour really starts and although these can be very exhausting, the pains might well be due to the fact that your baby is trying to turn from a posterior position into an anterior position. The best way to cope, if this is the case, is to try and get as much rest as possible during the night and to remain upright and active during the day. Leaning forward or going onto hands and knees during the pains will help both you and the baby.

A study published in the British Medical Journal January 2004 found that just going on hands-and-knees in late pregnancy (but not labour) was not enough to stop you having a posterior baby at birth.

Improving the baby's position during labour

Women instinctively know how to labour if they are left to their own devices. However, it is not always easy to tune in to your instincts. The best thing you can do during labour is to change position regularly to help your baby position more perfectly. This will have a positive influence on the whole labour process.

Keeping in mind that you should change into a new position every 30 to 40 minutes, here are some positions you could try:

- Kneel with pillows (for comfort) under your hands and knees.
- Walk around slowly or stand leaning forward, using your arms as support, onto a surface and rock your pelvis from side to side.
- Walk up and down stairs (slowly and sideways if you need to.) This can help the baby to re-position in your pelvis.
- Step on and off a small stool.
- If you get very tired during labour, lie on your left side with a pillow between your knees as this still allows the pelvis to expand to give your baby some space while you are resting.

BIRTH PLAN

A birth plan specifies the ideas and expectations that you have about the birth of your baby. Remember though, that birth is paradoxical: a very predictable yet unpredictable natural human passage. We cannot know the day or week labour will begin, how long it will last, exactly how it will feel, how it will progress or how we will react. What you can do, however, is educate yourself about the vast array of possibilities and learn about how to react in the various possible situations. In writing a birth plan you can decide what your ideal is and what you strive for, what the means are for you to create the most conducive environment for such a birth and which people can best help you to attain those birth arrangements.

A birth plan is used to help people, who come into contact with you during your labour and birth, to know more about you, how you have prepared for this birth and what your expectations are.

When making a birth plan be careful not to write only the best-case scenario. What if there are unexpected situations? For example, if you are planning a home birth and end up having to have an emergency Caesarean, you say that in the case of you having a Caesarean you would like to try and have baby placed on you for a few moments if possible or if it needs to be taken away that the father goes with the baby at all times.

Here are some headings you could use for a birth plan.

Birth companion

Write down whom you want with you during your labour. Do you want this/these person/s to stay with you all the time, or are there certain procedures or stages in labour when you'd prefer them to leave the room?

Positions for labour and birth

Mention which positions you would like try or how active you would like to be during labour and for your baby's delivery.

Pain relief
You might specify that you would prefer not to be offered any pain relief. On the other hand you may want to specify what kinds of pain relief you want to use, if any, and in what order. For example, you might prefer to try pethidine before an epidural.

Birthing pool
If you would like to use a birthing pool at the hospital or midwife-led unit or if you are hiring one to use at home, make sure it is in your birth plan so your caregiver knows you would like to try and give birth in water.

Monitoring your baby's heart rate
Say how you would prefer your baby to be monitored during labour. Write down whether you would like your caregiver to listen to your baby's heart intermittently using a hand-held device (Sonicaid or Doptone) or whether you want electronic monitoring using a belt strapped round your waist because you would feel more secure with constant monitoring – if you are in a hospital.

Episiotomy
Say whether you would like to try and avoid having an episiotomy.

Delivery position
Say whether you prefer to try and give birth kneeling, standing, lying on the bed, in water or squatting.

Third stage (delivery of the placenta)
You can choose to have an injection to speed up the delivery of the placenta, or you might want to say that you prefer to have a natural third stage without drugs if at all possible.

Keeping your baby with you
Specify that you would like to have skin-to-skin contact with your baby for the first hour after birth if possible.

Feeding the baby

Be clear about whether you want to breastfeed your baby. Also be clear about whether your breastfed baby is allowed to have any bottles. If you definitely don't want your baby to have bottles, say so.

Unexpected situations

Some women write down what they want to happen if their baby has to go the Special Care Baby Unit (SCBU.) They might want to be allowed to care for the baby as much as possible themselves, and to be transferred with him to another hospital if a transfer is necessary. You should specify that even though your baby is in special care that you want to express milk to prepare for eventually being able to breast feed. Mention that you would like to try and kangaroo (skin to skin contact with a SCBU baby) your baby if possible. Kangarooing has proved to aid miraculous recovery in SCBU babies.

Special needs: You may have very special needs that you want to mention in your birth plan. If you have a disability, write about the kind of help you will need in labour. Say whether there is any special equipment that would assist you. If you have particular religious needs, make sure that you include these. It might be important for you to have certain rituals carried out when your baby is born. Or you might require a special diet during your hospital stay for health or cultural reasons. Write all of these things down.

An *example* of a birth plan for a hospital birth

Labour

I would prefer to avoid an enema and/or shaving of pubic hair.

I wish to be able to move around and change position at will throughout labour.

I would like to be able to have fluids by mouth throughout the first stage of labour.

I would prefer to keep the number of vaginal exams to a minimum.

Monitoring

I do not wish to have continuous foetal monitoring unless it is required by the condition of my baby.

Labour Augmentation/Induction
I do not wish to have the amniotic membrane ruptured artificially unless signs of foetal distress require internal monitoring.
I would prefer to be allowed to try changing position and nipple stimulation before oxytocin is administered.

Anaesthesia
I do not want any kind of anaesthesia *offered* to me during labour, though would like it available if I specifically request it.

Caesarean
If my primary caregiver determines that a Caesarean delivery is indicated, I would like to obtain a second opinion from another physician if time allows.
I would like my partner present at all times if my baby requires a Caesarean delivery.
I prefer to have an epidural for anaesthesia if possible.
If my baby is not in distress, I would like him/her to be given to me immediately after birth.

Episiotomy
I would prefer not to have an episiotomy unless absolutely required for the baby's safety.

Delivery
I would prefer not to have my legs in stirrups but would like my partner and/or nurses to support me and my legs as necessary during the pushing stage.
I would like a mirror available so I can see my baby's head when it crowns.
Even if I am fully dilated, and assuming my baby is not in distress, I would like to try to wait until I feel the urge to push before beginning the pushing phase.
I would like to have my baby placed on my stomach/chest immediately after delivery.

After Delivery
I would like to have the cord cut by either me or my partner.
I would like to have my baby examined and bathed in my presence.
If my baby must be taken from me to receive medical treatment, my partner will accompany my baby at all times.

Breastfeeding
Unless medically necessary, I do not wish to have any bottles given to my baby (including glucose water or plain water.)
I do not want my baby to be given a pacifier.

Other
I will be having a doula to support my partner and I throughout my labour.

Extra birth planning
Prepare yourself to experience absolutely anything during your labour keeping in mind the flowing:

- **Be creative:** You might surprise yourself with what you want during labour. Labour can be a great opportunity to listen to your "inner voice" and let those creative juices flow. Just let yourself go you may feel like belly dancing, grunting or singing. I know of someone who swam endless lengths of her pool during dilation - something she Definitely had not planned on doing!
- **Express your feelings:** This is the one time you can just let go!
- **Ask for what you want:** Start doing this during your pregnancy. Ask your partner to please do the shopping or run you a bath, to get used to idea of "demanding" what you really want. During labour this can help to make you feel more comfortable thereby improving your labour.
- **Be positive:** Say out loud during labour that you are doing well or that you are doing the very best you can. Prepare your birth companions for the fact that you will need positive, encouraging statements during labour, for example; 'You are doing so well, keep going you are wonderful' etc.

- **Imagination:** Use your imagination during labour to visualise your cervix softening and opening to allow your baby to pass through. Imagine your entire body becoming soft and relaxed to increase the effectiveness of your contractions. Prepare your birth partners to repeat words like, softening, opening and relax to you during your labour.

BIRTH

By the time you reach 38 weeks your body is already fine-tuned for giving birth but it is still important that you and your caregivers understand how to work with, and avoid disrupting, your body's inborn knowledge.

It can be especially helpful to know about the following hormone "cocktail" involved with birth: oxytocin, endorphin and adrenaline. These three hormones play a major role in regulating the process of labour and birth.

Learning about these hormones can help you understand some of what is happening in your body during labour and birth. Women and caregivers can learn how to support the effective action of these hormones. Understanding how they work and how they are affected is important for making informed decisions.

The role of oxytocin during labour and birth
Oxytocin ("ahk-sih-TOH-sin") is often known as the "hormone of love" because it is produced during sexual intercourse, is needed for fertility, stimulates contractions during labour and birth and is produced during breastfeeding. It helps us to feel good; it triggers feelings of nurturing and influences social behaviour.
Receptor cells, which allow your body to respond to oxytocin, increase gradually in pregnancy and reach a high peak during labour. Oxytocin is a potent stimulator of contractions. These contractions help to open up your cervix, move your baby down and out of your body, give birth to your placenta and limit bleeding from the placenta

site. During labour and birth, the pressure of the baby against your cervix and then against tissues in your pelvic floor stimulates oxytocin and so thereby stimulates contractions.

Low levels of oxytocin during labour and birth can cause contractions to slow or stop and thereby lengthen labour or cause excessive bleeding at the placenta site after birth. This makes the possibility of necessary intervention higher.

The role of endorphins during labour and birth
Endorphins are calming and pain-relieving hormones that humans produce in response to stress and pain. The level of this natural morphine-like substance rises steadily and steeply during un-medicated labours. High endorphin levels during labour and birth can produce an altered state of consciousness that helps women flow with the process, even when labour is long and arduous. Despite the hard work of labour and birth, a woman with high endorphin levels can feel alert, attentive and even euphoric. A drop in endorphin levels in the days after birth may contribute to the "baby blues" that many women experience around the fourth day after delivery.

Low levels of endorphin can cause labour to be excessively painful, making the possibility of necessary intervention higher.

The role of adrenaline during labour and birth
Adrenaline is the "fight or flight" hormone that humans produce to help ensure survival. Women who feel threatened during labour (for example by feeling fearful, embarrassed or insecure) may produce high levels of adrenaline. Adrenaline can slow labour or stop it altogether.
Too much adrenaline can cause problems in labour and birth by:

- Causing distress to the unborn baby.
- Causing contractions to stop, slow or have an erratic pattern thereby lengthening labour.
- Creating a sense of panic and increasing pain in the mother.
- Causing caregivers to respond to this problem with Caesareans and/or other intervention.

The release of adrenaline during the pushing phase of labour has a positive effect. Its effect ensures that you gain energy, become more focused and obtain new strength and alertness. The baby also gets a burst of adrenaline; this allows it to be born alert with wide-open eyes and dilated pupils.

Steps you can take to help ensure that these hormones work well for you

- You may promote your body's production of **oxytocin** during labour and birth by:
- Staying calm, comfortable and feeling safe.
- Avoiding disturbances, such as unwelcome people or noise and uncomfortable procedures.
- Staying upright as much as possible. This helps because you are using gravity to apply the weight of your baby against your cervix and then, at a later stage during labour, against the tissues of your pelvic floor, both stimulate the production of oxytocin which in turn increases the effectiveness of your contractions.
- Both engaging in nipple stimulation in the first hours of labour and giving your baby a chance to suckle shortly after birth stimulate the production of oxytocin.

You may enhance your body's production of **endorphins** during labour and birth by:

- Staying calm, comfortable and confident.
- Avoiding disturbances such as unwelcome people or noise and displacement from a safe labour environment.
- Delaying or avoiding epidural or opioid as a pain relief method.

You may keep **adrenaline** levels low during labour and birth by:

- Staying calm, comfortable and relaxed.

The following may help you to keep the birthing-hormone-cocktail in balance:

- Going into labour being well informed as to how you (personally) can best achieve a calm and relaxed state.
- Having trust and confidence in your body and your capabilities as a birthing woman.
- Having trust and confidence in your caregivers and your birth setting.
- Being in a calm, peaceful and private environment and avoiding conflict.
- Being with people who help you with comfort measures, good information, positive words and other support.
- Avoiding intrusive, painful and disruptive procedures.

Although it is impossible to predict how a birth will proceed here is a standard idea as to how a 1st birth could *possibly* go:

1st Stage – early or latent phase:

- Your cervix will go from 0cm to approximately 3cm
- Your contractions could be anything from 20 minutes to 5 minutes apart.
- You will be excited and happy to be in labour – hold onto this feeling it is a very special moment and it will ban all feeling of fear!

1st Stage – active phase:

- Your cervix will go approximately from 3cm to 7cm.
- You will be more serious and concentrating on the contractions and they could be anything from 5 minutes to 2 minutes apart.

Transition Phase:

- Your cervix will go from 7cm to 10cm.
- Your contractions may be coming as close as one minute apart.
- You could be tired, restless and doubting your ability to cope.
- You may need to make noises during your contractions to help you cope.

2nd Stage – pushing to birth

- Your cervix will be fully dilated.
- Your contractions may be further apart.
- You will be working hard at pushing out your baby during contractions but you may be clear headed and present between contractions.

3rd stage:

- You will push the placenta out.
- You will be getting to know your baby – you will be fully awake and aware.

⦸ **Exceptions**

A second or following birth can take on any shape. A second birth is often seen to "skip" the first early stage and the third stage tends to be shorter. Having said that it is very important to remember that **any** birth (including a first) could be the exception!

BLADDER INFECTION

Being pregnant makes you more susceptible to urinary tract infections. Higher levels of the hormone progesterone relax the muscles of the ureter's (the tubes that carry the urine from your kidneys to your bladder) causing them to stretch. Your growing uterus may compress the ureter's, making it difficult for urine to flow through them as quickly and freely as it normally does. Later in pregnancy the baby presses on your bladder making it hard to empty it completely. These changes make the urine take longer to pass through your urinary tract, giving bacteria more time to multiply and take hold before being flushed out.

Symptoms of a bladder infection (cystitis)

Remember that your symptoms may vary but they could include:

- Pain, discomfort or a burning feeling when urinating.

- Pelvic discomfort or lower abdominal pain (often just above the pubic bone.)
- A frequent or uncontrollable urge to urinate, even when there's very little urine in the bladder.
- Foul-smelling urine and/or cloudy urine.
- Blood in the urine (usually hard to see with the naked eye.)
- An increase in Braxton Hicks contractions.
- Pain or discomfort during sexual intercourse.
- Backache.

Since the frequent urge to urinate is common during pregnancy it may be difficult to know for sure whether you have cystitis, especially if your symptoms are mild.

☠ **Warning!**
Some bladder infections during pregnancy are asymptomatic (no symptoms) or they only manifest themselves as chronic lower back pain, Braxton Hicks contractions or bellyache.

If your caregiver diagnoses a bladder infection you will be given a course of antibiotics that are safe to take during pregnancy. Please always tell your doctor if he is the one to discover the bladder infection that you are pregnant, as certain antibiotics may not be taken during pregnancy.

THERAPIES AND TIPS for a bladder infection

Golden Tip

Drink barley water, it discourages the bacteria from attaching to the walls of the bladder and therefore makes it easier to flush it out of your system.
To make barley water: One cup of barley to fifteen cups of water and bring it to the boil. Turn down the heat and simmer for thirty five to forty five minutes until the barley is soft and the water has turned milky-like and creamy. SAVE the barley water and sieve out the barley. Drink the barley water warm or at room temperature throughout the day. It is important to make a fresh batch of barley water each day.

Drink the barley water until you feel/know that the bladder infection is over.

Nutrition

- Drink plenty of water, at least eight 8 glasses a day.
- Drink cranberry juice that is 100% pure and not mixed with a sweetener. Studies show that pure cranberry juice can reduce bacteria levels and discourage new bacteria from taking hold in the urinary tract.

☑ Supplements

If you have taken antibiotics for the infection please ensure that you take Probiotics after finishing the course of antibiotics to help restore your good intestinal flora. If you don't you could have recurring bladder infections. See Probiotics for more information.

Homeopathy

- Solidago Complex D6 taken immediately if you feel any symptoms or even taken preventatively throughout pregnancy can help you avoid bladder infections if you know you are susceptible to them.
- Belladonna 6c is also commonly recommended for bladder infections.

Take the recommended dosage suggested by the product you buy.

Lifestyle

- Don't ignore the urge to urinate and always try to empty your bladder completely when you do urinate. Sometimes lifting your bottom while leaning with your hands on your knees as if you are about to get up, "lifts" your uterus off your bladder a little and you might find you can urinate just a little more.
- After a bowel movement make sure you wipe yourself from front to back to prevent any bacteria from your stool getting near the urethra.
- Try to avoid sex if you have a bladder infection. If you do have sex, urinate before and after having had sex.

- Avoid feminine hygiene products (sprays or powders) and strong soaps that can irritate your urethra and genitals and make them a better breeding ground for bacteria. Also don't use douches during pregnancy.
- Wear all-cotton underwear and cotton-crotch pantyhose/ tights.

Reflexology

Reflexology can relieve a few of the uncomfortable symptoms of a bladder infection.

When to consult your caregiver:

If you suspect that you have a bladder infection call your caregiver immediately.

Warning!

Look out for signs of the infection having spread to your kidneys, as this would require immediate medical attention.

Signs of a kidney infection:

- A high fever often with shaking, chills or sweats.
- Pain in your lower back or in your side just under your ribs on one or both sides and possibly accompanied by pain in your abdomen.
- Nausea and vomiting.
- Puss or blood in your urine, which may be hard to see with the naked eye so if you suspect a kidney infection you could urinate into a clear glass and hold it up to the light.

BLEEDING AND SENSITIVE GUMS

Bleeding sensitive gums are a common complaint during pregnancy. High hormone levels cause your gums to swell and react more to the bacteria in plaque. That, along with an increased blood supply to your mucous membranes can result in swollen, tender gums that bleed when you floss or brush. This is called “pregnancy gingivitis” and it affects about half of all pregnant women.

You may even develop a nodule on your gums that bleeds when you brush. This kind of nodule is called a "pregnancy tumour" or "pyogenic granuloma," and is relatively rare. (These nodules can actually pop up anywhere on your body during pregnancy but are found most often in the mouth.) A pyogenic granuloma can grow quite large and is more likely to appear in an area where you have gingivitis. It is generally painless and harmless and usually disappears completely after delivery.

THERAPIES AND TIPS for bleeding and sensitive gums

Lifestyle

Prevention is key, practice good oral hygiene and get regular, preventive dental care:

- Brush at least twice a day (or after every meal if possible), using a soft-bristled brush.
- Using an Aloe Vera toothpaste often helps to reduce sensitivity.
- Use a toothpick and floss daily to clean between your teeth (the toothpick will clean what the fine floss misses and the floss will get to places the toothpick can't.)
- Rinse your mouth well with water after brushing and flossing.
- Rinsing with sea salt-water (spitting out the salt water afterwards) may help to reduce any inflammation.

Nutrition

- Eat plenty of vitamin-C-rich foods, such as citrus fruits, strawberries, blackcurrants, potatoes, broccoli and cabbage.
- Make sure you get enough calcium in your diet. Calcium is essential for strong teeth and therefore better gum-health.
- Although dairy products are promoted as being the best source of calcium there is a controversy about the body's ability to assimilate calcium from pasteurized, homogenized milk. My preferred food sources of calcium include small fined boned fish like sardines and mackerel, seaweed (especially kelp) sesame salt (gomasio), tahini (a paste made from sesame seeds) and dark leafy greens like broccoli, fresh parsley, watercress,

cabbage, rocket leaves, turnip greens, pakchoi. The following fruits also contain some calcium: dates, figs, raisins, prunes, papaya and elder berries.

Homeopathy

For red, swollen and inflamed gums: Kreosotum 6C.
For bleeding gums: Phosphorus 6C.

When to consult your caregiver

If your gums and teeth are giving you constant discomfort and none of the above remedies help then you should consult your caregiver or your dentist.

BLEEDING

When you're pregnant even a small amount of vaginal bleeding can be scary. Sometimes bleeding does signal trouble but not always. In fact, many pregnant women experience light vaginal bleeding at some point during pregnancy, particularly during the first trimester. Often, such bleeding is the result of a normal event during pregnancy, such as the embryo's implantation into the uterine lining around one week after conception.
Try not to panic if you have a little bleeding but do take it seriously by monitoring it closely and taking note of possible symptoms, such as cramping. By understanding the most common causes of bleeding during pregnancy, you'll know what to look for and when to call your caregiver.

Depending on the seriousness of your symptoms, your caregiver may order laboratory tests or an ultrasound to assess the status of your pregnancy.

Bleeding in the first trimester

Many women have spotting or bleeding in the first 12 weeks of pregnancy. In most cases women who experience light bleeding in the first trimester go on to have normal, successful pregnancies.

Common causes of early pregnancy bleeding include:

Implantation bleeding. You may notice a small amount of spotting or bleeding very early in pregnancy about seven to eleven days after fertilization. This is known as implantation bleeding, it happens when the fertilized egg attaches to the lining of your uterus. It is usually a little earlier than a normal menstrual period, and it doesn't last long. Some women actually mistake this light bleeding for an early light period and don't realize they're pregnant.

Hormonal breakthroughs. Sometimes women continue to have a very slight period around the time they normally menstruate. This is very rare but does happen, if your pregnancy symptoms continue even though you think you have had a period, double check to see if you aren't pregnant.

Additional information: If you have been taking your BBT (Basal Body Temperature) before pregnancy your temperature could help you to determine if you are (still) pregnant even though you have had some bleeding. Your BBT should stay high and not drop to the usual follicle phase temperature.

Cervical changes. When you're pregnant, there's an increase in the blood supply and blood flow to your cervix. So you may experience light spotting after contact to this area, such as after sexual intercourse or a pelvic exam. This type of light bleeding shouldn't last for more than 24 hours.

Molar Pregnancy

Molar pregnancies are rare cause of early bleeding and involve the growth of abnormal tissue instead of an embryo. It is also referred to as gestational trophoblastic disease (GTD).

Signs of a Molar Pregnancy are vaginal bleeding, blood tests revealing unusually high hCG levels, absent fetal heart tones and grape-like clusters seen in the uterus by an ultrasound.

Vanishing twin

Bleeding in assisted pregnancies (IVF) where two or more embryos have been replaced may be caused by a "vanishing twin". This means that only one embryo manages to implant and the remaining embryo/s are rejected.

Miscarriage

Bleeding in the first trimester could unfortunately be a sign of miscarriage. Miscarriage does occur in 15 percent to 20 percent of known pregnancies, most often before 12 weeks. If you are losing a lot of blood accompanied by cramping you should contact your caregiver.

Ectopic pregnancy

Also called a tubal pregnancy, this condition occurs when the embryo implants somewhere outside the uterus, usually in a fallopian tube. It is much less common than miscarriage. However, an embryo implanted outside the uterus can't develop into a normal baby and it can cause serious internal bleeding. Other possible symptoms of ectopic pregnancy include abdominal pain, which is usually worse on one side, light-headedness and an urge to have a bowel movement. Ectopic pregnancies must be removed/terminated to save the life of the mother.

Bleeding in the second or third trimester

Conditions such as cervical growths or inflammation can cause minor bleeding in the second half of pregnancy. The most common cause of heavy vaginal bleeding in late pregnancy is a problem with the placenta, such as placenta previa or placental abruption.

Possible reasons for bleeding in the second or third trimester

Problems with your cervix.

A cervical infection, inflamed cervix or growths on your cervix can cause vaginal bleeding in the second or third trimesters. Occasionally, light bleeding from the cervix may be a sign of cervical incompetence, a condition in which the cervix opens spontaneously, leading to preterm delivery. This condition occurs most frequently between 18 and 23 weeks of pregnancy and requires prompt medical care.

Placenta previa.

Moderate to heavy bleeding in the late second or third trimester may indicate placenta previa. This a problem in which the placenta lies too low in the uterus and partly or completely covers the opening to the birth canal. The main sign of placenta previa is painless bright red vaginal bleeding. The bleeding may stop by itself at some point but it nearly always reoccurs days or weeks later. This is a rare but serious condition that requires immediate care.

Placental abruption.

In this condition, which affects only 1% of pregnant women, the placenta begins to separate from the inner wall of the uterus before birth, causing bleeding within the uterus. The bleeding from placental abruption may be scant, heavy or somewhere in between, but it is usually accompanied by abdominal pain. This condition usually occurs during the last twelve weeks of pregnancy.

Uterine rupture.

In women who have had a previous Caesarean birth a disruption of the surgical scar in the uterus is a rare but dangerous cause of vaginal bleeding usually accompanied by intense local abdominal pain or abdominal tenderness around the scar. It is very uncommon and if it happens it tends to be during labour.

Preterm labour.

Light bleeding from 20 to 37 weeks may indicate preterm labour, especially when accompanied by pelvic or abdominal pressure, dull backache, abdominal cramps or uterine contractions. If you have any signs or symptoms of labour before 36 weeks you need to call your caregiver right away.

A sign of possible labour (bloody show.)

During pregnancy a thick mucus plug seals the opening of the cervix to prevent bacteria and other germs from entering the uterus. As your body prepares for labour the cervix begins to thin out and soften and the mucous plug is dislodged. When this happens you may notice a thick or stringy discharge that may be tinged with blood. This is known as the "bloody show".

Bleeding throughout pregnancy

A main reason for bleeding throughout pregnancy could be fibroids. If you were unaware that you had fibroids then you will most probably find out when you have your first pregnancy scan.

When to consult your caregiver:

If you have slight spotting during the first trimester that goes away within a day you should tell your caregiver at your next visit. If you have any spotting or bleeding that lasts more than a day call your caregiver.

Contact your caregiver **immediately** if you have:

- Moderate to heavy bleeding.
- Any amount of bleeding accompanied by pain, cramping, fever or chills.

NB! Immediately call your caretaker if you experience blood loss during the last twelve weeks of your pregnancy.

BLOATING

You may experience more gas than usual during pregnancy. Don't be surprised if you find yourself belching like a champion beer drinker or having to unbutton your trousers weeks before you even begin to grow a pregnancy belly.

The primary reason is that during early pregnancy your body produces large amounts of progesterone, a hormone that relaxes smooth muscle tissue throughout your body including your gastrointestinal tract. This relaxation slows down your digestive processes, which can cause increased gas, bloating, burping and flatulence. Sometimes leaving you feeling miserable after eating, especially after a big meal. Another reason for bloating and belching is the fact that pregnancy can cause extreme hunger and that in turn causes bad eating habits. These eating habits include gobbling down of food (and air!) and overeating.

THERAPIES AND TIPS for bloating

Golden Tip

Probiotics, also known as intestinal flora, can improve digestion tenfold! Taking a good Probiotic supplement before bedtime every evening can relieve all kinds of digestive problems including bloating, wind, burping, heartburn and constipation. It is important to know that you could have a little *extra bloating* for two days when you first start taking Probiotics, this can be confusing but keep taking them you'll find that the symptoms will soon improve.

☑ **Supplements**

Supplementing with digestive enzymes can make a huge difference to bloating and especially burping during pregnancy. Enzymes are essential for normal digestion and taking extra plant enzymes can give you a helping hand during pregnancy when digestion tends to be sluggish. See "Digestive Enzymes" for more information. Take the recommended dosage of the product you buy.

Nutrition

- Try to avoid eating too many of the following due to the fact that they tend increase gas: onions, cabbage, fizzy drinks and sweetened fruit drinks.
- Try to reduce the amount of air you swallow by not eating too fast, take your time and chew your food thoroughly.
- Eat several small meals throughout the day instead of a few large meals. Large meals are difficult to digest and they will just cause more indigestion and bloating.
- Avoid drinking from a bottle or straw, don't gulp while drinking and limit your fluid intake during meals - you can make up for it between meals.
- Avoid chewing gum. You tend to take in a lot of air when chewing gum.
- You may want to avoid very fatty or fried foods. They don't cause wind, but they can make you feel more bloated because they slow down digestion.

Lifestyle

- Sit up while you're eating or drinking, even if it's just a small snack.
- Wear loose, comfortable clothing; avoid any tightness around your waist and belly.
- A brisk walk fifteen minutes after eating can help your sluggish digestive tract.
- Consider practicing yoga for relaxation and good breathing techniques to help relax your diaphragm. People tend to swallow more air when they're anxious and tense and digestion is impaired when you are stressed.

BLOCKED (CONGESTED) NOSE

Higher levels of oestrogen during pregnancy can contribute to swelling in the mucous membranes lining the nose and even cause you to make more mucous. What's more, the amount of blood in your body increases and your blood vessels expand during pregnancy, which can lead to swollen nasal membranes as well. You may even have occasional nosebleeds, particularly during the winter months. These symptoms often begin towards the end of the first trimester and may continue until a month after delivery.

THERAPIES AND TIPS for a blocked nose

Lifestyle

- Use a humidifier to moisten the air in your home. Sleep with a humidifier on in the bedroom to help ease congestion if it is keeping you awake at night.
- Drink plenty of fluids. This will help keep your nasal passages moist.
- Use steam; take a warm shower or bath before bedtime to help you breathe more easily while trying to fall asleep.
- Use saline drops to help moisten your nasal passages. You can find these at the drug store. Don't use medicated nose drops, sprays, or decongestants without first checking with your caregiver.
- There is a natural remedy referred to as a 'neti' pot or a rhino horn. A neti pot/rhino horn is a small stainless steel or ceramic pot that you can find online or in most health food stores. Most contain a conical tip that you insert into a nostril. You fill the neti pot/rhino horn with warm sea-salt water and flush each nostril with the solution. It works along the same lines as saline nasal drops, but it generally lasts longer and is much more effective because you also rinse out the sinuses. While it may take some getting used to, once you try a neti pot/rhino horn you may never want to try anything else!

- Try to avoid blowing your nose and if you do, blow it very gently. Blowing your nose hard can aggravate the membranes and lead to more stuffiness or nosebleeds.

Nutrition

Avoid eating any cow's milk product. Cows milk is a mucous forming food. If you are afraid that you aren't getting enough calcium don't worry, calcium is not easily absorbed from milk products and you would be better off eating the following foods for your calcium intake: goat's milk and cheese, salmon, sardines, mackerel, seaweed (especially kelp) sesame salt (gomasio), tahini (a paste made from sesame seeds) and dark leafy greens like broccoli, fresh parsley, watercress, cabbage, rocket leaves, turnip greens and pakchoi.

☑ Supplements

Probiotics (intestinal flora) can be taken as an adjunct treatment for sinusitis and congestion. Probiotics improve digestion and that often clears up the excess mucous formed by bad digestion. Take the recommended dosage suggested by the product you buy.

☯ Acupuncture

There are some good acupuncture points that help open up a blocked nose.

☛My experience: Acupuncture is excellent for relieving a blocked nose. You could have an un-blocked nose for as long as a week after visiting your acupuncturist.

When to consult your caregiver

If your congestion is not eased by any of the suggestions above, or if congestion is so bad that it keeps you from getting a good night's rest.

Talk to your caregiver before taking any type of over-the-counter cold remedies for a stuffy or runny nose.

BLOOD SUGAR DURING PREGNANCY

It is common for pregnant women to develop some loss of glucose tolerance during pregnancy. With an increase in circulating blood volume, the pancreas often has difficulty with the increased demands to supply insulin to help maintain proper blood sugar levels. It is therefore not uncommon for blood sugar levels to fluctuate during pregnancy.

Fifteen percent of all pregnant women will develop a condition known as gestational diabetes. This means that blood sugar levels are too high. This condition requires careful medical monitoring and diet control.

It is more common for women to suffer from a blood sugar level that drops too low during pregnancy. This is called hypoglycaemia.

Symptoms of hypoglycaemia:

- The occurrence a few times a day of excessive sweating, hunger and general weakness.
- Headaches.
- Feeling suddenly faint or dizzy.
- Fast heartbeat.
- Vision problems.
- Trembling and shakiness.
- Feeling sleepy or confused.
- Irritability and crankiness.
- Numbness or tingling around the mouth.

It is advisable to keep blood sugar levels within a safe range during pregnancy.

THERAPIES AND TIPS hypoglycaemia

Golden Tip

Research has shown that 500mcg Chromium Picolinate taken daily throughout pregnancy significantly reduces foetal and maternal problems related to blood sugar problems (hyperglycaemia and gestational diabetes.)

Nutrition

- Avoid sugar and foods high in sugar, during pregnancy sugar is rapidly absorbed into the blood and your body requires a larger release of insulin to maintain normal blood sugar levels. Check all packaging and if sugar appears near the top of the ingredient list of a product, you should avoid that product.
- Eat unsweetened breakfast cereals and breads without added sugars.
- Avoid pies, cakes, cookies, sweetened yoghurt, fruit drinks, sodas, candy, ice cream, syrup, brown sugar and corn syrup. Ingredients that end in "ose" contain sugars (e.g., sucrose, dextrose and glucose), should also be avoided. Although some fruit juices contain no added sugar, they still have lots of naturally occurring sugars that are readily absorbed into your blood stream. Therefore, limit your fruit juice intake if you have fluctuating blood sugar. It may be better to drink vegetable juices such as tomato juice or V-8.
- Whole fruit is a better choice than fruit juice, because it contains fibres, which will help slow the absorption of sugar. Be sure to avoid tinned fruit because it is generally preserved in syrup and contains little fibre.
- Vegetables are a wonderful snack. They are lower in sugar than fruit and once again they contain fibres.
- Concentrate on eating mostly complex carbohydrates, these include vegetables, whole-grain cereals and breads and whole grains such as brown rice and barley. Also, eat legumes, such as soybeans, black beans, lentils and chickpeas. The carbohydrates in these foods will supply you with plenty of energy, but require a longer time to digest and be absorbed into the blood stream, keeping your pancreas from being overloaded and your blood sugar level.
- Emphasize foods that are high in dietary fibre like fresh vegetables, beans and cereals. Fibre decreases the amount of

insulin your body needs to keep blood sugars within a normal range.

- Keep your diet low in saturated fats. Insulin becomes less efficient in a high-fat diet. Some fat is needed to help with the absorption of certain vitamins, and to provide the essential fatty acids necessary for foetal growth. However, you should avoid saturated fats like fatty meats, butter, cream, whole milk, full fat cheeses and foods such as crackers made with coconut, palm or palm kernel oil. Consume foods that contain unsaturated or mono-unsaturated fats such as fish and vegetable oils.
- Eat six small meals and healthy snacks throughout the day. By eating small meals and snacks that are evenly spaced you are more likely to keep your blood sugar level even.
- Be sure to include a bedtime snack that offers fibre, protein and complex carbohydrates. A good choice might be an apple and wheat-free crackers and a small bowl of live organic yoghurt.

***Example* of three meals and three snacks a day:**
Breakfast
One small glass of any of the following juice: orange, cranberry, berry or grapefruit – these fruits contain less fructose.
A bowl of oatmeal made with skim milk, rice milk or soymilk.
Two slices of whole-wheat (or wheat-free) toast with avocado salsa, hard goat's cheese or almond spread.

In between
Water and herbal tea, nuts (preferably raw.)

Morning snack
Organic live yoghurt with a grated apple and some sesame, sunflower and pumpkin seeds mixed in.

Lunch
Tuna salad with whole-wheat (or wheat-free) bread. Cranberry or vegetable juice.

Afternoon snack
Whole-grain crackers (or wheat-free) crackers with nut butter (not peanut) and a plum or apricot.

In between
Water and herbal tea, nuts (preferably raw) with raisins or rice crackers.

Dinner
Mixed salad, skinless chicken breast, a baked potato and steamed broccoli.
Fresh fruit, at east half an hour after dinner.
OR
Grilled mixed vegetables and roast chicken on a bed of brown rice with a green salad.
Baked apple.
OR
Couscous salad made with grilled mixed vegetables, avocado, cucumber, tomato and fresh coriander.
Fruit salad, at east half an hour after dinner.
Also see the "Recipes" chapter for more dinner recipes.

Bedtime snack
Some plain popcorn and a few squares of goat's cheese or a grated apple in a small bowl of live organic yoghurt and some whole-grain (or wheat-free) crackers.

☑ **Supplements**
Research has shown that 500mcg Chromium Picolinate taken daily throughout pregnancy significantly reduces the foetal and maternal problems related to blood sugar problems (hyperglycaemia and gestational diabetes.)

Lifestyle
Thirty minutes of daily aerobic exercise will help maintain a better blood sugar level.

When to consult your caregiver

Your caregiver should be aware at all times if you suspect that you are suffering from fluctuating blood sugar levels.

BONDING

Bonding with your baby begins during pregnancy. I encourage pregnant women to see themselves as mothers from the moment that they are pregnant. For some parents this becomes easier once they begin to feel the baby move. It has been proven that parents who are able to bond with their baby while it is still in the womb find it easier to bond with the baby once it is born.

Here are some tips to increase bonding with your baby during pregnancy:

- Give your baby a "working title", in other words refer to it by an intimate nickname that only you and your partner use to make it seem more real.
- You and your partner should stroke and caress your belly as often as possible.
- Create a moment around the same time each day to spend time "playing" with your baby. See if you can encourage a little kick or a prod as a response to what you are doing.
- Play your favourite music regularly especially if it makes you feel good. Your endorphins (feel good hormones) reach your baby via the placenta.
- Talk to your baby.

NOTE: Birth is a dialogue between mother and baby. It is important that you have good contact with your baby before birth to encourage this dialogue, which in turn could improve your chances of natural childbirth.

FATHER-NEWBORN BONDING

Most of the bonding research has focused on mother-infant bonding, with the father given only honorable mention. In recent years fathers, too, have been the subject of bonding research and have even merited a special term for the father-infant relationship at birth, namely, "engrossment." We used to talk about father involvement; now it's father engrossment, meaning involvement to a higher degree. Engrossment is not only what the father does for the baby like holding and comforting but also what the baby does for the father. Bonding with baby right after birth brings out sensitivity in dad.

Fathers are often portrayed as well meaning, but bumbling, when caring for newborns. Fathers are sometimes considered secondhand nurturers, nurturing the mother as she nurtures the baby. That's only half the story. Fathers have their own unique way of relating to babies, and babies thrive on this difference. Fathers will find that the baby will respond to his voice because she/he's heard it all along from within the uterus. In fact, studies on father bonding show that fathers who are given the opportunity and are encouraged to take an active part in caring for their newborns become just as nurturing as mothers. A father's nurturing responses may be less automatic and slower to unfold than a mother's, but fathers are capable of a strong bonding attachment to their infants during the newborn period.

BRAXTON HICKS CONTRACTIONS

A British doctor named John Braxton-Hicks first described the practicing action of the uterus preparing for labour some time in the late nineteenth century; this is why they carry his name. A Braxton Hicks is when the muscles of your uterus flex to strengthen themselves and (later on in the pregnancy) to gradually soften (or efface) the cervix in preparation for the actual birth. This spontaneous and irregular contracting of these muscles begins early on in pregnancy, but you will probably only become more aware of this contracting from about week 28. For some women they start as early as week 18.

Braxton Hicks contractions feel differently for each woman. Some find that they are not bothered by these contractions, while others feel very uncomfortable. Typically, Braxton Hicks contractions are described as causing more discomfort than pain. Some women experience Braxton Hicks as indigestion because the tightening of your uterus can cause your stomach to react.

A Braxton Hicks makes your abdomen feel rigid and hard because of the muscles that are tightening. This should only last for a few minutes (sometimes seconds). You may feel some discomfort in the centre of your belly, which then radiates downwards. These "practice contractions" are normally more of a sensation than actually painful, which differentiates them from false labour or actual labour. They generally become more frequent and more pronounced towards the end of the pregnancy.
Normal, healthy Braxton Hicks will be felt mostly in the evenings and at night. Unfortunately though sometimes Braxton Hicks come so frequently that you are uncomfortable most of the day and night if this is the case then you can try to relieve them slightly with the following advice.

THERAPIES AND TIPS for Braxton Hicks

Lifestyle

- Early or constant Braxton Hicks contractions can sometimes be brought on by too much exercise or exertion so it is important to rest as much as is needed.
- Stress can bring on Braxton Hicks so try to alleviate the stress that could be causing this.
- A full bladder can cause Braxton Hicks so make sure you empty your bladder when you feel the need. Make sure that your Braxton Hicks are not being caused by a bladder infection.

Nutrition

- If your Braxton Hicks contractions become too frequent and painful you could be lacking magnesium. Magnesium is important in the correct functioning of muscles and nerve impulses. Foods containing magnesium are: Bananas, oats, whole grains, meat, apricots, curry, cocoa, nuts (not roasted!) leafy green vegetables and dried apricots.

- Dehydration is often another cause of Braxton Hicks so it is important to keep drinking plenty of fluids.

☑ **Supplements**

Take a magnesium (oxide) supplement of 400mg per day or liquid magnesium (concentrated mineral drops) taken as recommended by the product you buy. Magnesium is best taken in the evening.

✿ **Bach Remedies**

Rescue Remedy can help to calm and relax you.

When to consult your caregiver

Braxton Hicks are sometimes caused by a bladder infection. If you are experiencing frequent and painful Braxton Hicks your caregiver should be told so that a bladder infection can be ruled out or detected.

If you are not yet 37 weeks and the Braxton Hicks contractions become regular and more painful or are accompanied by any type of discharge you should contact your caregiver immediately as you could be going into early labour.

☯ **Acupuncture**

Visiting an acupuncturist can help to de-stress you and thereby reduce your Braxton Hicks.

☛My experience: I have had good success with treating women who have extreme Braxton Hicks but I find that the effect of the treatment only helps for three to four days so I often need to treat these women every 3 to 4 days.

⃠ **Exceptions**

In subsequent pregnancies, Braxton Hicks tend to start a little earlier in the pregnancy. They can even begin as early as 15 weeks.

BREAKFAST – THE MOST IMPORTANT MEAL OF THE DAY

During pregnancy skipping breakfast altogether, or eating a breakfast of nothing but refined carbohydrates, is a disaster recipe for blood sugar imbalance, food cravings, nausea and fatigue. According to Dr Brewer and expert on high blood pressure during pregnancy, eating a protein-rich breakfast will drastically help you to avoid high blood pressure later on in pregnancy. Remember that this is a *protein-rich* breakfast, not a pure protein one, so you need to include some complex carbohydrates too.

A healthy protein-rich breakfast should keep you going for around 3 hours, at which time you can then eat an in-between-meals-snack in order to sustain your energy and blood sugar levels.

Protein-rich breakfast ideas

Fruit Smoothie
Two handfuls of any fruit, such as strawberries, blackberries, raspberries, plums, apricots, peaches, nectarines, or mangos with two tablespoons of organic live yoghurt – either cow's, sheep's or goat's. Topped with a tablespoon of seeds, such as linseeds, pumpkin seeds, sesame seeds or sunflower seeds.

Classic cereal
Four tablespoons of (unsweetened) muesli, bran flakes or barley flakes plus two tablespoons of mixed raw nuts, such as Brazil nuts, pecans, walnuts, hazelnuts and almonds then cover with either cow's milk, goat's milk, sheep's milk unsweetened rice milk or unsweetened soya milk (although you should limit your use of soya milk.)

Nut butter on toast
Two to three slices of toast, made from pumpernickel, whole meal or rye bread spread with sugar-free nut butter: either cashew, mixed nuts or almond butter (no peanut!)

Cheese or meat with bread

Two to three slices or bread, such as rye, whole meal or pumpernickel topped with a few slices of any hard cheese, such as cheddar or hard goats' cheese or a few slices of lean meat, such as chicken or turkey.

Eggs with toast or crackers

Two eggs poached, scrambled or boiled (make sure that the eggs are well done.) with two thick slices of toast, made from pumpernickel, whole meal or rye bread or a couple of crisp-breads, oatcakes or rice cakes – if you use mayonnaise make sure it is shop bought and not homemade due to the use of raw eggs in homemade.

BREASTFEEDING PREPARATION

Breast milk is the best food you can offer your new baby because each mother uniquely and naturally produces breast milk for her own baby. Breast milk contains antibodies and other immune factors and has the right amount of nutrients to suit your baby's first nutritional needs. It is also gentler on your baby's digestive system, so there's less chance of constipation, diarrhoea and allergies. Early breastfeeding nurtures maternal feelings and feelings of attachment between a mother and her baby.

Although many women realize all these benefits of breastfeeding it doesn't mean that to some mothers breastfeeding won't feel strange, even awkward at first. And, more likely than not, most mothers encounter a few bumps, if not major roadblocks, on the road to feeding their baby. You cannot prepare your baby but you can prepare yourself for breastfeeding.

Physical Preparation

Before your baby arrives, and maybe even before you have made the decision to breast-feed, your body has been preparing to feed your child. In fact, your body starts preparing the minute you get pregnant. You may have noticed that your nipples are getting darker and your breasts appear to be getting bigger. Your breasts are enlarging as your milk-producing cells multiply and your milk-carrying ducts develop. In addition, your body is storing extra fat to provide excess energy that you'll need for lactation.

Beginning to breast-feed

In a perfect world, you might be feeding within 10 to 60 minutes after you have given birth. Sometimes, it just doesn't work that way. If you're completely exhausted from delivery, groggy from medication, in pain from cramping or there were delivery complications, it's likely that your first breastfeeding session will be delayed. Never fear, although breastfeeding is recommended as soon as possible after birth, your ability to nurse your child won't be harmed if the first feeding is delayed a while. The bond between a mother and child starts during the pregnancy, but only fully develops over time. You'll have plenty of time after you or your baby have recovered, to cuddle, nurture, and feed your child, even if breastfeeding doesn't start as soon or go as smoothly as you had expected.

The First Few Days

For first few days after birth, your breasts will be soft to touch as the blood supply increases, and milk-producing cells start to function efficiently. Eventually, your breasts will become firmer. When you first start feeding, your breasts won't actually be producing milk, they'll first produce a substance called *colostrum,* a rich, yet, thin-appearing, orange-yellow substance that contains protein, salt, disease-fighting antibodies, and other important nutrients.

What to Expect

Once your baby begins sucking at your nipples, your breasts will receive a signal to make milk and increase the flow to the nipple. This is called *the letdown reflex*. In the very beginning, newborns eat little per feed, however, they feed frequently - usually every 2 hours. By the third or fourth day of feeding/nursing your breasts will begin to produce both colostrum and milk and they will feel fuller. By this time your baby will have increased his or her intake per feed.

You may feel cramping in your uterus the first few days each time you nurse. This is because the hormones that stimulate your milk flow also cause uterine contractions, helping your uterus to return to its normal size and position - yet another advantage to breastfeeding. In addition, your breasts may feel painful because they are engorged or overly full of milk. Some women use their hands or a breast pump to express a little milk from their breasts to relieve this pressure.

Emotional Preparation

Some babies "latch on and catch on" right away, with others it takes more time and patience and some infants never really get the hang of breastfeeding. This can be because they have an under-developed sucking reflex, or the shape of their mouth or jaw makes it hard for them to latch on to your breast, and sometimes, infants simply don't show much interest in feeding at the breast. Some mothers have "difficult" nipples for the baby to latch onto.

Don't panic if breastfeeding doesn't go smoothly at first. It can take several days before your baby latches on properly and feeds well. These are days that leave many new mothers feeling frustrated and uncertain of themselves. Here are some suggestions that may make those first few days a little easier.

Believe you can do it. Women have been breastfeeding successfully since the beginning of time, even though many have experienced the challenges mentioned earlier. So there's every reason to expect that you will also succeed. Your body is set up to provide all the nutrition your baby needs and your baby is born with the reflexes needed to latch on and get that nutrition from you.

Granted, it may take some practice before nursing becomes second nature to both of you and it may not always feel pleasant and rewarding, but hang in there. Many women before you that have breast-fed their baby have experienced the frustrations that you may experience and survived. Always talk to your lactation coach or nurse if needed.

Try to relax. Trust your body. Its been preparing for about nine months now and is ready to begin milk production once your baby is born, although remember that it usually takes three or four days for your milk to come in.

Here are a few practical suggestions to help you relax and take care of yourself when you want to nurse your baby:

- Find a quiet corner or room where you won't be disturbed.
- If possible, especially at first, have someone (husband, partner, relative, friend) take care of things such as phone calls, answering the door, etc., while you are breastfeeding.
- Take long, slow, deep breaths to help you relax during feeding.
- Drink a lot of water or breastfeeding herbal tea to help give your body extra fluids to produce breast milk.
- Sit in a comfortable chair with good support for your back and arms.
- Listen to soothing music.
- Wear loose clothing.
- Make contact, cuddle and caress your baby with your hands, eyes and voice.
- Take cues from your baby. Your baby will both let you know when he or she is hungry and when he or she is full. Your baby will also teach you cues so your body learns when to start and stop producing milk. Usually, if a baby is hungry, he or she will cry, nuzzle, or make sucking motions and fuss. Babies are also generally happy and content when they've finished nursing. Fussiness during feeding can be a sign that the baby is still hungry or has gas. Some babies are fussy about having a dirty diaper.
- Learn to calm your baby down before starting a feeding. Although you can use the clock as a general guideline of when to feed the baby - most babies eat every two to three hours-, pay more attention to your baby's signals to help determine when its time to eat and try to offer your baby the breast before he/she is distressed and crying. Granted, in the beginning, these signals can be tough to figure out and trying to figure out what a fussy baby wants can be one of the most frustrating experiences of parenting.
- Burp your baby several times while nursing because babies suck in air as well as milk. Burping brings up the excess air.

Sometimes a baby who is fussy while nursing may just need to burp.

- Find a breastfeeding class that you can attend at the end of pregnancy. Don't wait until you are already breastfeeding!

The La Leche League is a not-for-profit organization that offers breastfeeding classes and support worldwide. Their mission is to help mothers worldwide to breastfeed through mother-to-mother support, education, information and encouragement. They promote a better understanding of breastfeeding as an important element in the healthy development of the baby and mother.

BREASTS

Blood flow to your breasts increases very early on in pregnancy because they are already beginning to make milk producing glands and ducts. You may notice a significant increase in size in the first few weeks, which is often accompanied by tenderness. Your breasts may feel itchy as the skin stretches and you may even develop stretch marks on them.

You may be able to see veins under the skin of your breasts and you may find that your nipples are getting bigger and darker. After the first few months, your areola, the pigmented circles around your nipples, will also be bigger and darker.
You may not have noticed the little bumps on your areolas before, they are small oil-producing glands called Montgomery's tubercles, which become much more pronounced during pregnancy. Your breasts are going through these changes in preparation for nursing your baby.
Around your third month of pregnancy your breasts start producing colostrum the special milk your baby will get when she/he first starts nursing. During the last few months of pregnancy you may even begin to leak a small amount of this thick yellowish substance.
For increased comfort you may need to buy new, bigger and better fitting bras during pregnancy.

⃠ Exceptions

In a second or subsequent pregnancy some women find that they secrete a little milk or colostrum throughout their pregnancy.

BREATHING AND RELAXING EXERCISES FOR DURING LABOUR

It is important to read through the following information before going into labour so that you can practice the techniques during the last few months of pregnancy. It is best to practice with your birthing partner so that he/she can guide and remind you of the techniques during your labour.

STAGE 1 - latent phase.

What you could do *between* contractions to ensure total relaxation:

During the latent stage of labour you will most probably feel elated and excited to be going into labour. The knowledge that you will soon be holding your baby in your arms can be euphoric. Don't suppress this feeling but at the same time do try to encourage your body to be as relaxed as possible. The more relaxed you are the better your birth will go.

Walking, showering, sitting on a birthing ball, being on hands and knees, standing and generally moving around during the first stage has a positive effect on labour. It increases oxygen flow to the baby, helps with rotation of the baby and uses gravity to encourage the baby to move downward into the pelvis. Although you will be fairly active doing any of the above it is still important to try and relax the body and mind in between contractions. The following relaxation technique can be used.

If you are in a stationary position (birthing ball, hands & knees etc):

Take long deep breaths while doing this exercise by breathing in through your nose and out through an open, slack mouth.

Open your eyes wide then let them fall closed, next relax the muscles on your forehead, around your eyes, cheeks, jaw and mouth then move downward relaxing the muscles of your neck and throat. Do this until all the muscles in your face and neck are slack and relaxed. Drop your shoulders and then relax your arms and lastly relax your hands and fingers.

Now move down your body relaxing your chest, your abdomen, your cervix, vagina, anus and finally your legs and feet. Feel your whole body turn to a soft, jelly-like consistency.

If you are walking around: Walk slowly and calmly taking deep breaths and count to ten while inhaling and then count to ten again when exhaling. Even though you have your eyes open ask your birthing partner to walk beside you to keep you from walking into things so that you be totally relaxed; just breathing and counting.

Alternative to the counting: Take a deep breath in through your nose and while breathing out through your mouth you say (either out loud or in your head): AAA, BBB, CCC, DDD, EEE, FFF, GGG, HHH etc…

Saying something like the alphabet or counting needs no concentration and it works like a meditation or a mantra, which can quiet (empty) the mind.

STAGE 1 - Active phase & transition – *during* contractions:

Once the contractions become stronger and closer together it is important that you try to breathe deeply during each contraction. Breathing gets oxygen to both you and the baby and by controlling your breathing you can help your body to relax and allow the contractions to do their work – if you tense your abdomen and cervix and tighten your vagina or anus the labour will be more painful and longer.

Practicing slow, deep breathing will not only give you confidence about your ability to stay calm and cope during labour, it will also help your body to relax. A tense mother is a tense cervix and this will increase both the pain and the length of your labour.

As soon as a contraction begins you should take a long, deep breath in through your nose while keeping your shoulders, your arms and your hands as relaxed as possible. You should exhale in a long, slow breath

through your open, slack mouth. Try to imagine your out-breath going down towards your baby and out via the cervix (this is just a visualisation because of course your exhale is obviously leaving via your mouth.) Imagine your breath bringing oxygen to your baby and to your uterine muscles and then imagine it softening and opening your entire pelvic region. Sometimes making a low sound as you breathe out can help direct the energy down and outwards.
Try to repeat these slow deep breaths until the contraction has passed. When a contraction has ended (also as an indication for those around you that the contraction has ended) you take a deep breath and let it "explode" out through your mouth. Then breathe quietly and calmly relaxing your face, shoulders, arms, hands, abdomen, back and legs until the next contraction. Relax, no talking, no organising and discussing **between** contractions, try to withdraw into your own world as much as possible. Let your birthing partner do all the thinking!

Remember to tackle each contraction as it comes and that each contraction has a purpose. Each contraction does its work (opening your cervix) then goes away. It does NOT come back!
Try to stay calm and trust in your body. The more you relax between contractions the more oxytocin and endorphins your body will produce. Endorphins are your body's-own morphine and they help you to cope with the pain. Getting stressed, panicking or trying to take control will make your body produce more adrenaline. Adrenaline will suppress your body's ability to make endorphins. This will make it more difficult for you to cope with the contractions and it could slow contractions because adrenaline also suppresses the production of the hormone, oxytocin, which stimulates contractions.
If the contractions are not getting stronger or are becoming irregular or fading then you need to become more active (this means physically not mentally.) Move around more, take a shower or walk up and down the stairs or just stay upright. Nipple stimulation can also increase the intensity and efficiency of contractions.

Once the contractions become stronger the long slow breathing may become more difficult. You could try taking a deep breath in through your nose when a contraction starts and then breath it out in short puffs through your mouth. Blowing raspberries on an out-breath helps to relax the mouth, which in turn relaxes the cervix.

Transition

The last part of active labour when your cervix dilates from around seven or eight centimeters to a full ten centimeters is called the transition period because it marks the transition to the second stage of labour. This is the most intense part of labour. Contractions are usually very strong, coming about every one to two-and-a-half minutes and lasting a minute or more. During transition you may find yourself shaking and shivering and some women feel nauseated at this stage. During transition most women discover a breathing technique (often accompanied with much noise!) that works for them. Just try to remember to keep any noise you make low and guttural.

By the time your cervix is fully dilated and transition is over, your baby has usually descended somewhat into your pelvis. This is when you might begin to feel rectal pressure - as if you have to move your bowels. Some women begin to bear down spontaneously - to push - and may even start making deep grunting sounds at this point. There's often a little bloody discharge.

Additional information

Some babies descend earlier and the mom feels the urge to push before she's fully dilated. And some babies don't descend significantly until later, in which case the mom may reach full dilation without feeling any rectal pressure. It's different for every woman and every birth.

Transition can last anywhere from a few minutes to a few hours. It is much more likely to be faster if you've already had a vaginal delivery.

STAGE - 2 the pushing phase & STAGE - 3 delivery of the placenta.

Your caregiver will guide you through stage 2 and 3.

BREATHLESSNESS

During pregnancy, the increased levels of the hormone progesterone forces you to breathe more often. This can feel like shortness of breath but you actually have a larger lung capacity to allow your blood to carry larger quantities of oxygen to your baby.
Around the 31st week of pregnancy the uterus begins to press on the diaphragm - the flat muscle that moves up and down when you breathe - making it hard for your lungs to fully expand. This may cause more shallow breathing and you may feel short of breath.
During the last few weeks of pregnancy this feeling may lessen slightly when your baby moves deeper into the pelvis to prepare for birth.

TIPS AND THERAPIES for breathlessness

Lifestyle

- Sitting up straight will allow your lungs more room to expand.
- Try doing some deep breathing exercises a few times a day. Breathe in deeply through your nose, filling as much of your lungs as possible and allowing your abdomen to expand, hold your breath for a few counts and then breathe out slowly through your mouth, slightly pursing your lips to allow the air to escape slowly.
- Slow down! When you move more slowly, you lessen the work of your heart and lungs.
- If you are bothered by breathlessness at night, sleep propped up on some pillows to lessen the pressure on your lungs.

When to consult your caregiver:

It is normal to feel a mild breathlessness during pregnancy. Immediately contact your caregiver if your breathlessness becomes severe or comes on very suddenly and also if you are feeling dizzy or faint or if your breathlessness is accompanied by chest pain.

BREECH

Three to four weeks before the due date, most babies will move into a head down position. If this does not happen and either your baby's buttocks or feet or both are facing downward it is called a breech presentation. Breech presentation occurs in about 3% of all pregnancies.

Your caregiver will palpate (feel) your baby through your belly around 35 weeks to determine if your baby is lying head down. Sometimes an ultrasound may be necessary to confirm the baby's position.

If your baby is breech

Your main problem will be the limited time you have in which to consider your options. Breech babies are usually only diagnosed in the last weeks of pregnancy and there is sometimes little time to organise consultations or second opinions. Some caregivers will try to perform an external cephalic version (ECV.) An ECV is an attempt to turn the baby from the outside.

External cephalic version - EVC

Research indicates that manually massaging the baby into a better position is often successful for turning breech babies if done around 36 to 37 weeks. You will need to find a caregiver skilled in this procedure, as there is always a very slight risk that the cord will become entangled or the placenta starts to separate as the baby is turned. External cephalic version is therefore generally done in a hospital, where a Caesarean section is available in the unlikely event of such an emergency.

What can you do?

The breech tilt exercise

If the baby settles (engages) into the pelvis it will be difficult for the baby to turn. This exercise, done 3 times each day for 15 minutes discourages the baby from settling into the pelvis in a breech position.

Stop wearing a support belt or trousers. Give your baby plenty of room to turn.

Lie on your back, with your bottom against a wall with feet high up on the wall. You need to lift your hips higher than your shoulders so place some pillows or a firmly rolled towel under your bottom.
An alternative is to adopt a "knee-chest" position on hands and knees, with your bottom high in the air and your head and chest on the floor.
Visualising your baby turning while doing the exercises could help.
OR
Raise hips 30cm off the floor using large, solid pillows three times daily for 10-15 minutes each time. This is best done on an empty stomach and at a time when your baby is active. Visualize your baby turning and try not to tense your body, especially in the abdominal area.

☯ Acupuncture

Using moxibustion to encourage the baby to turn by itself

Acupuncturists have used Moxibustion for centuries to turn breech babies in China. It involves the use of a cigar-like herbal stick called moxa. The heat from burning moxa sticks is applied to two points on the ends of the small toes. It stimulates the baby's movements and encourages it to turn.
You need to visit the acupuncturist once so that they can show you how the technique is done then you can do it at home yourself. This simple treatment is best done just before bed, starting at 34 to 36 weeks.
It could take the baby some time to turn so it often happens at night. The moxa is done every evening for anything up to 3 weeks or until the baby turns.
A randomised controlled trial indicates that at approximately 70% of breech babies will turn using this method.
If, after trying the moxibustion and/or external cephalic version, the baby does not move into a head down position, there may be a good reason why the baby prefers to remain in the breech position, perhaps the placenta is positioned low down limiting the space for the baby's head in the lower part of the uterus or the uterus itself is shaped unusually and is restricting the baby's movements. If the baby does not turn easily, then it must be assumed that the baby needs to

stay where it is, and options for the birth (either by Caesarean or vaginally) will need to be considered.

☛ **My experience**: I have had very good results in the practice using moxa to turn breech babies. I also advice my pregnant women who have decided to attempt an external cephalic version (ECV) to use moxa for a week before the ECV because using the moxa often makes it easier to turn the baby.

Chiropractic Care

The late Larry Webster, D.C., of the International Chiropractic Pediatric Association, developed a technique, which enabled chiropractors to release stress on the pregnant woman's pelvis and cause relaxation to the uterus and surrounding ligaments. The relaxed uterus would make it easier for a breech baby to turn naturally. The technique is known as the Webster Breech Technique.

The Journal of Manipulative and Physiological Therapeutics reported in the July/August 2002 issue that 82% of chiropractors using the Webster Technique reported success. Further, the results from the study suggest that it may be beneficial to perform the Webster Technique as prevention for breech from 32 weeks.

Using Music

We know that babies can hear sounds outside the womb so many women have used music or taped recordings of their voice to try to get their baby to move towards the noise! Headphones placed on the lower part of your abdomen, playing either music or your voice, can encouraged your baby to move towards the sounds and so out of a breech position.

✜ Homeopathy

Pulsatilla is commonly given to turn a breech baby around 34 to 36 weeks. Always take the dosage indicated on the packaging.

Giving birth to a breech baby

Most women will be advised to have a Caesarean section for the birth of their breech baby, especially if it is their first child. Although Caesarean section carries its own risks and requires time to recover from the surgery afterwards, this may be the only option available, especially if your caregiver has little or no experience of vaginal breech birth.

Your chances of a safe vaginal birth will be increased if this is not your first baby, you have a small baby, you have given birth vaginally to a breech baby before, you labour without an epidural or an induction and you remain upright and mobile during the labour and birth. A caregiver who is familiar with breech birth and confident of their practice will also make this option much more successful.

If you decide to accept a Caesarean birth, it is advisable to wait until labour begins before the surgery is performed, as this will eliminate the risk of the baby being born too early and give the baby the benefits of the labour contractions, which are important for the final maturation of the baby's lungs in readiness for breathing on its own.

C

CAFFEINE

Caffeine is a stimulant and a diuretic. Since caffeine is a stimulant, it increases blood pressure and heart rate, both of which are not recommended during pregnancy. Caffeine also increases the frequency of urination. This causes reduction in your body fluid levels and can lead to both dehydration and oedema (water retention.) Caffeine is highly water-soluble so it easily crosses the placenta to your baby. Your baby's metabolism is still maturing and it cannot fully metabolize the caffeine. Any amount of caffeine can cause changes in your baby's sleep pattern or normal movement pattern in the later stages of pregnancy. Remember, because caffeine is a stimulant it can keep both you and your baby awake.

If you are a heavy coffee drinker try to cut down to one cup of coffee a day. If possible it is better for both you and your baby if you stop drinking caffeinated coffee and tea.

CALCIUM

Calcium is very important during pregnancy. Lack of adequate calcium during pregnancy is associated with muscle cramps, backache, high blood pressure, intense labour pain and afterbirth pains, pelvic pain, teeth problems and pre-eclampsia.

Your developing baby needs calcium to grow strong bones and teeth, a healthy heart, nerves and muscles, and to develop normal heart rhythm and blood clotting abilities. If you don't get enough calcium in your diet, your baby will leach it from your bones, which may cause problems to you during pregnancy and impair your health later on in life.

Calcium absorption is influenced by exercise, stress, acidity during digestion, availability of vitamin A, C, D and the availability of magnesium and phosphorous.

The best food sources of calcium are fish and dairy products, but there is controversy about the body's ability to assimilate calcium from pasteurized, homogenized milk. My preferred food sources include goat's milk and goat's cheese, salmon, sardines, mackerel, seaweed (especially kelp) sesame salt (gomasio), tahini (a paste made from sesame seeds) and dark leafy greens like broccoli, fresh parsley, watercress, cabbage, rocket leaves, turnip greens and pak-choi.
Fruits like dates, figs, raisins, prunes, papaya and elder berries are also sources of calcium.
Vitamin D (fish oil, see essential fatty acids) and magnesium are necessary to absorb calcium so make sure you get all three.
Some commercially prepared foods have added calcium. For example, there are now some brands of orange juices, cereals and tofu with added calcium.
Your body is also able to absorb calcium from Raspberry leaf and Nettle tea because they contain both calcium plus high levels of vitamins A and C and phosphorous.
Foods like spinach, chocolate, rhubarb and brewer's yeast are thought to interfere with the absorption of calcium and should be avoided.
A good calcium supplement could be taken during pregnancy and breastfeeding. Make sure it is a calcium carbonate supplement that includes magnesium. Take 200mg to 400mg a day.

CANDIDIASIS (CANDIDA)

Candida is a simple form of yeast that lives in harmony with the rest of our intestinal flora (a term used to describe the host of bacterial cultures living in the intestine.) The Candida is seen as a "weed", necessary in the fine balance of the intestinal environment and as long as our immune system is strong it stays the under-dog. When Candida rages out of control it overthrows the "friendly" intestinal flora and migrates from the colon to various other tissue in the body causing many different symptoms, both physical and mental.

Certain situations can trigger Candida overgrowth

- High blood sugar.
- The use of antibiotics.
- Pregnancy – some women are prone to Candida and pregnancy can then be a trigger due to the build up of mucous that occurs in the cervix and the high levels of oestrogen and progesterone, which make the mucous membranes softer and wetter during pregnancy.
- Stress, both emotionally and physically.
- A compromised immune system.

Symptoms of Candidiasis

There are many symptoms of Candida overgrowth in the body. During pregnancy the most important include:

- A vaginal infection with a red and irritated vulva and a white, cottage cheese-like discharge.
- Itching around the vagina.
- Chronic inflammation and irritation of the eyes.
- Extreme lethargy/tiredness.
- Digestive problems: constipation, diarrhoea, gas, bloating.
- Headaches.
- Athletes foot – yeast infection either on the feet or under the toenails.
- Lactose intolerance.
- Dry, itchy skin.
- Rectal itching.

- Sinus problems.
- Urinary tract infections.
- Pain during sexual intercourse.

THERAPIES AND TIPS for Candida

Golden Tip

- The most effective way to fight Candida is by restoring the amount of "friendly" intestinal bacteria (flora) in your body. You do this by taking Probiotics. Probiotics (are also known as the friendly intestinal bacteria/flora) give your intestine a boost to help restore the bacteria (flora) and thereby suppress the bad bacteria.
- Eating just one cup of live organic yoghurt helps as a backup after you have finished taking a course of Probiotics. Live yoghurt contains the friendly intestinal bacteria (flora) *Lactobacillus acidophilus,* better known as acidophilus. It is used to 'ferment' milk into yoghurt.
- Make a diluted douche with three parts organic apple cider vinegar and one part of warm water and "rinse" your vagina with it three times a day.

Nutrition

Candida is an organism. It has to eat to survive. Once Candida has established itself it sees to it that you feed it, and it does this by creating a craving for sugar and yeast in any form. You need to literally starve the Candida.

- **Avoid** the following foods: Refined carbohydrates like white flour products, cookies, cakes, refined sugars, marmite/ vegemite, brewer's yeast, milk and cheese (milk contains a lot of sugars in the form of lactose) and mushrooms.
- Eat garlic for its anti-bacterial properties. Odourless garlic tablets are also available but they must contain allicin to be effective.
- Eat yeast-free (sourdough) bread and avoid any stock cubes that contain yeast.

- **Increase** the intake of fresh vegetables especially those that contain Vitamin A: all yellow and orange veggies, broccoli, spinach, Brussels sprouts and dark green leafy vegetables AND Vitamin C: asparagus, peas, sprouts, broccoli, cauliflower, tomatoes, paprika and cranberry juice.
- Eat detoxifying foods like carrots (but not too many as they also contain a lot of sugar!), celery and parsley and drink green tea.
- Make fresh carrot and ginger juice to start your day!
- Eat a varied diet, which includes whole-wheat or wheat-free sourdough bread, fresh vegetables, pulses, free-range chicken, fish, seeds and nuts, brown rice, barley, quinoa, bulgar, avocado and olive oil. You can introduce dried and fresh fruit again after the first month.
- Although coconut is sweet it contains a substance called capriylic-acid, which aids the healing of the intestinal walls which the Candida has damaged so it can be eaten for its healing properties.
- Because of the imbalance in your intestine it is important to chew your food well to aid absorption.
- Take a pregnancy multi vitamin supplement to support your immune system.

The good news is that Candida has a difficult time proliferating in a healthy body so try to boost your immune system by eating a healthy balanced diet, avoiding sugars & yeast and take Probiotics.

♣ Phytotherapy/herbs

For vaginal Candidiasis use a tea tree spray locally twice a day.

Lifestyle

- If you are using panty-liners make sure they are cotton.
- Make sure your underwear is cotton. Avoid nylon and polyester, especially pantyhose.

Homeopathy

- Kali Muriaticum: is a tissue salt that is known as a blood conditioner. It is used to treat any thick white or yellow mucous excretions in the body. Always take the dosage indicated on the packaging.
- You can take Homeopathic Candida for relief from itching, burning and other symptoms associated with Candida yeast infections. For more information see the "Products" chapter.

Additional information

If your Candida is localized to your perineum, anus and vagina you could try having a Brazilian wax. This removes all your pubic hair around your perineum and anus and has been known to reduce Candida drastically in that area.

Warning!

Women are told to apply live yoghurt locally either inserted on a tampon or smeared on and in the vagina. Leaving yoghurt in the vagina for a few hours could result in the formation of Listeriosis. Listeria is bacteria that can cross the placenta, which could result in a miscarriage or premature birth.

When to consult your caregiver:

If you suspect that you have Candidiasis then you should let your caregiver know. He/she might need to give you a course of antifungal pessaries or creams if you are close to your due date to help get rid of the symptoms before you give birth.

CAREGIVER

Your caregiver during pregnancy will either be a midwife or an obstetrician gynaecologist (OBGYN.)

Your caregiver should be an important part of your support system and a trusted source of information throughout your pregnancy.

How to find a caregiver

Ask family and friends for recommendations.

Consult with your regular doctor and other medical professionals about possible caregivers in your area.

Contact the hospital or birthing centre that you would prefer and find out who its maternity caregivers are.

As you study your options, consider these questions

- Is the caregivers' office a convenient distance from your home or work?
- Can the caregiver deliver your baby in the place you want to give birth, for instance at a particular hospital, at home or in a birthing centre?
- Does the caregiver work in a solo or group practice? If it is a group practice, can you usually see your chosen caregiver or will you see all members of the group?
- Who will replace your caregiver if he or she isn't available when your labour begins?
- How much do the caregivers' services cost and does your insurance company cover this cost?
- What level of expertise does your pregnancy require and will your caregiver meet that need?

CARPAL TUNNEL SYNDROME (CTS)

The carpal tunnel is a bony canal formed by the wrist bones and a ligament in the wrist. Swelling and fluid retention that is so common during pregnancy can increase the pressure in this relatively narrow and inflexible space, compressing the median nerve that runs through it. Pressure on this nerve causes the following symptoms:

- Tingling or numbness in part of the hand, thumb, index, middle or ring fingers.
- Sharp pains that shoot from the wrist up the arm.
- Burning sensations in the fingers.
- Morning stiffness and cramping of hands.

- Thumb weakness.
- Frequently dropping objects.
- Waking at night with hand pain and numbness.
- Numbness in the whole hand.

THERAPIES AND TIPS for CTS

Lifestyle

- Sleep with your hand and arm propped up with a pillow or two.
- Try stabilizing your wrist in a neutral (straight) position with a splint. This position allows the carpal tunnel to be less compressed.
- Avoid sleeping on your hands. If you wake up with pain, try gently shaking your hands until the pain or numbness reduces.
- If possible, avoid jobs requiring forceful, repetitive hand movements, although they may not have caused your carpal tunnel, they can make your symptoms worse.

Nutrition

- Reduce or eliminate the foods in your diet that promote inflammation like saturated fats and fried foods.
- Incorporate foods containing Omega 3 into your diet, they can reduce inflammation.
- Turmeric, ginger and Bromelain (found in pineapple) are known to reduce inflammation.

☑ **Supplements**

- Riboflavin (Vitamin B2) can be helpful for reducing numbness and tingling and support the nervous system. Take 50mg a day
- Vitamin B6 can also reduce numbness and tingling. Take 50mg a day
- Omega-3 fatty acids are essential for reducing inflammation. Take 1,500 to 3,000 mg a day.
- Taking a plant enzyme containing Bromelain can reduce the inflammation

✣ Homeopathy
Apis mellifica for joints that are red, hot, or swollen. Take the recommended dosage suggested by the product you buy, or consult a homeopath.
Arnica montana for soreness; is especially effective if applied topically (in a gel or cream.)

☯ Acupuncture
Acupuncture sometimes works for carpal tunnel syndrome with regular sessions.
☛My experience: I have not had much success with CTS.

When to consult your caregiver
Consult your caregiver if the pain and numbness interfere with your sleep or daily routine and before taking any pain medications. Your caregiver may suggest wearing a wrist splint or hand brace. If your symptoms are constant and severe (constant numbness, muscle weakness, or loss of sensation), you may need to see an orthopaedist for treatment.

Carpal tunnel syndrome symptoms usually disappear, along with the swelling, after delivery. If pain persists after your baby is born, however, you need to mention it to your postpartum healthcare provider so they can refer you to an orthopaedist if necessary.

CERVICAL EXAMINATION

During labour your caregiver will be looking for signs that your contractions have caused changes in your cervix. These signs include position of cervix, effacement, dilation, station of your baby and sometimes the position of your baby.
Before labour begins, your cervix aims into your vaginal canal at an angle that makes it point toward the back (posterior). One sign of progress is that your cervix has become anterior, meaning that it's position has realigned to the front. This is generally a change that

happens a few weeks or days before labour and sometimes in second or subsequent pregnancies, early on in labour.
Dilation and effacement work together to open your cervix allowing your baby to move down and into your vagina enabling it to be born. During pregnancy your cervix lengthens and thickens to protect your baby inside the womb. During labour, your cervix softens and shortens to allow for birth. Effacement refers to the thickness or thinness of your cervix. Effacement is measured by percentage, with 0% being a thick and hard cervix and 100% being a very soft thin cervix that is “gone.”
During labour, your cervix opens wider to allow your baby to pass through. Dilation refers to how big the opening of your cervix is and is measured from 0 (closed cervix) to 10 (fully opened cervix). A cervix will need to efface before it will have any great progress in dilating.
The station of a baby refers to the progress of the head through the pelvis. Your caregiver will try to estimate where your baby’s head is in relation to the ischial spines of your pelvis (the narrowest part). Before your baby’s head reaches the ischial spines, the station is given in negative numbers for example -1. At the ischial spines the station is measured as 0. After the top of your baby’s head has passed through the area of the spines, the station is given in positive numbers for example +1.
Caregivers will also use a cervical exam to confirm the position of your baby in your pelvis. By feeling the position of the bones on the top of your baby’s head, the caregiver can determine which direction your baby is facing (to the front, back or leaning to a side).

CERVIX

Your cervix is the actual entrance to the uterus. It is the lower end of your uterus and the upper end of your vagina. During the last few weeks of pregnancy the cervix ripens by softening and shortening in preparation for childbirth. During labour your cervix dilates (opens) to allow your baby to pass down and into the vagina for birth.

CAESAREAN DELIVERY (C-SECTION)

Caesarean delivery remains one of medicine's most important and often lifesaving operations. However, a planned Caesarean delivery without a medical reason (indication) has not been proven to reduce any risk to either mother or baby.
Valid reasons for Caesarean delivery i.e.: when delivery is necessary but labour cannot be induced for medical reasons.

- When the baby's size or presentation precludes vaginal birth.
- In some multiple pregnancy (twins or triplets or more) cases..
- If the placenta is blocking the exit of the uterus (placenta previa.)
- If the umbilical cord falls into the birth canal ahead of the baby's head or other parts of the baby's body, this is called a prolapsed umbilical cord.
- If there is a history of uterine surgery or abnormalities.
- When labour fails to progress after 24 hours of contractions and/or two hours of pushing.
- Sometimes when diabetes mellitus or hypertension threaten the baby's welfare.
- If labour induction fails.
- When anatomical problems of the uterus or birth canal prevent successful vaginal delivery.
- Maternal or foetal emergencies.

Maternal or foetal emergencies necessitating immediate delivery include:

- Untimely separation of the placenta from the uterus.
- Bleeding from placenta previa.
- Prolapse of the umbilical cord.
- An active vaginal infection such as herpes or a life threatening bacterial infection.
- Any sign that the baby is in danger.

More than one-fifth of all births are by C-section, and roughly one-fifth of all Caesarean deliveries are prompted by an emergency condition.

Caesarean deliveries are classified by the type and location of uterine incision. The two most common incisions are a vertical cut in the upper portion of the uterus, often called a "classic" incision and the transverse, or "Kerr" incision in the lower portion of the uterus. The transverse is the preferred incision.
Although a variety of anaesthetic techniques are used, an epidural block is often the anaesthesia of choice for a Caesarean delivery. During a particularly difficult or emergency Caesarean, when there's no time to wait for an epidural aesthetic to take effect, the doctor will use general anaesthesia. Though it can slightly increase additional risks to the mother, the value of the surgery usually outweighs the risks of anaesthesia. In an emergency Caesarean delivery, the baby is usually not effected by the anaesthesia because delivery often takes place before the anaesthesia has had time to cross the placenta.

How a C-section is generally performed
Prior to surgery you will probably need a catheter to remove urine from your bladder during the operation and you will likely be given an intravenous (IV) line to provide you with additional fluid. If you have an epidural a drape will be placed so that you cannot see the procedure. Your birthing partner will sit near your head and keep you company. (If the doctor decides that you need to have general anaesthesia, your partner will be asked to wait outside.)
As the Caesarean delivery begins, the physician will cut open your abdomen and uterus in quick succession, rupture the membranes, and carefully guide the baby's head through the incision. You may feel a tugging sensation around your abdomen. The baby's mouth and nostrils will be suctioned and then the body gently delivered. The entire process can take less than five minutes and the remainder of the operation lasts about half an hour.
Once the doctor has checked the baby, you or your partner may be able to hold the infant while the doctor manually removes your

placenta, checks your uterus, and begins to stitch the incisions closed. The doctor will gently massage your uterus to expel any blood clots. Most women should begin walking within a day of their Caesarean delivery, when a urinary catheter is no longer necessary. You can usually start eating a soft diet on the day after the operation, and you'll probably leave the hospital approximately 3 days after delivery. During your recovery, you may have to use a stool softener and a mild pain reliever. You will probably need to visit your doctor 2 to 3 weeks after leaving the hospital so he or she can examine your incision and remove any sutures or staples.

After Delivery

Shortly after delivery and after mother-and-child bonding, the nurses will borrow your baby to check a few things, including respiration, pulse, reflexes, muscle tone, and colour. Each of these factors are rated (0, 1, or 2.) A healthy baby typically has a composite "Apgar" score of 8 or 9. If there is any concern about the baby before or after delivery a paediatrician may recommend a short stay in the paediatric intensive care unit or special care nursery for observation.

Meanwhile, you'll need to recover from what is, after all, major surgery.

The resulting bleeding (lochia) after birth is often shorter following a Caesarean delivery because the doctor will have at least partially removed any leftover tissue.

When to consult your caregiver postpartum after having a C-section

- If you develop a fever.
- If you become dizzy or faint.
- If you experience nausea and vomiting.
- If you become short of breath.
- If you have pain, swelling and redness at the incision site.
- If you think you have a urinary tract infection.

Planned Caesarean – the risks

If you are thinking of having a planned Caesarean delivery because you think it will be safer and less painful you might want to remember that a C-section is major abdominal surgery that carries major risks.

Risks to you

You have a four to eight times greater chance of dying from a Caesarean section than you do from giving birth vaginally. Even a routine, scheduled Caesarean delivery.

A Caesarean delivery carries the risk for many serious surgical complications such as the accidental cutting of your bladder or other internal organs and a twenty percent chance you will get an infection as a result of the surgery.

Having a Caesarean birth also affects your future reproductive possibilities because having a Caesarean section means you have a decreased chance of getting pregnant again. With a pregnancy after a C-section you have higher risk that your pregnancy will occur outside your womb, a condition that will never result in a live baby and is life threatening for you. You have increased risks in a birth following a C-section of the placenta detaching itself.

While some women might be willing to take risks with their own body, it would be very hard to find a woman willing to take risks with the life or health of her baby just for her own convenience or to avoid labour pain.

Risks to the baby

There is about a five percent chance that when the surgeon cuts into your body during a Caesarean section, the knife will accidentally also cut your baby.

Because all the water is not squeezed out of the baby's lungs as is normally done during a vaginal birth, more babies born after Caesarean section develop respiratory distress syndrome, one of the biggest killers of newborn babies.

Too often a Caesarean section is done too soon, because of the schedule of either the obstetrician or the mother, resulting in a premature birth. Premature newborn babies carry a higher risk of brain damage to the baby and foetal death.

Babies born via a choice C-section (when there have been no labour contractions to prepare the baby for birth) are known to have more digestive problems, more lungs problems and more difficulty in breastfeeding.

🖶Research & Facts

Obstetricians have jumped on the "woman's choice" bandwagon, which in many ways is a good thing except for the tendency to push women's choice only for things the obstetricians want to do anyway. For example, for years the scientific evidence has favoured vaginal birth after an earlier Caesarean section (called VBAC) rather than a repeat Caesarean section. Doctors, however, have never really pushed VBAC, but instead emphasize a repeat Caesarean. Pushing women to have the right to choose major surgery for which there is no medical indication is ridiculous as well as dangerous. It has been established legally and ethically that patients have the right to refuse treatment even when medically indicated, but patients have never had the right to choose medical or surgical treatment that is not indicated. Doctors are under no obligation to do unjustified major surgery. Womens' choices" are clearly limited to medically valid options.

(*Based on a report made by Marsden Wagner, MD.*)

The c/section rate has been steadily rising throughout the world. Currently the c/section rate in most South African public hospitals is about 20-35% with the rate in private hospitals reaching about 50%. South American countries like Brazil and Venezuela boast some of the highest c/section rates in the world reaching 70-80% in some private hospitals. In the USA the c/section rate is 30,2%. The WHO acceptable c/section rate is 8%

CHANGES IN YOUR BODY DURING PREGNANCY

Week 5-12

The earliest signs of pregnancy other than a missed period include tiredness, changes in smell and taste, breasts becoming fuller and slight menstrual cramping. Mood swings are also very common.

Nausea usually starts around week 5.

Your heart & metabolic rate both increase.

By week 9 your uterus has doubled in size since you conceived so you could be feeling "round ligament pain", which is caused by the stretching of the ligaments that hold your uterus in place.

Although you don't "show" a pregnant belly as yet you might notice that your waist is thicker. This is because your body acquires a layer of fat for both protection and warmth of the uterus when it "pops" up and out from behind your pubic bone.

Hormonal changes could cause you to be irritable, depressed or simply just not yourself.

You may be suffering with more frequent headaches as a result of the change in your hormone levels.

Due to the increase in blood volume you might find that you are beginning to feel warmer than you used to.

You may be thirstier than normal because your body needs extra fluid during pregnancy.

If you have been suffering from nausea you might begin to feel a little better around week 12 to 14.

You could be urinating more often and your urine could smell strongly.

Week 13-20

Week 13 ends the first trimester.

Around week 14 you could start to suffer from constipation. This is due to the ever-rising levels of progesterone.

Around week 15 your waist is really starting to thicken, you might need to begin changing your wardrobe. Your uterus is just higher than the top of pubic bone.

Around week 16, your caregiver may be able to detect your baby's heartbeat with a doptone.
For some women, nasal congestion and nosebleeds are an annoying side effect of pregnancy. This is due to altered levels of hormones, which may cause the mucous membranes in your nose to swell. You might notice that you have more vaginal mucous too.
If you have had a previous pregnancy you may feel your baby move anywhere from week 17.
Your placenta is now fully formed.
Around week 18 your energy levels may begin to improve.
You might find that the texture of your hair, skin and nails changes.
If this is your first pregnancy you may feel your baby move for the first time around week 20.
The top of your uterus (fundus) should be around the level of your navel from around week 20.

Week 20-27

Between week 18 and 24 your blood pressure could drop a little. This is called the "mid-pregnancy blood pressure drop" and because of this you could suddenly begin to feel dizzy or faint.
You could be perspiring more.
Some women's breasts begin to leak a little colostrum (your baby's first food.) You may notice small nodules around your nipples these are called Montgomery's tubercles.
Increased blood flow to the pelvic region could mean that it is easier to achieve orgasm.
Skin changes are common, you may notice darker patches of skin or changes in moles or freckles.
You may have indigestion as your uterus grows.
You could begin to feel backache, and pressure on you pelvis from around week 24.
Your uterus is about the size of a football around week 25.
From around 25 weeks you could be feeling Braxton Hicks.
Your uterus is pushing up against your ribcage, making your lower ribs spread out. This could cause some discomfort and breathlessness.
You may be leaking urine when you cough or sneeze.
Mood swings could disappear but you could be forgetful.

Depending on whether this is your first pregnancy, your build and the amount of amniotic fluid, you should now have an obviously pregnant belly.
Week 27 is the end of the second trimester.

Additional information

Do not be alarmed if when you wake up in the morning your pregnancy belly looks flatter than the day before. This is very normal! By the end of the day your belly will be larger due to the food you have eaten and because you have been upright all day.

Week 28-35

You might notice a sudden increase in weight.
Sometimes the pressure of your growing uterus and the high level of hormones can cause varicose veins.
You could have restless legs or cramps at night.
You could be feeling breathless.
Your haemoglobin count (Hb) could be a little low around week 30.
The weight of your growing baby could change your centre of gravity, which in turn puts a strain on your back.
Around week 32 your uterus will be reaching its highest position.
If this is your first baby it may have moved into a head down position around 33/34 weeks. Once this happens you may have less heartburn but you might feel more pressure in your pelvis and lower back and begin to feel pubic pain.
You could be retaining extra fluid from around 34 weeks.
You nipples could enlarge and your breasts become fuller with a visible, thin network of blue veins.
Around week 35 you may begin to feel as if your pelvic joints are loosened and they could therefore feel unstable.
Your baby could engage any time in these weeks. Some women experience "engaging contractions" as the baby moves deeper.

Week 36-40
You could be having vivid dreams.
Your Braxton Hicks could be getting stronger as the uterus prepares for birth.
Some women suffer from insomnia due to being uncomfortable and from needing to wake often to urinate.
Your weight is likely to plateau around 38 weeks.
Some symptoms from the first trimester like fatigue and nausea could return in the last few weeks.
You will be slowing down to prepare for birth.

CHILDBIRTH CLASSES

A childbirth class is a great way to prepare for labour and childbirth. Classes range from intensive courses beginning early in pregnancy and continuing through the postpartum period to short refresher sessions in the last few weeks of pregnancy.
A typical class includes up to eight weekly sessions and consists of lectures and exercises led by a trained childbirth instructor. While approaches vary, the goal is to provide you with information to minimize your fears, help you make informed decisions and to teach you techniques to help you relax both during pregnancy and labour. Childbirth classes are also a great opportunity to meet other expectant parents.
Classes usually cover:

- Relaxing techniques and exercises to help keep you healthy during pregnancy.
- How to recognize the signs of labour.
- The normal (possible) progress of labour and birth.
- Techniques for coping with pain.
- How your birthing partner can help you during labour.

Some classes also cover the basics of breastfeeding and immediate newborn care. If you're interested, you can usually take separate in-depth classes on these topics.

Some childbirth classes also discuss certain childbirth complications and how they might be handled.

Be sure to research the different classes available before you sign up in order to find one that meets your needs. If you plan to give birth without an epidural, for example, you'll want to be sure to find an instructor who spends a lot of time exploring all of the different natural methods of pain management. On the other hand, if you're not concerned about interventions and are sure you're going the epidural route, a course taught by a stringently anti-drug instructor will not support your choice.

Here are some well-known methods of childbirth instruction:

Lamaze stipulates that "birth is normal, natural, and healthy" and that "women have a right to give birth free from routine medical interventions." The curriculum emphasizes giving women the information and tools to feel confident about giving birth and empowered to give true informed consent about medications and other interventions.

The Bradley Method embraces the idea that childbirth is a natural process and that, with the right preparation, women may be able to avoid pain medication and routine interventions during labour and birth. The curriculum emphasizes the importance of diet and exercise during pregnancy, teaches deep breathing techniques to manage pain, and involves the husband or partner as an integral participant in the birth process.

Pre-natal yoga is a wonderful way to exercise, connect with yourself and your baby, and prepare for the journey of birth and motherhood. Pregnancy yoga can be an ideal way to stay in shape during your pregnancy, it keeps you limber, tones your muscles, and improves your balance and circulation, with little, if any, impact on your joints.
Yoga is also beneficial because it helps you learn to breathe deeply and relax, which will come in handy as you face the physical demands of labour, birth, and motherhood. Regular yoga practice will help

you fight the urge to tighten up when you feel pain, and show you how to relax instead.

COLDS

Pregnancy hormones cause your mucous membranes to swell. This can make it more difficult to get rid of coughs and colds. Prevention is key here. Eat well, and get plenty of rest and exercise. Also avoid people who are contagious, if possible.

THERAPIES AND TIPS for colds

Nutrition

Eat a well balanced diet to keep your resistance up. As a rule I always advise women to eat a green, yellow, orange and red vegetable or fruit each day!

In particular, you need to eat foods containing the following nutrients:

- Vitamin C: citrus, tomatoes, peppers, parsley, dark green vegetables, broccoli, strawberries, cabbage, potatoes, peas, lettuce, asparagus and kiwi.
- Zinc: lamb, alfalfa, eggs, beans, pumpkin seeds, avocado, beef, whole wheat, soy and watercress.
- Vitamin E: eggs, nuts (almonds, hazelnuts, and walnuts), sunflower seeds, mayonnaise, cold-pressed vegetable oils, including olive, corn & safflower, dark green leafy vegetables like spinach & kale, sweet potatoes, avocado, asparagus and yams.
- Eating garlic or onions can help fight infections.

Lifestyle

- Use a humidifier as it improves air quality and moisturizes the air. A warm and cool mist humidifier can help with problems caused by dry air such as dry swollen nasal passages and sinus problems.
- Use a something called a "neti pot" or "rhino horn", it is specially designed to rinse out your sinuses. Using a mixture

of warm water and sea salt you literally rinse out the sinus passages by allowing the mixture to flow in one nose passage (your head is tilted upside down and you are leaning over a basin) and out the other.

✳ Aromatherapy

Lavender, lemon and chamomile: Add no more than one drop of each oil to a bowl of boiling water and inhale the infused steam for ten minutes.

☑ Supplements

- Vitamin C is good for your general resistance and it promotes a better recovery. Take an Anti-acid Vitamin C 1000mg per day.
- Take a pre-natal multivitamin making sure it contains the following: Zinc, Vitamin E and Vitamin C to help boost your immune system and B vitamins to help if you are under stress.

✚ Homeopathy

- Use Aconite 6X every two hours for 24 hours at the first sign of a cold.
- Allium Cepa 6C three times daily for a streaming head cold.
- Take Echinacea for general immune support.

♣ Phytotherapy/herbs

Herbal Decoction for colds:

Four cloves, one teaspoon of coriander seeds, half a teaspoon of sea salt, half a teaspoon of turmeric, the juice of half a lemon and a teaspoon of honey. Boil one litre of water. Add the spices to the water and simmer for ten minutes. Add the lemon and strain. Sweeten with honey. Drink a hot cup of this every four hours.

☯ Acupuncture

Acupuncture can help with congestion and it also helps to boost your immune system.

☛My experience: I find that acupuncture helps to decongest a blocked nose and will support the immune system by relaxing and calming you. Stress has a very negative effect on your immune system.

COMPLEMENTARY THERAPIES IN PREGNANCY

Aromatherapy

Using aromatherapy for pregnancy and birth is an age-old process. Essential oil is used for aromatherapy. Essential oil is highly fragrant and concentrated. When undiluted it can be a skin irritant so it is important to use essential oils in the correct way.

You can blend an oil or combination of oils together with almond or jojoba as carrier oils for a great aromatherapy massage.

You can place a few drops in an air freshener or a burner

You can use the oils in a misting bottle with distilled water.

Some basic oils and their uses

Lavender: restores unbalanced states to a more harmonious state. In other words it relaxes you.

Chamomile: is the "Matriarch" of oils. It is very gentle, soothing and calming to the mind and body.

Neroli: is one of the most effective anti-depressant oils, it is useful for insomnia, hysteria, anxiety and other stress-related conditions.

Bergamot: is wonderfully uplifting, light and refreshing.

Clary Sage: is used during labour only. An aroma therapist told me that Clary Sage 'gives you wings'. She explained that it is used to stimulate contractions because it helps women overcome their "fear of the unknown".

Use aromatherapy oils during pregnancy at your own risk or consult an aromatherapist.

Aromatherapy and Birth

The use of aromatherapy during birth is an age-old therapy. Remember though that whatever smells may work in early labour, might change as the birth progresses to another scent. Birth partners should be open to change and listen to your preference at the time. These aromatherapy massage oils can be used on the back throughout labour, but use it only once or twice on the abdomen during the first stage. The essential oil will help the uterus to do its job, but you don't want to overdo it because the baby will have to do his/her part of the job during the second stage.

What the different aroma's do:

Rose

Uterine relaxant.

Helps ligaments to soften, enabling the pelvic bones to expand and to regain elasticity after the birth.

Natural antiseptic.

Slight analgesic effect.

Good cardiac tonic.

Neroli

Works on the nervous system and facilitates easy breathing, especially during panting (if this is used to stop pushing). Its calming effect increases the oxygen supply to the blood and brain and helps the woman to avoid hyperventilation.

In low doses (1-2 drops on a diffuser) it has a sedative and calming effect; in higher doses, it is a stimulant.

Antiseptic, disinfectant.

Confidence.

Antidepressant.

Lavender

Circulation stimulating.

Slight analgesic effect.

Calming.
Antiseptic and slight antiviral properties.
Promotes healing of open wounds - can be used instead of antiseptics.
Generally accepted by everyone.
Good for headaches, fainting, and bringing around after shock.

Clary sage
This essential oil must not be confused with sage. Don't use sage for the baby's sake - it leaves too high toxic residues in the body. Clary sage is a milder version, although it still should be used with care.
Helps respiratory, muscular, and uterine systems.
Mild analgesic.
Facilitates birth as it is a uterine tonic.
Euphoric.
Helps breathing.

Geranium
Circulation-stimulating.
Contractive effect - pulls together dilated tissues, so excellent for after the birth.
Good for the whole female reproductive system.
Antidepressant, known for its uplifting effects.

Jasmine
Improves strength and efficiency of contractions.
Reduces labour pains.
Increases breast-milk supply.

TRADITIONAL CHINESE MEDICINE & ACUPUNCTURE - *Featured in Pregnancy™ August 2004*

For the mother, pregnancy can be a time of depletion. Acupuncture can help to sustain your energy, supporting and maintaining chi through the natural cycles of pregnancy as well as building the foundations of good emotional & physical health for your baby. If disharmonies, which can manifest as both emotional and physical symptoms, have not been addressed before conception, then various conditions that make pregnancy uncomfortable can arise.

Traditional Chinese Medicine (TCM)

Traditional Chinese Medicine (TCM) is a complete system of healing that developed in China about 4,000 years ago and has changed very little over the centuries. The idea that all of nature including Man is governed by Yin/Yang and the Five Elements (Wood, Fire, Earth, Metal and Water) lies at the heart of Chinese Medicine. Good health, like the universe at large, is subject to constant battling between opposing forces such as yin and yang which can be seen as hot and cold, male and female, joy and sadness, light and dark, full and empty etc and the Five Elements. An imbalance between these forces can cause a blockage in the flow of the Qi (pronounced chee) or vital energy travelling through the body along invisible pathways known as meridians. TCM practitioners typically use acupuncture, massage, moxa, cupping, nutrition and herbs to encourage the Qi to function optimally hereby helping the body back into harmony and wellness. TCM sees the person as an integral mind/body organism and thereby does not treat just symptoms/diseases; it ventures to stimulate the body's natural healing potential by treating root causes rather than just symptoms.

Acupuncture

As more women seek drug-free treatment for the conditions of pregnancy, this ancient Chinese healing art has much to offer.

Acupuncture treatment during pregnancy benefits both baby and mother. Regular treatments throughout pregnancy enhance the health of the mother, relieve pregnancy symptoms that have become debilitating, prevent complications and positively influence the development of the baby.

Acupuncture can also aid fertility and it is also used to support couples during fertility treatments like IVF, ICSI and IUI.

What acupuncture can treat in pregnancy, childbirth and the postpartum period:
Anxiety.
Allergies.
Backache.
Blood pressure whether it is too high or too low.
Breech.
Carpal tunnel syndrome.
Delayed labour.
Depression.
Digestive problems.
Oedema.
Fatigue.
Heartburn.
Haemorrhoids.
Encourage the release of the placenta.
Insomnia.
Pain management during labour.
Preparation for childbirth.
Nausea.
Stimulate contractions ('induce' labour) in the case of post due date - as from 9 days past the woman's due date (41weeks, 2 days.)
Stress.
Post-partum: mastitis, pain, too little breast milk, backache, depression and anxiety.

The treatments

While some acupuncture treatments may cause a slight increase in foetal movements, no treatment, unless intended to start labour, should significantly increase uterine activity. If there are no specific complaints during pregnancy, treatments are normally given once monthly until the last month, when weekly sessions help prepare the women for labour.

A question often asked in my practice is, "Does it hurt?" My answer is that it is more a sensation than that it is painful. Of course you feel it but it should not be painful.

To establish a diagnosis, questions are asked and the pulses and tongue are observed.

An average first session lasts 60 minutes and the following sessions last 50 minutes.

Acupressure

An alternative to using needles to stimulate the acupuncture points is acupressure. Acupressure has the capacity to restore and balance the body's energy so that changes can be made to the way the body functions. In traditional Chinese Medicine terms, acupressure can encourage the body to work more efficiently. From a medical model, acupressure during childbirth can be seen a way of promoting the release of endorphins, blocking the pain receptors to the brain, dilating the cervix, and increasing the efficiency of the contractions

Chinese Herbs

Herbology evolved into a healing art in China through observation and usage. This knowledge was compiled and passed down for refinement through the centuries. Herbs, like everything else in Chinese Medicine, are classified according to their energetic qualities and functions. They are defined with terms like warming, cooling, tonifying or purging which describes the overall energetic configuration of the herb.

Chinese herbs can be used to treat a variety of symptoms and ailments. During pregnancy herbs are used with caution and should only be taken under the careful advice of a qualified practitioner.

Herbs are used in the following instances:

Nausea.

Insomnia.

Threatened miscarriage.

To stimulate contractions ('induce' labour) - as from nine days past the woman's due date (41weeks, 2 days.)

Post partum convalescence.

Bach Flower Remedies

The Bach remedies are particularly useful because they act directly on the emotions, which are often in turmoil during and after pregnancy. Being completely safe they can be a first choice when physical and

mental demands get too much. Bach Remedies help us to cope with stressful situations on an energetically emotional and mental level. Bach Flower Remedies are holistic, which means that they are designed to treat the whole person and, in principle, treat the internal imbalances that cause physical or psychological problems. Bach Remedies are excellent as a self-help therapy. They can be bought at any chemist or health food shop and there are no contra-indications known in the use of Bach Remedies. Some women worry about the fact that they are based on alcohol but the amount you will be ingesting is minute. You would have drink two to three bottles in one sitting to receive a damaging amount of alcohol, so don't worry!
There are 38 Bach flower remedies, named after their originator, Dr Edward Bach; there is also the Rescue Remedy (made up of Impatiens, Star of Bethlehem, Cherry Plum, Clematis and Rock rose) - this is a useful standby in times of shock, injury or trauma.

Bach remedies, which might be useful during pregnancy and/or labour include:
Aspen — feeling apprehensive for no apparent reason.
Elm — feelings of overwhelming responsibility.
Larch — fear of failure, lack of self-confidence.
Olive — feeling exhausted and drained of energy.
Rescue Remedy – for all shock and stressful situation.
Walnut — assists in adjusting to transition or change.
Wild chestnut — persistent anxiety or worry.
Wild oat — being unsure of a direction in life.

Chiropractor

Many women who have never seen a chiropractor before are understandably anxious about what an adjustment is like, and especially how it is done during pregnancy. Pregnancy specialised chiropractors have a drop table (the special table that chiropractors work with) that is specially designed for pregnant women. Parts of the drop table can be tilted up slightly at an angle to the rest of the table. When the chiropractor does an adjustment, the tilted part of the table drops a little, hence the name. The adjustment plus that small drop (usually not very jarring) is often enough to realign the part of the body being worked on. Not all chiropractors use a drop table, but it's often a good tool with pregnant women because of limited ability to do other manoeuvres. Some chiropractors work with other techniques depending on their training and background.

Chiropractor & pregnancy

Your spine and pelvis undergo many changes and adaptations to compensate for your growing baby and the risk of interference to your nervous system is increased. Specific chiropractic care throughout pregnancy works with enhancing nervous system function providing greater health potential for both you and your baby Along with providing a boost for general health, chiropractic can be very helpful with situations such as sciatica, breech positioned babies, posterior babies and after your baby is born a chiropractor could help in the case of colic.

Cranio Sacral Therapy

Cranio Sacral therapy helps at all stages of pregnancy by deeply relaxing both mother and baby. In pregnancy your body needs to be able to function as best it can. Trauma, anxiety and fear that may be held in the body causing pain and discomfort, should be addressed. Cranio Sacral treatment helps to gently release the body of these burdens, allowing mother and baby to thrive. A well-balanced and relaxed pelvis can greatly ease the process of childbirth. Relaxing the pelvic area may also help create space for breech babies to turn. Pregnancy is a time for new insights and perspectives, and cranial can help to enhance this process bringing you more in touch with your own body and also facilitating a deeper connection with your baby.

After the Birth: On its journey into the world, a baby moves through the narrow tunnel of its mother's pelvis. At this stage, an infant's skull is only partly formed. As a baby's head passes along the birth canal, it is squeezed into shapes that are determined by the contours of its mother's pelvis. As the labour progresses these strong forces of compression can often last for several hours. This is a very stimulating time for the baby, but during this time, some babies may also become traumatised. This may then be reflected in the early months as colic, or difficulty settling or feeding, or simply a preference in which side the baby prefers to lie or feed. In Caesarean section, the moulding that occurs when the baby passes through the birth canal does not occur. However a sudden change in pressure is exerted on the baby, as it is moved from the environment of the womb to the outside world, and this can create a sense of shock in the baby's tissues. Many infant problems, like colic, suckling problems, breathing difficulties, restlessness and irritability, may result from Cranio Sacral imbalances caused during the birth process. Treatment of young infants may help to relieve such problems.

Homeopathy

Homeopathy is ideal for treating various symptoms of pregnancy, as it carries no known side effects. During pregnancy, any conventional medication feels like a threat to the unborn. However, the gentle and ancient system of homeopathy suits pregnancy because it does not introduce harmful substances into the body. With homeopathy the treatment tends to be more holistic, this means that not just your symptoms but also your entire body is being treated.

Visiting a homeopath

Remedies are chosen after a consultation, which can include bewildering questions about whether you have hot feet and what you like best to eat. This is in order to establish a complete picture of you as a patient, to which the homeopath can match a correct remedy. The same symptom can be treated with a wide variety of different remedies, depending on your unique susceptibility. Once the remedy has been identified, it works by stimulating your healing potential and in doing so restores equilibrium.

Nutrtional Therapy

What we take into our body during pregnancy has long lasting effects. Poor nutrition during pregnancy can be responsible for Spina Bifidia, low birth weight, childhood illness and allergies as well as an increased tendency to heart disease and diabetes later in life.

Your baby gets first pick of any nutrients in your body, so it is vital for your own health that you receive the nutrients you need to ensure a healthy pregnancy and strong recovery. Certain dietary recommendations can be helpful in dealing with cravings, morning sickness, blood sugar imbalances, pre-eclampsia and digestive disturbances. Low levels of certain nutrients are indicated in miscarriage, and diet has been used to successfully rebalance hormones and avoid postnatal depression.

Osteopathy

Pregnancy is a time of great change at a physiological, mechanical and emotional level. Right from the early stages of pregnancy the pelvis starts to change its position in relation to the rest of the body as all the ligaments in the body begin to soften. These changes combined with previously entrenched postural, biomechanical and stress factors can predispose to discomfort anywhere in the body, especially back, neck, head and legs. Also these mechanical factors can drain the body's resources and cause fatigue. They can also contribute to a difficult birth. The pelvis is vulnerable to strain during birth which can then affect the whole body, leading to lower back and pelvic pain, recurring headaches, pelvic floor problems and post natal 'blues'.

Osteopathy is a gentle way of helping the body be more comfortable during pregnancy. It can also help to ensure that the body is in the best possible condition for delivery and a check-up after birth can help prevent many problems that could occur as a result of the strain of birth.

Phyto Therapy – Western herbal medicine

Herbal medicine, also called botanical medicine or phyto medicine, refers to the use of any plant's seeds, berries, roots, leaves, bark, or flowers for medicinal purposes. Long practiced outside of conventional medicine, herbalism is becoming more mainstream because up-to-date analysis and research show their value in the treatment and prevention of disease.

Phyto therapy during pregnancy

Although there are many herbs that may not be used during pregnancy there are also a few that are safe to use:

Alfalfa is a plant containing a good source of vitamin K necessary for blood clotting. Alfalfa can be eaten or taken as an infusion in the last 4 weeks of pregnancy to possibly help avoid excess blood loss.
Black Haw is used in the early stages of pregnancy to help prevent miscarriage
Blessed Thistle is used in the latter stages of pregnancy as a liver tonic and builder, as well as a stimulant of blood flow to the breasts and used to increase milk production. Thistle also reduces haemorrhaging during childbirth.
Chamomile is a great calming agent and helps with nausea and also contains some anti-inflammatory properties. It should not be used in large quantities until week 37 of the pregnancy.
Dandelion tea is used for digestive disorders, oedema, water retention and constipation.
Fennel tea can alleviate heartburn.
Ginger is safe and can be effective for the treatment of nausea and vomiting. It can be taken in a capsule, as a tincture or as tea.
Kelp is high in vitamins and minerals, aids thyroid function
Nettle contains high levels of calcium and iron and is also used to reduce oedema.
Peppermint tea is used for heartburn and nausea.
Red Raspberry Leaf is rich in iron that has also been effective in helping in the production of milk, decreasing nausea, preventing miscarriage and easing labour pains. It can be taken as a capsule or as tea.
Slippery Elm soothes a cough, sore throat, and bronchitis as well as easing gastrointestinal symptoms.
Spirulina is high in many vitamins and minerals and is used as one of the plants to treat anaemia.

***Avoid* the following herbs completely during pregnancy:**
Angelica - stimulates suppressed menstruation, **Black Cohosh** - uterine stimulant - mostly used during labour, **Blue Cohosh** - a stronger uterine stimulant, **Borage oil** - a uterine stimulant - use only during the last few days of pregnancy, **Comfrey** - can cause liver problems in mother and fetus - use only briefly, externally only, for treating sprains and strains, **Dong Quai** - may stimulate

bleeding, **Fenugreek** - uterine relaxant, **Goldenseal** - too powerful an antibiotic for the developing fetus, also should not be used if nursing, **Henbane** - highly toxic, **Horsetail** - too high in silica for the developing fetus, **Motherwort** - stimulates suppressed menstruation, **Mugwort** - can be a uterine stimulant, **Nutmeg** - can cause miscarriage in large doses, **Pennyroyal Leaf** - stimulates uterine contractions (NOTE: Pennyroyal essential oil should not be used by pregnant women at any time!) **Rue** - strong expellant, **Shepherd's Purse** - used only for haemorrhaging during/after childbirth, **Uva Ursi** - removes too much blood sugar during pregnancy and nursing, **Yarrow** - uterine stimulant.

Reflexology

The balancing nature of reflexology lends itself well to the discomforts experienced during pregnancy. Anxiety, indigestion, constipation, poor circulation and swollen ankles are all conditions that have been helped by reflexology. Treatments are especially useful towards the end of pregnancy in preparation for the birth and during labour. Stalled labour or overdue dates can prove to be anxious times, therefore, by relaxing the mother and stimulating certain reflexes, labour often progresses naturally.

CONSTIPATION

During pregnancy, your body produces more female hormones than normal. It is the job of these hormones to make sure that your pregnancy develops normally but unfortunately they also automatically slow down your intestinal movements. Progesterone acts by relaxing all smooth muscle tissue. The wall (outside) of the bowel is made of muscle and it therefore relaxes, making it less able to move your bodily waste along.

What are the signs of constipation?

- More than four days between each bowel movement.

- Your faeces are hard and dry, which makes them difficult to pass.
- There is a feeling that not all the faeces are being passed.
- If the faeces are very hard, they may cause bleeding from the rectum and possibly piles.
- Constipation can also be giving you lower abdominal pain.

THERAPIES AND TIPS for constipation

Golden Tip

- Eat one Umeboshi plum or drink Umeboshi tea every morning.
- Drink 3 to 4 cups of prune juice a day.

☑ **Supplements**

- Taking Probiotics helps restore intestinal flora and can help to treat constipation. It will not change the reduced function of your intestine but it certainly improves overall digestion and therefore often solves constipation.
- Try to avoid taking chemical iron supplements as these cause constipation.
- Taking a digestive enzyme supplement can help "speed" up your digestion.
- Take one tablespoon of Linseed oil every morning and evening but do not exceed this dosage and keep your linseed bottle stored cool and dark. Linseed oil should always contain Vitamin E and don't use the linseed if the bottle has been open for longer than four weeks or begins to taste bitter.

Nutrition

- Start your day with a large glass of warm water with a squeeze of lemon in it to help "kick-start" your digestion and improve your pH.
- Eat enough natural fibre: fresh fruit, vegetables, whole-grain bread, breakfast cereals sprinkled with broken linseed and prunes.

- Drink at least two litres of liquid a day - especially water.
- Dandelion tea can sometimes help to combat constipation.
- Eating dried fruit especially prunes could help a sluggish bowel but take care not to eat too much dried fruit in one sitting as it will give you terrible wind and possible cramps.

Lifestyle

- Make sure you are getting enough exercise. A gentle stroll in the morning sometimes gets the bowels moving.
- Place a small footstool under your feet when sitting on the toilet, this is a better position in which to empty your bowel without having to push too hard.
- Don't delay going to the toilet if you feel the urge to 90 a bowel movement.

Reflexology

One or two sessions a week of foot reflexology regulates bowel movements like no other therapy.

Acupuncture

An acupuncture session once a week will help regulate your bowel movements.

☛My experience: Acupuncture definitely helps to improve digestion during pregnancy but I always combine the treatment with reflexology and nutritional advice.

Massage

Gently massage your entire abdomen in an **anti-clock-wise** direction (around the outer perimeter of your uterus) with some lavender oil in bed each morning and evening. You can also use the abdominal massage while sitting on the toilet. Although your faeces travels through your intestine in a clock-wise direction the peristaltic movement of your intestine is in fact anti-clockwise and so with this massage you are stimulating your intestine instead of just "moving" the faeces out.

✳ Aromatherapy

Grapefruit, lemon and mandarin oils are said to help relieve constipation. You can "burn" these oils so that you can inhale their smell or you can place them in carrier oils to use for massaging your abdomen with.

When to consult your caregiver

If you are not able to pass a bowel movement for more than a week or if you are suffering from abdominal pain and/or headaches.

CONTRACTIONS

The onset of contractions is an indication that your labour has begun. Contractions thin out and open your cervix, which is the "exit" of your womb where your baby passes through during labour. Experts believe that because of the pressure of the baby on the cervix, the hormone Oxytocin is made and this in turn causes the womb to contract. The contraction of your womb forces your cervix open from 0 to 10 cm so that your baby can pass through it and into the birth canal.

Every labour is different and each woman will experience her contractions differently. Most women will experience practice contractions called Braxton-Hicks in the last two to three weeks of their pregnancy. When real labour begins these contractions will become regular and more painful. As labour progresses the contractions will become longer, - at least forty five to seventy five seconds each - stronger and progressively more frequent, going from one contraction every ten to fifteen minutes to one every five minutes and eventually to one every two to three minutes. As the dilation nears ten centimetres the contractions could be as frequent as one every minute.

Once the contractions become stronger and more regular they will begin to come in waves. They will have a beginning, a peak and an ebbing away.

Having said that, contractions could begin suddenly and could already be only three minutes apart OR they can be very irregular and very painful from the start or some women hardly feel their contractions until they are almost one minute apart!

The question most asked in my practice is 'HOW WILL I KNOW THAT THE REAL CONTRACTIONS HAVE STARTED?' The answer I normally give is that if you are in doubt then they probably aren't real contractions. For more about contractions see the "True or False Labour" chapter.

CORD CLAMPING

Adaptation to life outside the womb is a major physiological task for your baby once it is born. Inside your womb, the placenta fulfils the functions of lungs, kidneys, intestine and liver for your baby. Blood flow to these organs is minimal until your baby takes a first breath. To bridge the moment of placental function and first breath Mother Nature ensures that there is a reservoir of blood in the cord and placenta that provides the additional blood necessary for a newborn baby.
The transfer of this reservoir of blood from the placenta to your baby happens in a step-wise progression, with blood flowing into your baby with each third-stage contraction and with some blood returning to the placenta between contractions. Crying slows the intake of blood, which is also controlled by constriction of the vessels within the cord (*research done by Gunther 1957*) - both of which imply that your baby may be able to regulate the transfusion of blood from the cord according to its individual need. The cessation of cord pulsation (typically five minutes, but can be as long as half an hour) signals that the transfer of reserve blood is complete.

Research & Facts
Waiting to clamp the cord: This elegant and time-tested system, which ensures that an optimum, but not a standard, amount of blood is transferred, is rendered inoperable by the current practice of early

clamping of the cord, usually within thirty seconds of birth. Early clamping has been widely adopted in Western obstetrics as part of the package known as active management of the third stage.

In one study, premature babies experiencing delayed cord clamping the delay was only 30 seconds- showed a reduced need for transfusion, less severe breathing problems, better oxygen levels, and indications of probable improved long-term outcomes, compared to those whose cords were clamped immediately. (Kinmond 1993.)

The recent discovery of the amazing properties of cord blood, in particular the stem cells contained within it, heightens the need to ensure that a newborn baby gets its full quota. These cells are unique to this stage of development, and will migrate to the baby's bone marrow soon after birth, transforming themselves into various types of blood-making cells, which could make a difference in the development of the immune system.

CRAMPING

Slight lower abdominal cramps at the very beginning of pregnancy are normal. As soon as a healthy egg has been fertilised it makes its way down the Fallopian tube to the uterus and there are tiny contractions that aid this. Also the blood supply to the uterus increases dramatically, even at this early stage the uterus starts to increase in size and this can cause cramps very similar to those you may get just before your period. Try not to panic! What you often aren't told is that cramping and strange pains may be felt all the way through your pregnancy. These pains are caused by the fact that the womb doesn't just float in your abdomen but is held in place by connective tissue and tendons and that he tissue has to stretch to accommodate your expanding baby. Don't forget that your entire lower abdomen gets completely rearranged by your expanding uterus so that all your organs are literally "squashed" into any available space.

CRAVINGS

Many women are already familiar with strange cravings from when they are pre-menstrual but the cravings that can occur during pregnancy can be very extreme. During pregnancy the blood has a tendency to become more acidic. By eating the craved foods, you could instinctively be trying to alkalize your blood. Another reason you might have cravings during pregnancy is that you are deficient (lacking) in a certain vitamin or mineral. The most common are the minerals, iron and zinc. A craving is called *pica* in medical terms. The word *pica* is Latin for magpie, which is a bird notorious for eating almost anything. Most pica cravings involve non-food substances such as sand, clay, chalk, burnt matches, stones, charcoal, ice, cornstarch, toothpaste, soap, plaster, coffee grounds, baking soda and cigarette ashes.

Can Pica be harmful?

If you give into pica cravings and eat non-food substances it could be potentially harmful to both you and the baby. Eating non-food substances may interfere with the nutrient absorption of healthy food substances and actually cause a deficiency. Pica substances are also a concern because non-food items may contain toxic or parasitic ingredients. Some pica craving substances may actually create weight gain. Other pica craving substances may wear down teeth or create bowel obstructions and constipation.

THERAPIES AND TIPS for cravings

Nutrition

- If you are craving non-food substances like sand, chalk or ice cubes there is a strong possibility that you are anaemic. Check the information about anaemia.
- If you are craving pickled foods, lemon, grapefruit or sauerkraut you may be trying to alkalize your blood. Solve these craving by sucking on an umeboshi "pill" or taking a ¼ teaspoon of umeboshi paste three times a day.

- Check any food cravings you are having by looking up which nutrients are found in those particular foods and then supplement your diet with foods containing those substances.

✎ Anecdote

I was treating a pregnant woman in my practice who suffered from leg cramps and insomnia plus she told me that she had become obsessed by bananas and that she was eating at least ten a day. This is not a very healthy thing to be doing – anything in excess is not healthy! But if you look at what bananas supply nutritionally you'll find that they supply Tryptophan, which is necessary to make Serotonin, which in turn naturally enhances sleep. Bananas also contain a good ratio of magnesium/calcium/phosphor, which are all needed for proper muscle function and muscle relaxation.

I advised her to take 400mg of magnesium per day (in a supplement which also included a good ratio of calcium & phosphor), to exercise more and to go for a massage once a week. She stopped craving bananas after just four days, began to sleep better and her legs cramps disappeared completely!

When to consult your caregiver

If you're having very strong cravings for non-food items even after having followed the advice for anaemia and supplementing accordingly, you will need to consult your caregiver so that they can check your blood status.

D

DEPRESSION

Although pregnancy is often portrayed as a time of great joy this is unfortunately not the case for all women. At least one in ten pregnant women suffer from bouts of depression throughout and after their pregnancy.
Depression during pregnancy could be caused by a number of things:

- The rapid increase in hormone levels at the start of pregnancy can disrupt brain chemistry and lead to depression.
- A history of depression, either your own or that of your mother or a sister during their pregnancies.
- Circumstance.
- Unresolved emotions and/or conflicts.

Some of the symptoms below, such as fatigue or trouble sleeping, are also common among healthy women during pregnancy, but when they're combined with a sense of sadness or hopelessness or they interfere with your ability to function, depression is probably at least partly to blame.
Symptoms of depression:

- A sense that nothing feels enjoyable or fun anymore.
- Waking up feeling blue, sad, or "empty" and staying that way for most of the day, every day.
- You find it hard to concentrate.
- Extreme irritability or agitation.
- Excessive crying.

- Trouble sleeping or sleeping all the time.
- Extreme or never-ending fatigue.
- A desire to eat all the time or not wanting to eat at all.
- Inappropriate feelings of guilt or worthlessness or hopelessness.

THERAPIES AND TIPS for depression

Lifestyle

Depression and anxiety can be a "natural" symptom of the first few months of pregnancy and they often just resolve and disappear by 16 weeks. If you are prone to depression and/or anxiety you may not be able to avoid them altogether.

Try following some of the following advice:

- Take it easy. Resist the urge to pack in as many chores as you can before the baby comes. You may think you need to set up the nursery, clean the house, or work as much as you can before you go on maternity leave, but you don't, your priority should be your well-being.
- Pencil *yourself* in at the top of your to-do list. You won't have as much time for yourself once the baby has been born. Read a book, have breakfast in bed, or go for a nice long walk around the neighbourhood. Try to find something that makes you feel good. Taking care of yourself is an essential part of taking care of your developing baby.
- Bond with your partner, try spending plenty of time with him/her to nurture your relationship and talk with them about how you feel.
- Take a break or holiday if at all possible.
- Air out your fears and worries about the future with your partner, friends, family or caregiver.
- Try to manage your stress or find someone to help you with that.

☑ Supplements

- During pregnancy, a woman's body can become depleted of Omega 3, which is automatically transferred for use to your fetus. A deficiency of Omega-3 can lead to depression.

Statistics show that women who have pregnancies that are close together often suffer from depression due to the lack of Omega 3. Take 2000mg to 3000mg Omega-3 per day.

- Research has shown that there is also very often a deficiency of the mineral zinc in women who become depressed during and after pregnancy. Taking a Zinc supplement can help. A liquid zinc supplement has proven to show quicker results. Take the recommended dosage suggested by the product you buy.

☯ Acupuncture

Acupuncture can help treat depression.

☛My experience: Acupuncture is excellent for treating depression. It encourages the release of neurotransmitters in the brain that help relieve depressive symptoms.

Nutrition

Eating a healthy, balanced diet can help eliminate feelings of depression and anxiety. Vitamin and mineral deficiencies have been linked with depression and anxiety, vitamin B, zinc and magnesium in particular. So make sure you eat enough of the following:

- Foods containing vitamin B: Whole grains, seeds, beans, nuts, meat, milk, wheat germ, broccoli, eggs, avocados, soy products and meat.
- Foods containing magnesium: Bananas, oats, whole grains, meat, apricots, curry, cocoa, raw nuts leafy green vegetables.
- Increase the amount of foods containing zinc: The richest sources of zinc are in meat, fish, oysters, shellfish, prawns (or shrimps), crab, turkey, chicken and ham. Zinc is also present in live yoghurt, ricotta, beans (green, kidney, baked), nut butters, nuts, tofu, lentils, eggs, breads, cereals, pasta, rice, wheat germ, bran, onions, ginger and sunflower seeds.

Yoga

Yoga can lead to physical relaxation and improved spiritual wellbeing.

When to consult your caregiver

If you feel unable to handle your daily responsibilities or are having thoughts of harming yourself, call your caregiver for a referral to a counsellor.

Mood swings with cycles of depression alternating with periods of an abnormally high spirits, including increased activity, little need to sleep or eat, racing thoughts, inappropriate social behaviour, or poor judgment are signs of a serious condition called bipolar disorder, which requires immediate attention. Call your caregiver if you have those symptoms.

DEVELOPMENT OF YOUR BABY DURING PREGNANCY

The development of your baby in the womb is a wonderful process. I have compiled a month-by-month timescale of what happens in the womb. But keep in mind that different pregnancies do develop at different rates. Also, bear in mind that the method caregivers use to date your pregnancy means that you could be anything up to two weeks out from this timescale.

Although we talk about a pregnancy spanning nine months it is actually calculated by weeks rather than months. I have looked at both months and weeks.

Week one, when we're talking about the typical 40 weeks of pregnancy, starts on the first day of your last period. It is true that you're not actually pregnant *yet*, but most caregivers count everything from this day. The number of weeks passed, based on the 40 week term from your last menstrual period (also known as your "LMP" date), is called "menstrual age."

Two weeks later, when one or more of your eggs are fertilized, "gestational age" begins to mark time from baby's conception. This term lasts about 38 weeks, which is the amount of time your baby is actually developing.

First month

After the egg has been fertilised by the sperm, it starts to divide into more cells. This happens while it is carried along the Fallopian tube to the uterus. By the time it reaches the uterus the fertilised egg has become a cluster of cells that float in the uterine cavity until it embeds in the wall of the uterus. This implantation in the wall of the uterus is when conception is complete. This is roughly **4 weeks** after the first day of your last menstrual period if you have a 28-day cycle. (Add or subtract the number of days according to your own cycle if you want a very accurate estimate.)The egg is now called an embryo.

Second month

At **5 weeks** the embryo is the size of a grain of rice (about 2mm long) and would be visible to the naked eye. It has the beginnings of a brain with two lobes and its spinal cord is starting to form. At **6 weeks** (three to four weeks after fertilisation) the embryo has a head with simple eyes and ears. Its heart has two chambers and it is beating. Small buds are present that will form arms and legs later. The beginnings of the spine can be seen and the lower part of the body looks like a tail.

At **7 weeks**, the limb buds have grown into arms and legs. Nostrils can be seen on the embryo's face. The heart now has four chambers.

At **8 weeks**, the eyes and ears are growing, and your baby is about 2cm long from crown to rump. The head is large and out of proportion with the body and the face is developing. The brain and the blood vessels in the head can be seen through the thin skin. The bones in the arms and legs start to harden and elbows and knees become apparent. Fingers and toes can also be seen.

Third month

What is known as the embryonic period finishes at the end of **week 8** and the foetal period begins. This period sees rapid growth of the fetus, and the further development of the organs and tissues that were all formed in the embryonic period.

At **9 weeks** the head is almost half the crown-to-rump-length of your fetus. Then the body grows substantially in length until by **12**

weeks, the head is more in proportion. By the time you are **12 weeks** pregnant, your baby is just over 5cm long from crown to rump. Its body is fully formed, including ears, toes and fingers complete with fingernails.

Fourth month

By **14 weeks** your baby will be about 9-10cm long. Its body is now covered with a layer of fine hair called lanugo. The external genitals begin to appear in **week 9**, and now, by **15 weeks**, have fully differentiated into male or female genitals. By **week 15** the eyes have moved to the front of the face and the eyelids remain closed.
By **16 weeks** its face is becoming more human in appearance, although the chin is small and the mouth is quite wide. Between **16** and **24 weeks** you should feel your baby move for the first time - it may at first feel like butterflies.

Fifth month

The rapid growth that your baby has been experiencing now begins to slow a little. By **week 20** your baby measures about 18cm from crown to rump and is half as long as it will be when born. The legs are now in proportion with the body well developed. Faint eyebrows are visible. At this stage, you will feel your baby moving about a lot, often when you lie down or rest.

Sixth month

By **24 weeks** your baby's organs are fully formed. Your baby now has the face of a newborn baby, although the eyes are rather prominent because fat pads are yet to build up in the baby's cheeks. The eyelids are fused until **weeks 25 to 26** when they open. Your baby drinks amniotic fluid and may get hiccups.
The skin is wrinkled, red and thin with little underlying fat. The skin is covered with a waxy substance called vernix, which protects it while it is floating in the uterus. The body is well muscled, but still thin. Your baby has become better proportioned, with the size of the body catching up with the size of the head.
Your baby's hearing is also well developed by this stage; it will respond to noise.

Seventh month

By **28 weeks** fat is being deposited under the skin of your baby. Your baby now uses the senses of vision, hearing, taste and touch. He can recognize your voice among other voices.

Eighth month

Your baby is becoming plumper and plumper. By **30 weeks** the toenails are present and by **32 weeks** the fingernails have grown to reach the ends of the fingers. Your baby's eyes will be open when its awake.

By about **32 weeks** your baby will have settled into a head down position. There is no longer enough room left in the womb to move about freely. Your baby's antibodies increase, and your baby absorbs about a gallon of amniotic fluid per day. Your body replaces amniotic fluid every 3 hours. You will feel occasional vigorous jabs from your baby's arms and legs. If your baby is a boy, his testes will have migrated down into the scrotum somewhere in the eighth month.

Ninth month

Sometime between **36 and 40 weeks**, your baby's head will engage, this means that the baby's head will be lying just on top of your cervix. Some babies only engage at birth.

By **40 weeks**, your baby should be plump and healthy. The lanugo hair that had covered your baby has now mostly disappeared, although some hair may remain low on the forehead, in front of the ears and down the centre of the back.

Full term

By full-term, your baby should weigh around 2.7 to 3.5kg, although full-term babies can weigh anything from 2.5 to 5kg. From **38 weeks** after conception, your baby has all its organs and body systems ready for the big moment when it is born into the world.

DHA (OMEGA 3)

There are three major types of omega 3 fatty acids that are ingested in foods and used by the body: alpha-linolenic acid (ALA), eicosapentaenoic acid (EPA), and docosahexaenoic acid (DHA). Once eaten, the body converts ALA to EPA and DHA, the two types of omega-3 fatty acids more readily used by the body.

An adequate store of DHA is important for any adult, but it is crucial for the development of a baby, and its brain in particular, which undergoes its biggest growth spurt during the third trimester of pregnancy. Cells increase rapidly and brain development absorbs seventy percent of the nourishment that your baby gets from you. At birth, a baby's brain contains more cells than at any other time in his or her life - at least twice the amount he or she will ever need. To allow the brain (and eyes) to grow and develop properly, DHA is vital. It is essential for all the functions and activities of the brain's neurons and synapse functions and plays an important role in the development of the nervous system and the improvement of IQ.

If you are lacking in essential fatty acids, your baby will obtain the DHA it needs from your body's richest source, your brain. This could account for the slight shrinkage (two to three percent) that occurs in some women's brains during pregnancy, causing vagueness, forgetfulness, and poor concentration. These are all common complaints towards the end of pregnancy.

Taking an Omega-3 supplement, which should include around 500mg of DHA, will help both you and your baby throughout pregnancy and breastfeeding.

You can read more about fatty acids in the Omega 3 chapter.

DIGESTION

You might find that your digestion is sluggish during pregnancy. This is because your body produces large amounts of progesterone, a hormone that relaxes smooth muscle tissue throughout your body, including your gastrointestinal tract. This relaxation slows down your digestive processes, which can cause increased gas, bloating, burping, constipation and flatulence and create generally miserable sensations in your gut, especially after a big meal.

THERAPIES AND TIPS for digestion

Nutrition

- Start each day with a glass of warm water with a squeeze of lemon to help kick-start your digestion.
- Try to reduce the amount of air you swallow while eating, don't eat in a hurry, take your time, chew your food thoroughly, and don't talk while chewing.
- Eat several small meals throughout the day instead of a few large meals. Large meals are difficult to digest and they will just cause more indigestion and bloating.
- Avoid drinking from a bottle or straw, don't gulp while drinking and limit your fluid intake during meals. You can make up for it between meals.
- Don't eat when you are angry or upset.
- Avoid eating very cold foods or drinking cold drinks while eating.
- Don't eat too much at one time.
- Don't skip meals.
- Avoid very fatty or fried food as it tends to slow down digestion.

☑ Supplements

- Supplementing with digestive enzymes can make a huge difference to bloating during pregnancy. Enzymes are essential for normal digestion and taking extra enzymes can give you a helping hand during pregnancy when digestion tends to be sluggish. Take the recommended dosage suggested by the product you buy.
- Probiotics, also known as intestinal flora, can improve digestion tenfold! Take the indicated dosage of the product you buy.

Lifestyle

- Sit up straight (don't slouch or lie down) while you're eating or drinking, even if it's just a small snack.
- A brisk walk can activate your sluggish digestive tract.
- Some people tend to swallow more air when they're anxious and tense. If this applies to you, you could consider practicing yoga for relaxation and good breathing techniques to help relax your diaphragm.

DILATION

Dilation is the opening of the cervix during labour in preparation for childbirth. Dilation is measured in centimetres or, less accurately, in "fingers." "Fully dilated" means that the cervix has dilated 10 centimetres and that you are ready to push your baby out.

DOULA

The word, "doula," comes from the Greek word for the most important female slave or servant in an ancient Greek household, she was the woman who helped the lady of the house through her childbearing. The word has come to refer to "a woman experienced in childbirth who provides continuous physical, emotional, and informational support to the mother before, during and just after childbirth".

Labour support doulas are trained and experienced labour support persons who attend to the emotional and physical comfort needs of labouring women to aid the labour process. They do not perform clinical tasks such as heart rate checks, or vaginal exams. They use massage, aromatherapy, positioning suggestions, etc., to help labour progress as well as possible. A labour support doula joins a labouring woman either at her home or in hospital/birth centre at the beginning of her labour and remains with her until a few hours after the birth.

In addition to emotional support, a doula works as an advocate to their client's wishes and may assist in communicating with medical staff to obtain information for the client so that her client can make informed decisions regarding medical procedures during her labour.

Postpartum doulas are trained to offer evidence-based information and support in breastfeeding, emotional and physical recovery from childbirth, infant soothing and coping skills for new parents. They may also help with light housework, fix a meal and help incorporate an older child into this new experience.

Community doulas play an important role for women at risk for complications, and those facing barriers to prenatal care. These doulas will combine the roles of labour support and postpartum doulas to offer continuous encouragement and reassurance to pregnant women who have little social support, like teenagers. Community doulas can encourage self-advocacy, teach parenting skills and motivate a teenager to feel in control of her pregnancy.
Goals of social support models like the Community-based Doula Initiative include preventing subsequent pregnancy and increasing the quality of the mother-infant bond directly after birth in order to increase the chances of secure mother-infant attachment throughout early childhood.

In general a doula provides

- Explanations of medical procedures and interventions.
- Emotional support.
- Advice during pregnancy.
- Exercise and physical suggestions to make pregnancy and childbirth more comfortable.
- Help with preparation of a birth plan.
- Facilitation of communication between members of the labouring woman's birth team.
- Massage and other non-pharmacological pain relief measures, aromatherapy, acupressure, acupuncture, breathing and any other non-medical comfort techniques she may be trained in.

- Positioning suggestions during labour.
- Support the partner so that s/he can provide support and encouragement to the labouring woman.
- Help to avoid unnecessary interventions.
- Help with breastfeeding preparation.
- Some doulas offer a written record of the birth (birth story.)
- Is present during entire labour and afterwards as long as is needed by parent(s.)

Women supported by a doula during labour have been shown to have

- 50% reduction in Caesarean rate.
- 25% shorter labour.
- 60% reduction in epidural requests.
- 30% reduction in analgesic use.
- 40% reduction in forceps delivery.

Six weeks after birth, mothers who had doulas were

- Less anxious and depressed.
- Had more confidence with baby.
- More satisfied with partner (71% vs. 30%.)
- More likely to be breastfeeding (52% vs. 29%.)

These statistics appear in "A Doula Makes the Difference" by Nugent in Mothering Magazine, March-April 1998. For detailed results from multiple studies, see: http://www.dona.org/positionpapers.html

For more information on the study of the effectiveness of doula support, please look on the following website: http://maternitywise.org/pdfs/continuous_support.pdf

DREAMS

You might find that you have incredibly vivid, sometimes crazy dreams during pregnancy. Although it is not known why the speculation is that because pregnancy is a time of enormous change you tend to process all your anxieties, worries and practicalities while sleeping causing restlessness and extreme dreaming. Progesterone also causes you to sleep very lightly during pregnancy, which means you wake easily and maybe because of that you remember your dreams more easily.

DUE DATE

Even though our mothers seem baffled by the fact that this generation count the length of their pregnancies by weeks and not by months, the length of pregnancy was defined as early as the 1800's by Naegele as ten lunar months (280 days/40 weeks) estimated from the first day of the last menstrual period until the due date 40 weeks later.

Things to think of when estimating your due date

Your caregiver will generally recommend an ultrasound around the 12th week of your pregnancy to estimate more precisely how many weeks pregnant you are.

Your caregiver can also estimate how far along you are by checking the height of your fundus (the top of your uterus.) Maturation can differ though and some say that a female fetus can be more mature than a male at the same gestational stage – *Kline 1989.*

If you had menstrual cycles longer than 28 days you should add a day onto your due date for every day that your cycle was longer. Ovulation could have been later than you thought in which case the gestation would be longer. Your caregiver will often take this into account too.

Statistics show that:

- 4% of all women give birth on their due date.
- 5 to 10% of pregnancies last around 42 weeks.
- An average of first time pregnancies (primipara) last for 288 days, this is 8 days past the due date.

- Pregnancies of women having their second/third/fourth etc (multipara) baby lasts an average of 283 days, this is 3 days past due date.

E

EATING & DRINKING DURING LABOUR

It's usually best to be guided by what you *feel* like eating while you are in early labour. However, it is worth remembering that meat and foods with a high-fat content can be heavy on the digestive system. Complex carbohydrates are especially good for labour because they guarantee a long, slow release of energy to help you through contractions. So it might be a good idea to choose from: Whole wheat bread, toast or crackers. Cereals, pasta, potatoes and rice are also good.
Sugary foods are easy to eat, and they do give you an energy boost, however, the energy quickly dissipates and leaves you feeling quite low, quite quickly. So avoid too many sweet snacks. Fruit is a good way to give you quick energy boosts.

Eat only as much as is comfortable; it's not a good idea to overload your stomach. Try to eat small amounts, regularly. A little snack every hour while you are in early labour, before you go to the hospital or call the midwife, will store up plenty of energy for the work ahead. Once you're in strong labour, you will probably find that you don't want to eat.

Midwives and childbirth educators sometimes recommend dextrose tablets and sports-drinks for women in labour. You may wish to avoid the fizzy variety of sports drinks as they may make you feel nauseous.

Labour is thirsty work, and birthing rooms need to be nice and hot. So you will certainly need to drink plenty of water. Make sure you buy some bendy straws to make it easier to drink no matter what position you are in. Don't worry about needing to urinate because of drinking a lot, walking to the toilet is an excellent way of keeping mobile during labour, and it could help make your contractions more effective. If you'd prefer your water flavoured, put a little squash in it. Stick to clear juices.

Examples of foods to eat during early labour

Small meals & snacks:

- Small baked potato.
- Sandwiches.
- Sardines on toast.
- Pasta with a light sauce (not creamy.)
- Rice with soy sauce.
- A bowl of cereal.
- Dried fruit.
- Fresh fruit particularly bananas, grapes and orange segments.
- Pieces of fruit dipped into honey for extra energy.
- Celery & carrot sticks.
- Cereal bars.
- Raisins.
- Crackers.
- Chicken soup – it is sometimes nice to just drink the clear bouillon of chicken soup and to save the more hearty part for after the birth.
- Vegetable soup.

Warm drinks

- Tea
- Also see my "Hot Chocolate Drink".

EMBRYO

From conception until eight weeks your developing baby is called an embryo. From eight weeks on it becomes a fetus. Remember that the first day of your pregnancy is counted from the first day of your last menstruation.

EMPOWERMENT

Empowerment is a process. It shouldn't be confused with an end product i.e., medicated or un-medicated delivery, home or hospital birth, etc. A woman's positive feelings about the birth of her baby could come from whether she felt supported, safe, encouraged and whether all the decisions made were in her and her baby's best interests. There is no right and wrong birth story.

Note: Empowerment often comes as a result of being able to make an informed choice. An informed choice is a voluntary, well-considered decision that an individual makes on the basis of options, information, and understanding.

ENDORPHINS

The biological necessity for pain in labour is mediated by the body's ability to produce endorphins. The beneficial effects and protective nature of endorphins are helpful for enhancing performance; they are nature's natural painkillers, they are similar to opiates in their chemical structure and action.

Endorphins offer a number of benefits for you during labour

- They are natural painkillers, produced in response to the pain caused by the dilating cervix and the contraction of the uterus.
- They create a sense of wellbeing and promote positive feelings.
- They may be an important link in mother-baby attachment; creating a positive emotional climate for the first meeting with the baby.

For your baby
From the baby's perspective, endorphins also work as painkillers during labour.

You are able to influence how effectively your body is able to produce endorphins during labour by being as relaxed and calm as possible. Techniques such as massage and acupressure also increase the amount of endorphins your body makes.

ENGAGING - BABYS HEAD

Your caregiver will externally check the position of your baby in the last few weeks of pregnancy and will be able to tell you whether or not your baby's head is engaged.
From about 33 weeks onward of your pregnancy you may experience your baby moving lower down into your pelvis. This process is known as "engagement" and simply means that the leading part of the baby has "engaged" into the pelvic brim. This helps to position the baby in preparation for the birth later. Your caregiver will usually record when this has occurred during one of your antenatal checks. Women often experience "engaging contractions" when the baby engages. These can be quite painful and are often experienced as a false start to labour. Many women report feeling more physically at ease following the head engaging. You may feel it is easier to breath, sleep and walk around. On the other hand the babies head engaging may lead to increased pressure on your bladder and you may feel a sensation of fullness and pressure between your legs.

Additional information
In first pregnancies the baby's head tends to engage during the last month. However in second pregnancies it is not unusual for the head not to engage until very late in pregnancy or even as late as the onset of labour.

ENZYMES - DIGESTIVE

An important part of a healthy pregnancy is providing you and your baby with good nutrition. In order to achieve this goal, you need to eat a healthy diet and you may possibly need to add supplementation to provide you with any nutrition that is lacking from your food sources. Once you're providing your body with these, you need to make sure you are properly absorbing your nutrients. The old saying, "you are what you eat", should really be changed to "you are what you absorb". Proper absorption gives your body the nutrients it needs to be healthy and to stay healthy.

Digestive enzymes are necessary for effective absorption. Digestive enzymes breakdown the food we eat so it can be used as a source of nutrients and energy.

Digestive enzymes come from two sources

- Internally, the pancreas produces digestive enzymes.
- Externally, raw food is the primary source of enzymes with sprouted seeds, grains and legumes as the most powerful source.

Foods and enzymes

The body has a difficult time digesting fried, pasteurized, barbecued, dried, and other over-processed and over-cooked foods, as their enzyme content is zero. So eat fresh raw fruits and vegetables and sprouted seeds. When cooking your vegetables, lightly steam or stew them. Slow stewing "traps" the enzymes in the vegetables.

During pregnancy digestion is also impaired due to the hormones that relax the smooth muscle of the digestive tract and because of your growing baby, which crowds your abdominal cavity.

Enzymes as a supplement

By taking digestive enzymes you:

- Accelerate the stomach's emptying of food improving your absorption.
- Reduce stomach acid.

- Reduce gas.
- Reduce abdominal cramping.
- Reduce heartburn.
- Lessen the possibility of allergies.
- Lessen any irritation along your digestive tract.

The most prominent plant based enzymes found in a supplement

- Papain, extracted from papaya fruit and Bromelain, extracted from pineapple both aid in the digestion of protein.
- Amylase, for the digestion of starches and carbohydrates.
- Lipase, to digest fats.
- Cellulase, breaks down fibre cellulose into smaller units.
- Lactase, helps in the digestion of dairy products.

Take a plant source digestive enzyme complex before or during each meal. Take the recommended dosage suggested by the product you buy.

EPIDURAL

During the active phase of labour you may begin to long for pain relief. Though an epidural is an obvious solution for your discomfort, it is important to know everything there is to know about epidurals before choosing to have one.

An epidural and your Baby

The drugs cross the placenta and affect the baby, making his/her heartbeat and breathing more sluggish during labour and after delivery.

An epidural and you

Many physicians do consider the epidural block to be the optimal method of pain relief for uncomplicated labour or non-emergency Caesarean births because it allows a woman to remain fully alert. Nevertheless, the anaesthetic requires up to twenty minutes to take full effect and may leave a painful "hot spot" after delivery. In addition, it may diminish uterine contractions, increasing the need for Pitocin, a chemical form of the natural hormone, oxytocin that stimulates contractions. The risk of an episiotomy with a forceps delivery is hereby also increased, and in about one out of hundred women, a severe, chronic headache will develop after having an epidural.

EPISIOTOMY

An episiotomy is a surgical cut made just before delivery in the muscular area between the vagina and the anus (the area called the perineum) to enlarge your vaginal opening.
Obstetricians used to cut episiotomies routinely to speed delivery and to prevent the vagina from tearing, particularly during a first birth. Many experts believed that the "clean" incision of an episiotomy would heal more easily than a spontaneous tear. But a great many studies over the last twenty years have disproved this theory, and most experts now agree that the procedure shouldn't be done routinely.
Research has shown that women with spontaneous tears generally recover in the same or less time often with fewer complications than those with episiotomies. Women who have episiotomies tend to lose more blood at the time of delivery, have more pain during recovery, and have to wait longer before having sex without discomfort.
Sometimes an episiotomy damages the anal sphincter increasing the risk of anal incontinence, which means trouble controlling bowel movements and gas.

Why you may need an episiotomy
In a few situations, an episiotomy may be necessary for your own or your baby's wellbeing:

- If your baby's heart rate shows that he isn't tolerating the last minutes of labour and needs to be born as quickly as possible.
- If your baby is very large and your caregiver feels he/she needs a little extra room to be able to be born.

- If your practitioner needs a little extra room when using forceps or a vacuum extractor to help deliver your baby.
- If your tissue is starting to bleed or looks like its about to tear in multiple places as your baby's head begins to crown. The idea here is that being cut in one place may allow you to avoid tearing in more than one place. That said, a few shallow tears may still be preferable to an episiotomy, even so your caregiver will have to make the call.

How to make sure you don't have an unnecessary episiotomy
Talk to your caregiver early on in your pregnancy about your feelings regarding the procedure. Ask them how often and under what conditions they would perform an episiotomy, and how they might help you avoid tearing as well.
Studies show that, in general midwives tend to do far fewer episiotomies than obstetricians.
Research also shows that if you do perineal massage starting around four weeks before your due date it decreases the likelihood that you'll tear or need an episiotomy.

🖶 **Research & Facts**
Episiotomy is NOT recommended for routine delivery by the American College of Obstetricians and Gynecologists.

EXCESSIVE URINATION

Excessive urination is a normal symptom of pregnancy because of the fact that your kidneys need to process much more liquid due to the extra blood in your system and your body constantly makes new amniotic fluid leaving the "old" fluid which your kidneys need to flush out. By the end of pregnancy your bladder is literally squashed by your growing uterus triggering a feeling of pressure, which has you making endless trips to the toilet both day and night.

THERAPIES AND TIPS for Excessive Urination

☯Acupuncture

Acupuncture sessions will help balance your water metabolism and you might find that you will be waking less at night to go to the toilet.

☛My experience: many women find that after a session of acupuncture they still need to urinate often during the day but that their sleep is less disturbed by the fact that they are not having to urinate so often at night.

Lifestyle

- Don't reduce your drinking because you think it may lessen your trips to the toilet. You need to consume at least 1,7lt of liquid a day. I say, "consume" because you also get a fair amount of liquids from eating fresh fruit and vegetables. If you are up frequently at night to urinate it may be best to drink a good amount during the day and then cut down in the hours before bedtime.
- Avoid drinking caffeinated drinks because they are diuretic and will cause you to urinate more.
- Try to make sure you have emptied your bladder completely every time you have been to the toilet. When you think you are finished, stand up slightly with your bottom jutting out over the toilet while leaning on your thighs with your hands, this tilts the full weight of your uterus off your bladder and you will often find that you can dribble out a little more!

When to consult your caregiver

Unfortunately a urinary tract infection during pregnancy doesn't feel exactly the same as when you aren't pregnant. Any of the following symptoms could indicate a possible a urinary tract infection and you will need to contact your caregiver immediately:

- Frequent Braxton Hicks.
- Abdomen pain and or lower back or flank pain.
- You feel that you need to urinate directly after just having been or you get a stinging or burning sensation when urinating.

- Your urine is dark and you only manage small amounts each time you feel the urge.

EXERCISING DURING PREGNANCY

If complications don't limit your ability to exercise throughout your pregnancy there is no doubt about it, exercise is a big plus for both you and your baby. At a time when you wonder if this strange body can possibly be yours, exercise can increase your sense of control and boost your energy level. Not only does it help to make you feel better by releasing endorphins (the feel good hormones) it can:

- Relieve backaches and improve your posture by strengthening and toning muscles in your back, butt and thighs.
- Reduce constipation by accelerating movement in your intestine.
- Prevent excess wear and tear on your joints (which become loosened during pregnancy due to normal hormonal changes) by activating the lubricating synovial fluid in your joints.
- Help you sleep better by relieving stress.
- Helps you to look better because exercise increases the blood flow to your skin, giving you a healthy glow.
- Prepare your body for birth by strengthening your muscles and heart and increasing your endurance to support you during labour and delivery.
- Help you gain control over your breathing which in turn can help you manage the pain during labour.
- Regain your pre-pregnancy body more quickly because you will gain less fat weight during your pregnancy if you exercise. Remember though that the goal of exercising during pregnancy is to maintain fitness, not to loose weight.

Many women enjoy dancing, swimming, water aerobics, yoga, pilates, biking or walking as their particular exercise during pregnancy. Swimming is especially appealing because of the weightlessness you feel in water. Many experts recommend walking. Walking is great because it is easy to vary your pace and to do it whenever you have the time. Whatever type of exercise you decide on, the key is to listen to your body's warnings. Many women can become dizzy and as the baby grows, their centre of gravity changes so it may be easy for you to lose your balance, especially in the last trimester.
Your energy level may also vary greatly from day to day. And as your baby grows and pushes up against your lungs, you'll notice a decreased ability to breathe in more air (and the oxygen it contains) when you exercise.

Stop exercising if you feel:

- Fatigue.
- Dizziness.
- Heart palpitations (your heart pounding in your chest.)
- Shortness of breath.
- Pain.

You should keep your heart rate below 160 beats per minute.
It also isn't good for your baby if you become overheated because temperatures greater than 102.6 degrees Fahrenheit (39 degrees Celsius) could cause problems with the developing fetus - especially in the first trimester - which can potentially lead to birth defects. So don't overdo exercise on hot days.

Exercises you should avoid

It is recommend that pregnant women avoid weight training and sit-ups. Lifting reduces the blood flow to the kidneys and uterus, and exercises done on your back (including sit-ups and leg lifts) cause your heart rate to drop and also decrease the flow of oxygenated blood to your body and the baby. Its better to tone your abdominal muscles while on all fours by relaxing your muscles while you inhale and then tightening your muscles as you exhale.

It is generally a good idea to avoid any activities that include:

- Bouncing and jarring.
- Leaping and jumping.
- Sudden changes in direction.
- Any sport where there is a risk of abdominal injury.

Typical limitations include contact sports, downhill skiing, scuba diving, and horseback riding because of the risk of injury they pose.

F

FAINTING & DIZZINESS

Fainting is common during pregnancy because your cardiovascular system undergoes dramatic changes: Your heart rate (pulse) goes up, your heart pumps more blood per minute and the amount of blood in your body expands by an average of forty to forty five percent. The capacity of your circulatory system also increases as blood flows to your enlarging uterus and placenta. Because of this your blood is more likely to pool in the lower body and your brain may become temporarily deprived of enough oxygen, causing fainting or dizziness. During the second trimester, maternal blood pressures usually falls below early pregnancy levels. This is known as the mid-pregnancy blood pressure drop. This drop in blood pressure could lead to dizziness or light-headedness. During the third trimester, blood pressure usually goes back up to the early pregnancy level.

Practical suggestions

- Lie down on your **left** side this will maximize blood flow to your heart and thus to your brain, and will likely keep you from actually fainting and probably relieve the sensation of light-headedness altogether.
- Avoid standing for long periods of time.
- While standing practice contracting and relaxing your leg and buttocks muscles to help your blood to return to your head.
- When resting lay on your side as opposed to your back.
- When sitting return to standing slowly.

- Don't get out of a hot bath too quickly – also remember that very hot baths are not advised during pregnancy.
- Keep cool in hot weather.
- Take a few drops of Bach Rescue Remedy as soon as your start to feel faint, this doesn't treat the cause of feeling faint, it just helps you to cope.
- Make sure your blood sugar doesn't get too low by eating small protein-rich snacks throughout the day.
- Take three deep, slow breaths to increase the amount of oxygen in your system.

When to consult your caregiver

Feeling light headed from heat, hunger, or getting up too fast can just be a part of being pregnant. However, if you are feeling dizzy for no apparent reason you should alert your midwife. You could have anaemia or very low blood pressure.

Call right away if dizziness is accompanied by severe headaches, blurred vision, impaired speech, palpitations, numbness or tingling, bleeding or if you actually do faint. Any of these symptoms could be a sign of a more serious problem that could affect you or your baby.

FEAR

Extreme pain in labour is often caused by fear and tension. A tense woman means a tense cervix. All caregivers know the effect of a tense cervix: pain, resistance at the outlet and prolonged labour with possible complications involving intervention.

Ensuring that you are well informed as to what happens to your body and your baby when you are in labour and having the confidence that your body is capable of birthing your child can help eliminate unnecessary fear and tension.

The practice of physical relaxation introduced in the last few months of pregnancy and during labour shows that women experience their labours in a more positive and gratifying way.

Each woman is different but if you understand what labour involves and what the best way is for you to relax both your mind and body during labour, you have a better chance of having a natural birth.

FEET

While pregnant, you have more blood and other fluids circulating in your body and because of gravity, some of that fluid settles in your feet. Many women notice some swelling throughout pregnancy, but most only experience it during their third trimester.
Swelling is often worse during the summer months because of the heat. Feet also tend to be slightly bigger during pregnancy due to hormones that help loosen your pelvic joints; unfortunately the body is unable to isolate this loosening function to the pelvis only and so all joints become looser and more flexible. Because of this flexibility and the extra weight the feet tend to "spread out", causing them to become wider, bigger and sometimes very sensitive.

THERAPIES AND TIPS for feet during pregnancy

Lifestyle

- Because gravity plays a big role in swelling, elevate your feet at least three to four times a day. When lying on a sofa or in bed, prop your feet up on pillows; when sitting in a chair, place your feet on a footstool.

Additional information

If your baby is in a posterior position you will need to vary your feet up position with being on hands and knees from week 34.

- Vary between sitting with your feet up and moving around to improve circulation.
- Wear special support stockings and avoid socks with tight bands around the calf or ankle.

- Exercise helps; water aerobics are ideal because the "hydrostatic" pressure helps distribute fluids that have pooled in your feet.
- Ask your partner or a friend to give you a *gentle* foot massage. This will increase circulation and help disperse the swelling.
- Increase your fluid intake. It seems counterintuitive, but the more water you drink, the less swelling and water retention you'll experience.
- Don't squeeze your feet into ill-fitting shoes.

Feet after the birth

Fluid-related swelling will disappear a few days after your baby is born. Some women however find that their feet are a size larger following a pregnancy so make sure you have your feet professionally measured if it feels as if your shoes don't fit after pregnancy.

When to consult your caregiver

Some swelling in your feet during pregnancy is normal, but if it appears abruptly or if you notice that your hands are also swelling, call your caregiver immediately. These could be signs of pre-eclampsia, a type of pregnancy-related high blood pressure than can be very dangerous.

FETUS

From week eight of your pregnancy your developing baby goes from being called an embryo to being called a fetus.

FIBROIDS

A fibroid tumour is a mass of compacted muscle and fibrous tissue that grows on the inside wall (or sometimes on the outside wall) of the uterus. It can be as small as a pea or as large as a grapefruit.

Fibroid tumours occur in as many as fifty to eighty percent of all women.
Fibroids usually develop prior to pregnancy, though many women don't know they have one until they have an ultrasound or the fibroid is discovered during a pelvic exam.
Only ten to thirty percent of pregnant women with fibroids experience symptoms. The most common is abdominal pain, which may be accompanied by light vaginal bleeding. Further possible symptoms of fibroids during pregnancy are pelvic pressure, frequent urination, a belly that is larger than it should be for term and constipation.
Even if you do experience symptoms, they don't usually affect your baby. However, your risk of miscarriage and premature delivery does increase slightly if you have fibroids and they can occasionally cause the baby to be in an abnormal position for delivery. They can also stall labour, or, if they're located in or near the cervical opening, they may block the baby's passage. All of these (rather rare) problems can increase the likelihood of a Caesarean delivery.
Some women can experience a lot of pain from fibroids. The main treatment in this case is bed rest.
Fibroids often grow larger during pregnancy, due in part to pregnancy hormones. You will most probably be recommended to have regular ultrasound examinations during your pregnancy to determine any likely complications.

When to consult your caregiver

If you know that you have fibroids be aware of the signs of a possible early labour and call your caregiver immediately if any of these signs occur.

FLUID RETENTION- OEDEMA

Oedema is a puffy swelling, of the fingers, ankles, legs and feet it can occur during pregnancy due to the fact that your blood vessels dilate under the influence of hormones and your blood volume doubles during pregnancy. The result of both these factors is a 'pooling' of the

blood, especially in the lower extremities (feet and ankles.) Higher levels of oestrogen in the last part of pregnancy can cause even more puffiness. Hot weather, standing for a long time and high blood pressure make oedema worse, especially at the end of the day.
A certain amount of oedema is quite common and normal during pregnancy so don't be alarmed. However, if you experience severe and/or sudden swelling in your hands and face call your caregiver. Swelling in these areas are not usually associated with normal oedema and could be a sign of pre-eclampsia, a serious condition for both you and your baby.

THERAPIES AND TIPS for oedema

Lifestyle

- The best way to deal with excess fluid is not to restrict it but to mobilise it. Keep it from staying in areas that cause the most discomfort, such as in the legs, feet, fingers and abdomen. A good balance between rest and exercise is a good way to do so. So when you're not resting, exercise gently. Women who exercise tend to suffer less from the common ailments associated with pregnancy, including swelling. It seems to redistribute the retained fluids. Brisk walking is good exercise and you could try swimming when you are getting too heavy to walk briskly.
- Another way to help move excess fluid is by assisting kidney function. You can do this by drinking sufficient fluids.
- Keep your legs elevated whenever possible.

Additional information

If your baby is in a posterior position you will need to vary your feet up position with being on hands and knees from week 34.

- Don't cross your legs when sitting.
- In addition, you may find that wearing support tights especially designed for pregnancy could make all the difference. Make sure you are fitted properly and wear them according to the directions. Avoid socks with tight elastic tops.

- If it is your fingers that are swollen remember to take your rings off before they become too tight to remove.

Nutrition

- Celery sticks, asparagus, artichokes, grapes, blackcurrants and parsley are all natural diuretics.
- Eating the following foods that contain vitamin B6 help your body to rid itself of excess fluid: poultry, fish, eggs, beans, broccoli, cabbage, bananas and peas.
- Avoid refined forms of table salt and use natural sea salt instead.
- Include potassium rich foods such as bananas, unpeeled potatoes, fish, dates, avocado, dried figs, melon, carrot and prune juices and beans (black, kidney, lima) into your diet to reduce oedema.
- Young dandelion leaves eaten in your salads are an excellent source of calcium and potassium. It will vitalize your kidneys and help reduce oedema.
- Eating only steamed vegetables and fresh fruit for an entire day could reduce oedema drastically.

☑ Supplements

Take vitamin B6 50mg once day to aid your body with ridding its self of excess fluid.

Massage

- Gentle massage can help oedema. Be sure to find a masseur that is knowledgeable about both pregnancy and oedema.
- You can give yourself a gentle massage to increase your circulation in the groin and pelvic region, which in turn will decrease the oedema in your legs and feet. Using massage oil *gently* massage with your right hand starting from the midline of your lower tummy, just above the pubic bone, along the bikini line then up towards your left hipbone. Repeat this ten times. Now do the same but use your left hand and massage towards your right hipbone.

☯Acupuncture
Acupuncture does help reduce oedema but does so more easily if you visit your acupuncturist at the very beginning stages of oedema.
☛ **My experience**: I have successfully treated women with oedema but I feel that nutrition and lifestyle play an important role in addition to my acupuncture treatments.

✜ Homeopathy
You can take homeopathy to assist your kidney function during pregnancy. Visit a homeopath for exact advice.

♣ Phytotherapy/herbs
Drink four to six cups of nettle tea throughout the day to reduce oedema.

✳Aromatherapy
Edema aromatherapy massage
Ginger - 3 drops
Lavender - 2 drops
Cypress - 2 drops
Diluted in 2 tablespoons vegetable oil. Massage the feet, legs, fingers and hands towards the heart. Use once a day for not longer than ten consecutive days.

💣 When to consult your caregiver
If you have sudden swelling accompanied by headaches, blurred vision and possible abdominal pain you need to contact your caregiver immediately. These could be signs of pre-eclampsia.

FOODS TO AVOID DURING PREGNANCY

Cravings
Not all the foods that you crave during pregnancy are good for you. They often contain too many unsaturated fats, sugars and little if

any of the nutritional benefits. Try to keep cravings realistic. For many women pregnancy it is the only time they feel that binges and cravings are legitimate but remember a healthy diet during pregnancy isn't only about do's and don'ts its about taking care of a growing baby with nutritious, balanced food. There is no harm in eating something you are really craving every now and then, but if you know that whatever you crave is unhealthy it is better not to give into it. Go to "Cravings" for more information.

Caffeine and Alcohol

Caffeine is a stimulant and a diuretic. Since it is a stimulant, it increases your blood pressure and heart rate, both of which are not recommended during pregnancy. Caffeine also increases the frequency of urination. This causes reduction in your body fluid levels and can lead to both dehydration and oedema (water retention.)

Caffeine crosses the placenta to your baby and your baby's metabolism is still maturing and cannot fully metabolize the caffeine. Any amount of caffeine can also cause changes in your baby's sleep pattern or normal movement pattern in the later stages of pregnancy. Remember, caffeine is a stimulant and can keep both you and your baby awake.

Drinking alcohol during pregnancy can cause physical and mental birth defects.

Caffeine and alcohol actually prevent absorption of folic acid and iron, two essential nutrients during pregnancy, and leach calcium out of your bones. They both directly affect your fetus and can have long-term developmental effects.

Avoid Saturated (bad) Fats

You only need five percent fat in your diet to stay healthy. Make sure you avoid eating too many saturated fats: animal fats like cream, meat, pastry, cheese and milk. Also cut the fat off red meat because chemicals found in animal diets are often stored in the fat.

Eat unsaturated fats: seeds, olive oil, fish, shellfish and raw nuts.

Fish and Seafood

Sushi

It's fine to eat sushi when you're pregnant as long as any raw fish used to make it has been frozen beforehand. This is because occasionally fish contains small worms, which could make you ill if they are still alive when you eat the fish. Freezing kills worms and makes raw fish safe to eat.

Most of the raw fish used to make sushi in restaurants has generally been frozen at minus 20°C for at least 24 hours, although this is not a general rule so it may be better to find a restaurant that does so.

If you make your own sushi at home, freeze the fish for at least 24 hours before using it.

It is recommended that you avoid eating too much tuna due to its high content of mercury.

Shellfish

You should avoid oysters and other shellfish while you're pregnant, unless they are part of a hot meal and have been thoroughly cooked. This is because, when they are raw, these types of seafood might be contaminated with harmful bacteria and viruses. Proper cooking usually kills these. It's unusual for shellfish to contain listeria, a type of food poisoning bacteria that can harm unborn babies. Salmonella and campylobacter (the most common food borne illnesses) might make you ill, but it's unlikely that they will have any direct effects on your baby. If you're concerned about eating shellfish, you might choose to avoid them when you're pregnant.

Smoked fish

Some countries give the advice that pregnant women should not eat smoked fish because of the risk of listeria even though the risk is extremely low. The risk of listeria is much higher with soft mould-ripened cheeses (such as Brie and Camembert) or pâté, which you shouldn't eat during pregnancy.

Food Additives

Unfortunately many foods that we enjoy are full of preservatives, flavour enhancers, colouring and even hormones and antibiotics. Food additives help foods look better and last longer. Organic foods

and produce have the fewest chemical residues and additives and often taste much better too.
Most additives are said to be safe during pregnancy however, I advice you to avoid the following additive:
MSG – Monosodium Glutamate is a flavour enhancer and is used in many products especially, soups, crisps and is used the Asian and Eastern kitchens. It can cause headaches, a dry mouth, nausea, dizziness, skin rashes and stomach upset.

Artificial food colourings

Colourings are in many processed foods, and most are considered safe during pregnancy but try to avoid too many foods that have bright, artificial colours.

Saccharin

Saccharin is a sweetener and has not been shown to be safe in pregnancy and is known to be dangerous in large quantities outside of pregnancy.

Non-pasteurized foods and raw meat

Pasteurization eliminates bacteria in the processing of milk. Most milk and yoghurts are pasteurized. Although some products are not pasteurized:
Some bottled smoothie's and yoghurt drinks are often not pasteurized.
Many soft cheeses, like blue cheeses, Brie, feta, Camembert, soft French cheeses and some mozzarellas are not pasteurized. Non-pasteurized cheese and pates or raw meat can carry bacteria called Listeriosis or Toxoplasmosis, which are very dangerous for your developing baby.

Fruits and Vegetables

Always wash any fruits and vegetables thoroughly before eating them.

Uncooked eggs

Raw eggs are risky during pregnancy because they can carry salmonella. So stay away from runny eggs, sauces made with raw eggs and homemade mayonnaise.

Avoid dieting

If you are sensitive to weight gain normal gain weight during pregnancy can feel alarming. It could be tempting to start or continue dieting. Don't do it. Nourishing a healthy, growing baby is your responsibility, and an imbalanced diet is a bad idea. You actually need six small healthy balanced meals a day. And the healthier they are, the healthier your weight will be. You should to avoid eating the foods that increase significant weight gain like fatty foods, sweets, chocolates and cakes, creamy sauces etc.

If you are a vegetarian or on a vegan diet your diet should be safe as long as you take supplements to get the nutrients you will be missing such as vitamin B12, folic acid, iron, zinc, magnesium, calcium and vitamin D. Also make sure you get enough plant proteins with each meal.

FRIGHT, FLIGHT, FIGHT

The human body has an automatic survival system that allows us to take flight (run) or fight (defend) when we feel frightened or threatened. It is a natural reaction of the sympathetic nervous system, causing the body to produce huge amounts of adrenaline to equip us with the ability to run or defend.

When a woman is giving birth this system needs to be "put on hold" so to speak, to enable a woman to give birth. If a woman feels unsafe, judged, frightened or threatened her body will automatically produce adrenaline (it assumes that the woman needs the extra adrenaline to help her cope with her situation) and this in turn will halt the birthing process.

So in order for you to give birth to the best of your ability you need to make sure you are in a place in which you feel:

- Safe.
- Comfortable.
- Not judged.

And with people who:

- Won't judge you.
- Will support you.
- Will encourage you.
- Give you the feeling of safety.
- Understand what you need and want.

G

GINGER TEA

Ginger tea is used to quell nausea.
To make a litre of the ginger tea, add two teaspoons of grated ginger to one litre of water. Bring the ginger water to the boil in a well-covered non-aluminium saucepan. Simmer the mixture for about four minutes at low heat.
Drink four cups spread over the day.

GOOD FATS VERSUS BAD FATS

Your body creates some important substances out of fats and uses fat to transport vitamins. Nutritional fats are divided into good (healthy) fats and bad (unhealthy) fats. Think of fats as building bricks. The better the bricks (good fats), the stronger the building.

Good fats
Good fats tend to stay liquid at room temperature and often even in the refrigerator. They are the naturally occurring, traditional fats that haven't been damaged by high heat, refining, processing or other man-made tampering such as 'partial hydrogenation' and are these fat are the "good bricks". The best of these kinds of fats are found in fish, nuts, avocados and seeds. Extra virgin cold-pressed olive oil is also a good fat.

Certain essential fats such as omega-3's (found in oily, cold water fish) and the occasional omega-6 (found in evening primrose oil) have been used to treat everything from postnatal depression, skin problems and are essential for the development of your baby's nervous system.

Polyunsaturated Fats

Omega-3 Fatty Acids

- Fatty fish such as herring, sardines, salmon, mackerel and trout (tuna is also a fatty fish but has been linked to containing high amounts of mercury.)
- Flaxseed, walnuts and canola oil (all contain a less active form of omega-3.)

Omega-6 Fatty Acids

- Vegetable oils: corn oil, safflower oil, sesame oil, soybean oil and sunflower oil
- Soft (liquid or tub) margarine, ideally one that is trans fat-free
- Walnuts
- Sunflower seeds, pumpkin seeds and sesame seeds
- Soy "nuts" (roasted soy beans), soy nut butter and tofu

Monounsaturated Fats

- Vegetable oils: olive oil, canola oil and peanut oil
- Nuts: almonds, cashews, peanuts, pecans and pistachios
- Avocado
- Nut butter

Bad Fats - Saturated fats

Saturated fat becomes firm at room temperature. Animal fats are generally seen as bad fats and especially in combination with refined carbohydrates they are extremely unhealthy. Also, because of horrible factory farming methods, antibiotics and steroid use, fats from non-organically raised, non-free-range animals should be avoided during pregnancy. Among the worst of the bad fats are margarine and the fats found in anything fried. If it says 'partially hydrogenated' on a food label, avoid it like the plague. Refined vegetable oils are also on the bad fats list. These oils oxidize easily and have been processed with high heat, which removes all the healthy nutrients like Vitamin E.

Fats with negative health effects are known as saturated fats and trans fats.

Examples of these are:

- High-fat meats.
- Vegetable oils that have been partially hydrogenated.
- Fried foods.
- Margarine.
- Commercially prepared foods containing partially hydrogenated oils like crackers, cookies, cakes, pastries and microwave popcorn.
- Poultry skin.
- High fat dairy products: cheese, butter, whole milk, and reduced fat milk.
- Cream, cream cheese, sour cream and ice cream.
- Tropical oils: coconut oil, palm oil, palm kernel oil and cocoa butter.
- Lard.
- Fried foods: doughnuts, French fries and other deep fried fast food items.

H

HAEMORRHOIDS

Many pregnant women suffer from haemorrhoids (also called piles) during pregnancy. Haemorrhoids are varicose veins (swollen veins) that appear in your rectal area. They are often itchy or painful and can sometimes rupture and bleed. Your growing uterus can increase the pressure on the lower veins in your body plus the pregnancy hormones can cause the walls of your veins to relax, allowing them to swell more easily.

THERAPIES AND TIPS for haemorrhoids

Golden Tip

Dab pure Hamamelis (Witch Hazel) tincture onto your haemorrhoids. Readymade Hamamelis pads are also available in some chemists or drugstores. If the pads aren't available make your own pads by soaking cotton wool pads (the ones you use to remove make-up) in Hamamelis and store them in a Tupperware, ready for use.

Nutrition

Haemorrhoids and Constipation

- Haemorrhoids are not always but often caused by constipation so make sure you eat enough natural fibre: fresh fruit, vegetables, whole grain bread, breakfast cereals sprinkled with broken linseed and prunes.

- Drink at least two litres of liquid a day especially water. Dandelion tea and prune juice are also good liquids to help combat constipation.
- Eating dried fruit especially prunes could help a sluggish bowel but too much dried fruit in one sitting could give you terrible wind and possible cramps.
- One tablespoon of Linseed oil every morning and evening can help move a very sluggish bowel.

✳Aromatherapy

Add fifteen drops of geranium and five drops of cypress essential oil to the contents of a small tube of KY jelly. Simply squeeze the jelly into a small jar, add the essential oils, mix very well and rub around the anal area when required. This treatment will not only alleviate the symptoms but it also helps to prevent hemorrhoids occurring in the first place.

☯ Acupuncture

Acupuncture works very well to reduce the pain caused by swollen haemorrhoids.

☛My experience: I have had very good feedback from the women who I treat for painful haemorrhoids. The treatment seems to reduce both the pain and the size of the haemorrhoids.

Lifestyle

- Avoid long periods of standing or sitting if possible.
- Use unscented, unbleached brands of toilet paper – preferably use Hamamelis pads to wipe with.
- Keep your anal area clean and dry but avoid using soap as this may aggravate the problem.
- Use a Witch Hazel (Hamamelis) spray or a natural haemorrhoid cream on the haemorrhoids twice a day.
- Walking or swimming for at least 30 minutes per day aids your digestive system, thereby relieving constipation.
- Always go to the toilet as soon as you feel the urge.

☑ **Supplements**

Taking an intestinal flora supplement (Probiotics) daily could improve bowel function.

Remember that if you are taking a chemical iron supplement it could be the cause of your constipation so be sure to stop taking it once your iron levels are back to normal or switch to non-constipating iron sources.

Homeopathy

Aesculus Hippocastanum is used when haemorrhoids are sore and aching, with a swollen feeling.

When to consult your caregiver

Contact your caregiver if you have excessive bleeding.

HEADACHES

An increase in headaches during the first trimester are thought to be caused by the surge of hormones along with an increase in the blood volume circulating throughout your body. Headaches may be further aggravated by stress, poor posture, dehydration, changes in your vision, lack of sleep, low blood sugar and caffeine withdrawal. Try to avoid medication during pregnancy.

THERAPIES AND TIPS for Headaches

Lifestyle

- Relaxation techniques like meditation, yoga and biofeedback are helpful in reducing stress and tension headaches.
- Stopping for a catnap can also help.
- When you are at the office, give your muscles a break by getting up regularly, taking a few slow, deep breaths and having a good stretch.

- Headaches are more likely on hot days when the extra weight you are carrying makes you feel sticky and tired. On hot days drink plenty of fluids and make sure the room you're in is well ventilated.

✚ Homeopathy

- Gelsemium 6C – for band-like pain over the eyes made worse by heat and movement.
- Phosphorous 6C – for head pain brought on by atmospheric changes or shock and made better from rest and food.
- Nux vomica 6C – for headaches that occur first thing in the morning but get better as the day wears on.

☯ Acupuncture

Acupuncture is excellent for treating headaches during pregnancy.
☛ **My experience**: I find that just one or two treatments are sufficient to get rid of headaches completely!

☯ Shiatsu

Many headaches begin with muscle tension around the jaw and neck. This can be caused by stress or by just sitting in one position at a desk all day. Tense muscles restrict blood flow to the head, which can result in head pain. To lessen tension in body and mind consider a regular Shiatsu massage.

Reflexology

A reflexology session relaxes you and helps the body to rediscover balance giving it the possibility to resolve tension headaches.

Chiropractor

Sometimes headaches are caused by a misalignment of the vertebrae. A chiropractor that is used to working with pregnant women will be able to realign your spine.

Nutrition

- Dehydration can cause headaches make sure you drink at least 2 litres of water/liquids a day if you are suffering from headaches.
- You should try to prevent sudden low blood sugar, which is a common headache culprit. Try eating smaller, more frequent meals and avoid all refined sugars and carbohydrates.
- Certain foods are known to be headache triggers, so avoid the following: chocolate, nuts, caffeine, citrus fruit and hard cheese.

Massage

Ask you partner to give you a gentle neck and shoulder massage to relieve the tension or find a professional masseuse that is specialized in pregnancy.

✳ Aromatherapy

Peppermint oil contains a mild, local anaesthetic and several studies have shown that it is one of the most effective headache relievers. Several studies, including one published in 1995 in the Journal of Phytomedicine, have found that peppermint oil was the most effective aromatherapy remedy for headaches.

Mix 5 drops of peppermint with a base of 1 tbsp vegetable oil - preferably one that doesn't have a strong smell. Rub it on your temples, neck or wherever you feel the pain.

When to consult your caregiver

If you are in your second or third trimester and have a sudden headache or a headache for the first time in your pregnancy (which may or may not be accompanied by visual changes, sharp upper abdominal pain, sudden weight gain, or swelling in your hands or face), you will need to have your blood pressure and urine checked right away to be sure you don't have pre-eclampsia.

HEARTBEAT

The embryonic heartbeat starts beating around twenty-two days after conception, or around five weeks after the last menstrual period. The heart at this stage is too small to hear, even with amplification, but it can sometimes be seen on an ultra sound scan around 6 weeks.

The Doppler device

A ***Doppler*** device is a small sound device that is pressed against your abdomen to amplify the sound of your baby's heartbeat. It uses a form of ultrasound to convert sound waves into signals of your baby's heart so that you can hear them. Around the 9th or 10th week after your last menstrual period, you might be able to hear your baby's heartbeat at your prenatal appointment. Whether you actually hear the heartbeat at 9 or 10 weeks depends partly on luck. The Doppler device must be placed at just the right angle for it to detect the tiny heartbeat. It also depends on the position of your uterus and if you're slim or heavy. By the 12th week, the heartbeat can usually be heard consistently, using the Doppler device for amplification.

Heart rate

A normal heart rate for you is under 100 beats per minute, but your baby's heart rate should be between 120 and 160 beats per minute.

HEARTBURN

Heartburn is a burning sensation that you feel behind the breastbone, often accompanied with the taste of acidic regurgitated food. It is caused by both hormonal and physical changes in your body. During pregnancy, the placenta produces the hormone progesterone, which is needed to relax the smooth muscles of the uterus. Unfortunately it also relaxes the valve that separates the oesophagus from the stomach, allowing gastric acids to seep back up your oesophagus, causing an unpleasant burning sensation. Progesterone also slows down digestion and in later pregnancy, your growing baby crowds your abdominal cavity, slowing elimination and pushing up the stomach acids to cause heartburn.

THERAPIES AND TIPS for heartburn

Golden Tip

- If you also have other digestive problems like bloating, flatulence and constipation take Probiotics in powder form. Mix half a teaspoon in some warm water and swirl it around your mouth before swallowing it. In addition to this "swirling" also take the recommended dose of the Probiotics brand that you have.
- If you have no other digestive problems drink a small glass of warm water with a teaspoon of apple cider vinegar in it before eating in the morning and again before bedtime. Also drink this mixture anytime in the day each time you have heartburn. Although vinegar is sour in taste it is very alkaline and will cancel out the high acid accumulation in your oesophagus.
- Suck on an Umeboshi "pill" or take a quarter of a teaspoon of Umeboshi paste when you experience heartburn. Sucking on an Umeboshi pill can often keep heartburn at bay for a few days. For more information go to the Umeboshi chapter.

Nutrition

- Avoid carbonated beverages, alcohol (which you should avoid anyway during pregnancy), chocolate, caffeine, high-acid foods like citrus fruits and juices, tomatoes, spicy, fried and fatty foods.
- Cut out eating bread. This sounds quite drastic but if you have really bad heartburn you will be prepared to try anything and for many women this works immediately!
- Don't eat big meals. Instead, eat several small meals throughout the day.
- Don't eat too close to your bedtime, eat a light evening meal before seven pm. Give yourself two to three hours to digest before lying down. When you do lie down it may help to

sleep slightly propped up with several pillows or a wedge. Elevating your upper body will keep the acids from running up your oesophagus.

- Avoid drinking large quantities of fluids during meals; you don't want to distend your stomach and it dilutes the enzymes needed to digest your food. It is important to drink at least eight glasses of water daily during pregnancy, but drink them between meals.
- Take your time eating and chew each mouthful thoroughly.
- Make sure you eat enough raw fruit and either raw or lightly steamed vegetables every day. These are rich sources of enzymes. Enzymes are needed for the digestive system to work properly. They are necessary to break down food particles so they can be utilized for energy and they speed up digestion.

Lifestyle

Yoga

Doing particular yoga exercises can be helpful for women who have heartburn. Ask your pregnancy yoga teacher to show you exercises that may help.

☑ Supplements

- Digestive enzymes break down foods into nutrients, which your body can then readily digest. By accelerating the stomach's emptying of food you reduce stomach acid and lessen any irritation along the digestive tract. Take a pure, plant source digestive enzyme complex before each meal. Always take the recommended dosage suggested by the product you buy.
- Take Probiotics (see Golden Tip.) Always take the recommended dosage suggested by the product you buy.

☯ Acupuncture

Heartburn can be very successfully treated with acupuncture.

☛ My experience: I find that acupuncture works well if treated as soon as the symptoms begin. I also give a homework point called CV12 -Zhongwan (just below the sternum) so that you can apply gentle pressure to it three times a day for sixty seconds.

✚ Homeopathy
Nux Vomica 30C every couple of hours until you feel better.

♣ Phytotherapy/herbs
Teas can be made with the seeds of digestive herbs such as fennel, anise or dill to relieve heartburn.

Reflexology
Regular reflexology sessions will help to ease heartburn. You could ask your reflexologist to give you some homework reflexology, which your partner could do on you every evening.

HERPES

Most women suffering from herpes have usually contracted it before pregnancy. If this is true in your case then the good news is that your baby has received lots of antibodies against the herpes virus while he/she is inside you. The rate of transmission from mother to baby is very low when you have an old herpes virus infection even when there is an outbreak at the time of birth. This is because your baby has built up a good degree of immunity. The real problem occurs when you are infected for the first time while pregnant, especially if it is during the third trimester when you haven't had enough time to make antibodies and pass them on to your baby. Genital herpes is an infection caused by herpes simplex virus-2. It is a sexually transmitted and contagious disease. HSV-2 enters your body through small cuts, wounds or breaks in your skin. The HSV dies quickly outside the body so using something like a towel that has been previously used by an infected person cannot give you genital herpes.

Symptoms of genital herpes

Symptoms of genital herpes may include red bumps, small blisters, pain, ulcers or itching around the affected area. Symptoms usually begin within few days after exposure to an infected person. First small blisters, red bumps may appear and they usually become ulcers that bleed. After few days the ulcers heal and scabs form.

In men it can appear on the buttocks, penis and thighs or the inside of the urethra. In women it can appear in the vaginal area, buttocks, cervix or anus.

Headaches, fever, swollen lymph nodes in your groin and muscle aches could also be signs of genital herpes.

Genital Herpes is transmitted through unprotected sex.

Diagnosis

A blood test and a culture of the blisters or ulcers is the way genital herpes is diagnosed.

Treatment

Every country has a different protocol to treating herpes but most caregivers will treat herpes with antiviral creams and possibly oral antiviral drugs during the last weeks of pregnancy.

Your baby and Herpes

If you are infected with the Herpes virus there is always the possibility that you pass the infection onto your baby but the risk of passing it on if the infection is not active (no lesions present) is very low. Genital herpes in a newborn baby can cause seizures, meningitis, skin, or eye problems and sometimes brain damage.

THERAPIES AND TIPS for herpes

☑ **Supplements**

- Although there haven't been extensive studies on taking L.Lysine during pregnancy many caregivers prescribe L.Lysine capsules, 1000 mg three times a day for five days during an outbreak. It is more effective if taken at the first sign of an outbreak (tingling or pain.) You may then follow with L.Lysine 500 mg three times a day for the rest of the pregnancy to suppress the herpes.

- Herpes is a sign of a compromised immune system and taking a zinc supplement could boost your immune system. Supplement up to 50 mg per day. A liquid zinc supplement has proven to show quicker results. Take the dosage indicated advised by the product your purchase.
- Take 1000mg of an Acid-free Vitamin C for immune support.
- Use creams containing any of the following for local use on blisters and lesions: Propolis, which is a waxy substance that honeybees make, helps herpes sores to heal. Red Marine Algae can control and reduce the herpes viruses (including Oral Cold Sores, Genital herpes & Shingles) and is found in ointment or cream. Lysine is sometimes added to creams for treating Herpes.

Lifestyle

- Stress management is important because stress is definitely a trigger for an outbreak of herpes.
- Keep the area dry and wear cotton underwear. Also try to go without any underwear when possible to keep the area dry and aired.
- Taking *sitz baths containing two tablespoons of Epsom salts and two tablespoons of fine green clay can help ease the itching.
- After urinating, wash the area and then blow-dry it gently. The goal is to get the wet lesion to crust over, after which it will heal quickly and no longer be a risk to the baby.
- If you are prone to herpes having a Brazilian wax can help to keep your vagina and anus free of a herpes outbreak.
- Refrain from sex if you have lesions.

*A sitz bath (also called a hip bath) is a type of bath in which only the vagina and buttocks are soaked in water or a saline solution.

Nutrition

- Eat foods that contain lysine, these include meat, cheese (particularly parmesan), certain fish (such as cod and sardines), nuts, eggs, soybeans (particularly tofu, isolated soy protein, and defatted soybean flour), Spirulina and fenugreek seed.
- Eat foods that boost the immune system: fresh vegetables especially greens, fresh fruit especially berries but avoid eating any citrus fruits and drinking any juices containing citrus fruits during an outbreak.
- Avoid any food containing sugar, white flour and caffeine.

When to consult your caregiver

If you have herpes, or your sexual partner has herpes you should always inform your caregiver. Together you can make a plan to reduce your chances of the herpes becoming active. Babies who are born with herpes are successfully treated if the disease is recognized and treated early.

HIGH BLOOD PRESSURE (HYPERTENSION)

Your blood pressure is measured at each prenatal visit. The pressure in the arteries is measured as the heart contracts (systolic pressure) and when the heart is relaxed between contractions (diastolic pressure.) The blood pressure reading is given as two numbers; the top number represents the systolic and bottom number the diastolic pressure. A systolic reading of 140 or higher or a diastolic reading of 90 or higher is considered high blood pressure (hypertension.) As blood pressure can go up and down during the day, caregivers often re-check a high reading with one or more additional readings to determine if you truly have high blood pressure.

Five to eight percent of all pregnant women develop high blood pressure (hypertension) during pregnancy. This is referred to as gestational hypertension. Gestational hypertension generally goes away soon after delivery.

The effects of high blood pressure (hypertension) range from mild to severe. High blood pressure (hypertension) can harm your kidneys and other organs, and it can cause low birth weight and early delivery of your baby.

In a few cases gestational hypertension may progress to pre-eclampsia, so all women who develop high blood pressure (hypertension) in pregnancy are monitored closely. It must be said that most of these women have successful pregnancies so don't become too alarmed if your blood pressure is *slightly* high.

If you do seem to be developing signs of pre-eclampsia then ultrasounds and foetal heart rate testing may be recommended to check on your baby's well being. Complete bed rest may be recommended and you will be kept under constant observation.

Pre-Eclampsia

Pre-eclampsia is a potentially serious disorder, which is characterized by high blood pressure (hypertension) and protein in the urine and often symptoms such as headaches, blurred vision, dizziness, intense stomach pain and possible nausea. Pre-eclampsia also may be accompanied by swelling (oedema) of the hands and face and sudden weight gain (five or more pounds (3kg) in one week.) You should contact your caregiver right away if you develop any of these symptoms.

Pre-eclampsia usually occurs after about 30 weeks of pregnancy. Most cases are mild, with blood pressure around 140/90. Women with mild pre-eclampsia often have no obvious symptoms. If left untreated, though, pre-eclampsia can cause serious problems. All forms of hypertension can constrict the blood vessels in the uterus that supply the fetus with oxygen and nutrients. When this occurs before term, it can slow the fetus' growth.

Exceptions

Unfortunately some women develop pre-eclampsia very early in pregnancy, so even if you are not yet 30 weeks and you are experiencing any of the above symptoms alert your caregiver immediately.

THERAPIES AND TIPS for high blood pressure

Lifestyle

- Relaxation is important when you have high blood pressure. Although pre-eclampsia isn't strictly just high blood pressure it has been proven that if women stop working, relax more and reduce their levels of stress their pre-eclampsia can be controlled.
- Make sure you get plenty of sleep.
- Sometimes taking Bach Rescue Remedy helps to reduce stress temporarily.
- A little gentle exercise helps to improve circulation and thereby reduce blood pressure.

Nutrition

- The sodium/potassium balance in your body is very important so **do not restrict** your salt intake during pregnancy. When salt intake is restricted this balance is disturbed and the placenta may not grow sufficiently and it may stop functioning properly. Your body cannot make enough new blood for you and the baby without adequate salt. Salt restriction can actually cause high blood pressure and swelling, rather than prevent them. Use **natural sea salt** instead of table salt, which is iodized sodium chloride. **Do however restrict** table salt, processed, pre-packaged foods, which contain sodium chloride in abundance. Use your taste buds, this way you are more likely to eat the right amount of salt for you.
- Maintain a healthy, balanced diet, containing plenty of raw fruits and steamed vegetables.
- You may be missing some nutrients if you are showing signs of pre-eclampsia: Calcium rich foods: Goat's milk and cheese, salmon, sardines, mackerel, seaweed (especially kelp)

sesame salt (gomasio), tahini (a paste made from sesame seeds) and dark leafy greens like broccoli, fresh parsley, watercress, cabbage, rocket leaves, turnip greens, paksoi. There is controversy about the body's ability to assimilate calcium from pasteurized, homogenized milk so don't be lulled into thinking you are getting enough calcium if you are eating a lot of milk products.

- Omega-3 rich foods: fatty fish (herring, tuna, mackerel, sardines, wild salmon), flaxseed oil, seaweed, walnuts, leafy green vegetables and crustaceans
- Foods containing vitamin B6: eggs, chicken, carrots, fish, liver, kidneys, peas, wheat germ and walnuts
- Eat 80 to 100 grams of protein each day. Foods that contain protein: Organic buttermilk, organic live yoghurt, butter, cheese (preferably goats or sheep), eggs, fish, shellfish, chicken or turkey, lean beef.
- Even though the best protein is absorbed from animal products, non-animal proteins include: Rice, beans, cornmeal, tofu, nuts, whole meal, sesame seeds and sunflower seeds.
- Avoid caffeine (coffee, tea or cola) at all cost. Instead drink the following: raspberry leaf tea, nettle tea, dandelion tea, water and fruit juice.
- The juice of half a lemon or lime plus two teaspoons of cream of tartar in a half a cup of water once a day for three days, lowers your blood pressure, if needed, repeat after a break of two days.
- Foods to eat: anything with a high water content: watermelon, cucumbers and celery if you are also suffering from oedema with the high blood pressure.

☑ Supplements

- 200mg Calcium given in conjunction with 400mg magnesium can help to lower blood pressure.
- Vitamin B6, 50mg per day.
- Omega-3 has been associated with treating heart disease and high blood pressure outside of pregnancy and is recommended for women who have chronic hypertension even before

becoming pregnant. Most women are taking Omega-3 during pregnancy but for women with hypertension high doses are recommended (up to 4000mg per day.)

☯ Acupuncture

Seeing an acupuncturist throughout your pregnancy can help prevent high blood pressure.

☛My experience: I find that acupuncture can be beneficial in the treatment of high blood pressure but should always be in done in conjunction with conventional medicine if there are signs of pre-eclampsia. One of the reasons acupuncture can help reduce high blood pressure is that it helps you to relax. I find that a session will sometimes help reduce high blood pressure for three to four days. If caught early acupuncture will having a lasting effect on reducing high blood pressure.

♣ Phytotherapy/herbs

To help lower your blood pressure, take 2-4 capsules of Passionflower daily, or 15 drops of Passionflower tincture three times a day, continue for several weeks for the most benefit.

Reflexology

Regular reflexology treatments will help to keep you calm, which will possibly lower your high blood pressure for a few days at a time. Consult a qualified practitioner for treatment.

Massage with Aromatherapy therapy

A massage using essential oil given by a masseur/masseuse specialised in pregnancy could help to reduce tension and therefore temporarily lower your blood pressure.

When to consult your caregiver:

Occasionally pre-eclampsia develops very quickly. So, if you have any sudden swelling, or intense headaches accompanied by blurred vision or spots before your eyes or if you have severe pain in your abdomen, dizziness and possible nausea don't hesitate to call your caregiver. Early detection and care can make a big difference in the case of pre-eclampsia.

🖶 Research & Facts

Dr. Brewer is an obstetrician who has done research into high protein diets to combat pre-eclampsia and nausea. He is convinced that eating 80 to 100 grams of protein daily with no salt restriction prevents toxaemia. In thirty years of using this diet in thousands of patients he has seen no cases of eclampsia, anaemia, nausea, premature separation of the placenta, severe infections in lungs, kidneys and liver, low birth weight babies, premature babies and miscarriage. All babies were born healthy. *The American obstetrical profession continues to oppose the concept that malnutrition causes eclampsia*. Dr. Brewer has been able to instruct midwives in how to institute his high protein diet for eclamptic patients. *This diet leads to reversal of symptoms, which is unheard of when using conventional drug therapy.*

Dr Brewer recommends:

- One quart or more of milk daily.
- Two eggs **and** one or two servings of fish, chicken, lean beef or cheese daily.
- One or two daily servings of fresh green leafy vegetables (mustard, collard or turnip greens, spinach, lettuce, broccoli, or cabbage.)
- Five daily servings of whole wheat bread, corn tortillas or cereal.
- A piece of citrus fruit or a glass of orange or grapefruit juice.
- A large green pepper, papaya or tomato.
- Three pats of butter daily.
- Five servings of yellow vegetables weekly.
- Three baked potatoes weekly.
- No sea salt restriction.

HORMONES AND NATURAL CHILDBIRTH

There are four major hormones active during natural childbirth.
Oxytocin: The hormone of love, which stimulates the contractions and aids bonding directly after birth.
Endorphin: The hormone of pleasure, which acts as pain-relief and helps you to reach a trance-like state during labour.
Adrenaline and Nor-Adrenaline (Epinephrine and Nor-Epinephrine): The hormones of excitement, which aid your body to remain active during birth.
Prolactin: The mothering hormone, which triggers milk production.

These hormones, which are triggered at childbirth are common to all mammals and originate deep in the mammalian or middle brain. For natural birth to proceed optimally, this part of the brain must take precedence over the neo-cortex, or rational brain. This shift can be helped by an atmosphere of quiet and privacy. Dim lighting, little conversation, reassurance, gentle support and no expectations or rationality from you as the labouring woman can help achieve this. You will then intuitively choose the movements, sounds, breathing and positions that will help you to birth your baby most efficiently. This is your genetic and hormonal blueprint, which you can access via your middle brain only if your rational brain is "switched off".

HORMONES DURING PREGNANCY

Most hormones during pregnancy are produced or stimulated by the placenta from around the eighth week of pregnancy. Before that the corpus luteum (what is left of the follicle once you have ovulated) stimulates the production of hormones.

Human chorionic gonadotrophin – HCG

HCG is the hormone that triggers the positive result in pregnancy tests. The levels of HCG are high in the first three months and are suspected of being one of the causes of nausea. HCG stimulates the corpus luteum (what's left of the follicle once you have ovulated) to produce progesterone.

Relaxin

Relaxin has an effect similar to that of progesterone in relaxing especially the smooth (internal) muscles of the body, promoting growth and softening of the uterine cervix and transforming the pubic joint cartilage into being more flexible. Relaxin plays an important role at the beginning of pregnancy by inducing a healthy physiological response in blood vessels by increasing dilation and thereby benefiting blood pressure and kidney function.

Progesterone

Progesterone affects almost every aspect of pregnancy. It relaxes smooth muscle and decreases prostaglandin formation, which is especially important for the uterus so it is less likely to contract and cause a miscarriage. All the abdominal organs also become more flexible from progesterone, which is necessary for when they get squashed by the uterus in late pregnancy. Progesterone increases body temperature and the breathing rate and it causes blood vessels to dilate making it possible for them to carry more blood.

Other smooth muscle in the body may also be affected by the high levels of progesterone, such as the lower oesophageal sphincter; which can result in increased heartburn and acid reflux, especially in the later stages of pregnancy and the anal sphincter; which can result in haemorrhoids. Progesterone also softens cartilage and is therefore responsible for the commonly occurring hip and pubic bone pain. Progesterone can also cause tenderness in the breasts early on in pregnancy and the bloated feeling many women experience throughout pregnancy.

Oestrogen

Oestrogen plays a very important role in the development of the fetus. Without oestrogen, the lungs, kidneys, liver, adrenal glands and other organs of the fetus would never be triggered into maturation. In fact, the placenta itself would never grow and operate properly if not for oestrogen.

The following list shows some other known "jobs" undertaken by oestrogen:

It triggers the maturation of reproductive organs, helps in the development of sexual characteristics, assists in the lactation process, regulates bone density in the fetus, maintains the endometrium during pregnancy, promotes blood flow within the uterus, maintains, regulates and triggers the production of other hormones. Increased levels of oestrogen during at the end of pregnancy sometimes cause ankles to swell and the soft 'puffy' look some woman get.

Oxytocin

Oxytocin is a hormone that is released during labour, it causes your uterine (womb) muscles to contract, which in turn causes your cervix to become thin and dilate. Oxytocin also ensures the release of your placenta and is released into your bloodstream when your newborn suckles on your breast. The highest level of oxytocin you will experience is just after the birth of your baby. Oxytocin is the 'love hormone' and ensures that the mother and baby bond just after birth.

Prostaglandins

These are hormones that play a role in softening and preparing your cervix helping to get it ready for labour.

HOSPITAL BAG

When packing your hospital bag remember to include support items for both you and your husband.

Bring snacks, money, magazines, warm socks, a hot water bottle, sports drinks and "distraction material" (a favourite hobby, puzzle, game or a deck of cards.) Many fathers wish they had remembered basic things such as a camera, chewing gum, breath mints, dextrose, toothbrush and toothpaste and a change of clothes. Don't forget to bring clothes for the baby and a clean change of clothes for yourself!

HOT CHOCOLATE DRINK FOR DURING LABOUR

This quick and easy to make, delicious hot chocolate drink can boost a slow starting labour *or* get a stalled labour going again.

Hot Chocolate Recipe
1lt of water (NOT MILK!)
1 slab of 72% pure (bitter) chocolate
10 black peppercorns
1 sprig of fresh rosemary (or a large pinch of dried rosemary)
1 cinnamon stick (or half a teaspoon of dried cinnamon)
Honey to taste

Boil 1lt of water, add the chocolate, peppercorns and cinnamon stick and slowly bring back to the boil. Now add the rosemary and honey and gently simmer for 3 to 5 minutes.

- Rosemary is ideal for treating exhaustion and weakness and is anti-spasmodic.
- Pepper stimulates the circulation.
- Cinnamon is a uterine stimulant, acts as a tonic and is anti-spasmodic.
- Pure chocolate contains high amounts of magnesium and magnesium is a muscle relaxant, which can therefore decrease pain intensity. Chocolate also stimulates the release of endorphins (your body's natural painkiller) and is a stimulant.

HYPEREMESIS GRAVIDARUM

Pregnancy nausea is very common and affects around 70% of pregnant women ranging from a mild nausea to extreme nausea with vomiting. For a small percentage of women the vomiting and nausea can be so severe that it is impossible to keep any food or liquid down at all causing significant weight loss and dehydration. This condition is known as Hyperemesis Gravidarum.

Hyperemesis affects around three in every thousand pregnant women and is described as relentless vomiting and nausea, which leads to the loss of at least 5% of the body weight. Like pregnancy nausea, hyperemesis can vary greatly in degree and duration, but for some women it may mean substantial time off work, a huge disruption to normal life and frequent visits to the hospital to re-hydrate right up until birth.

Unlike morning sickness, Hyperemesis Gravidarum usually requires hospital treatment to prevent dehydration and malnourishment. Treatment usually involves special drugs to suppress vomiting plus intravenous feeding and re-hydration.

☑ **Supplements**

- The only vitamin that has been proven to help Hyperemesis Gravidarum is vitamin B6, which is given intravenously in hospital.
- You could try preventing Hyperemesis Gravidarum in subsequent pregnancies by taking a Milk Thistle supplement for at least 3 months prior to trying to falling pregnant and during the first three to four months of pregnancy. Take the dosage recommended by the product you purchase.

When to consult your caregiver

If you suspect you're suffering from this condition it is important that you contact your caregiver immediately.

I

INDUCTION OF LABOUR

Induction of labour is carried out when it is felt that your baby is better off out of the womb than in. The most common reason for inducing labour is that you have gone over your due date, usually by two weeks. Other reasons could include pre-eclampsia, poor growth of the baby, an infection or unexplained bleeding at term.

Natural Induction - if you go past your due date

Acupuncture

Acupuncture for induction involves the insertion of very fine needles into specific points of the body to encourage the body to take that last step towards going into labour. Acupuncture to induce an over-due labour will generally be started around forty-one weeks and three days and you may need two to three sessions on consecutive days. Acupuncture can help to relax you and get your mind off the waiting, which can be just the trigger your body needs to go into labour. Acupuncture will not induce labour if both your body and the baby are not ready for labour.

Nipple stimulation

Nipple stimulation is the gentle rubbing or rolling of the nipples to encourage contractions. The theory is that oxytocin, a hormone that causes contractions, is released when the nipples are stimulated. The usual recommendation is fifteen minutes of continual stimulation on each nipple each hour for several hours. Just be gentle and if your contractions do start and continue or get stronger then stop the stimulation.

Sex

Sex as means of getting labour started is thought to work in three ways: firstly the physical movement may help to stimulate the uterus into action; secondly, sex can trigger the release of oxytocin, the 'contraction' hormone; thirdly, semen contains a high concentration of prostaglandins which help to ripen (soften) your cervix. Sex is safe as long as your waters have not broken. Not enough studies have been done to prove that sex works as a labour-starter but, if nothing else, it will take your mind off the waiting!

Borage Oil

Either Borage oil (also known as EFA or GLA) or Evening Primrose Oil (EPO) are used by many midwives to help ripen the cervix in the last few weeks of pregnancy. A 500mg capsule is taken daily and two gel capsules (each 500mg) are inserted vaginally and pushed up against the cervix before bedtime from 40 weeks onwards. Remember that you need to use clean fingers and make sure the capsules are also clean. Inserting anything into the vagina during pregnancy increases the risk of infection.

Reflexology

Reflexology is often said to induce labour and is used in many countries.

Homeopathy

Homoeopathic remedies use highly diluted versions of more potent substances used to treat the body.

Caulophyllum 30c is a well-known homeopathic medicine used to induce labour. Take one dose every 20 minutes until labour kicks in then stop unless labour slows down again.

Cimicifuga 30c can be a great aid for when your labour starts up but the contractions are irregular and painful but don't get longer or stronger. Take one dose every 20 minutes until the contractions become regular.

Walking

Walking is said to trigger labour, the explanation appears to be that the pressure of your baby's head pressing down on the cervix from the inside stimulates the release of oxytocin. Also, just being upright gets the forces of gravity working for you, encouraging the baby to move down onto the cervix. Be careful not to wear yourself out though. Labour can be exhausting and you don't want to use up all your energy before you've begun. Just take gentle stroll every evening before bedtime.

Castor oil

There are reports of castor oil being used to bring on labour as far back as the Egyptians, though how it works is poorly understood. The most commonly given explanation is that it acts as a powerful laxative and when it stimulates the gut it also stimulates the uterus and so "kick starts" labour. The second theory is that castor oil contains prostaglandins; these are hormones, which soften and prepare the cervix for birth. Be aware that nausea will most likely be the immediate effect of castor oil, followed by a bad case of diarrhoea. Beware! If the diarrhoea persists it can lead to dehydration, make sure you drink enough water to compensate the loss of liquid if you decide to go down this route.

4 fl oz of castor oil mixed with orange juice is the usual dose and if you are brave enough a second dose can be taken 12 hours later! I do not recommend taking castor oil in my practice.

Eating curry

Spicy food is often suggested as a means of bringing on labour. There are no scientific theories relating to this, but it may be that it stimulates the bowel and so encourages the uterus to get going by mechanical means.

Eating fresh pineapple

Fresh pineapple (especially the core!) contains the enzyme bromelain, which is thought to help to soften the cervix and so bring on labour. Each pineapple contains only very small amounts of bromelain so you would need to eat as many as twenty to have any effect. The most likely side effect of eating large amounts of pineapple would be a severe case of diarrhoea.

Red raspberry leaf

Raspberry leaf does not actually induce labour it prepares your uterus for labour and also has a positive effect on labour. An Australian study has shown that it will speed up the second stage of labour and reduce forceps delivery.

Start at 36 weeks with one cup of tea a day and build up gradually to four cups of tea daily. The tea can be sipped freely during labour to aid efficient contracting of the uterus.

Situations when the caregiver will decide that it is safer for a woman to give birth due to a risk to the baby or to the mother:

- Hypertension (high blood pressure.)
- Certain medical conditions such as diabetes in the mother.
- Ruptured membranes without contractions - the time given for labour to start spontaneously once your waters have broken varies from country to country, anything from twenty-four to seventy-two hours.
- Evidence of diminished foetal wellbeing.
- Diminishing amniotic fluid.
- Going well over the due date (at least 42 weeks in most countries) also known as 'post maturity'.

All inductions carry a risk

Most labours start naturally thereby allowing your body the chance to move from one stage of labour to the next. In this way your body is able to release endorphins so that you are able to cope with the ever-increasing intensity of your contractions. With chemical induction this natural succession is by-passed. The pain often comes more quickly and acutely and most women need pain relief to cope (usually an epidural.)

Induction by your caregiver

Membrane sweeping

Some caregivers try to induce your labour by sweeping your membranes. This has been shown to increase the chances of labour starting naturally within the next forty-eight hours and can reduce the need for other methods of induction of labour. Membrane sweeping involves your caregiver placing a finger just inside your cervix (if they can get into it) and making a circular, sweeping movement to separate the membranes from the cervix. It can be carried out at home, at an outpatient appointment or in hospital.

If you have agreed to induction of labour, you will generally be offered membrane sweeping before other methods are used. The procedure may cause some discomfort or bleeding, but will not cause any harm to your baby and it will not increase the chance of you or your baby getting an infection. Membrane sweeping cannot be done if your membranes have ruptured (waters broken.)

Using prostaglandins

Prostaglandins are drugs that help to induce labour by encouraging the cervix to soften and shorten (ripen.) This allows the cervix to open and contractions to start. Prostaglandins are normally given as a capsule or gel that is inserted into the vagina. This is usually done in hospital. More than one dose may be needed to induce labour. Doses are normally given every six to eight hours.

If you go past your due date and your membranes have not yet ruptured (waters broken) then prostaglandins are often the recommended method of induction.

Foley catheter.

A catheter with a very small un-inflated balloon at the end of it is inserted up into your cervix. The balloon is then inflated with water putting pressure on your cervix, stimulating the release of prostaglandins thus causing the cervix to open and soften. When your cervix begins to dilate, the balloon falls out and the catheter is removed.

Using Oxytocin

Synthetic oxytocin is a drug given in hospital to stimulate contractions.

Oxytocin is given through a drip and enters the bloodstream through a tiny tube into a vein in the arm. Once contractions have begun, the rate of the drip can be adjusted so that your contractions occur regularly until your baby is born.

Whilst being given the oxytocin your caregiver will monitor your baby's heartbeat continuously. Often if your waters have not broken, a procedure called an amniotomy may be recommended. This is when your caregiver makes a hole in your membrane to release (break) the waters. This procedure is done through your vagina and cervix using a small instrument. This will cause no harm to your baby, but the vaginal examination needed to perform this procedure may cause you some discomfort.

Oxytocin is given by a drip and being attached to this will limit your ability to move around. Whilst it may be okay to stand or sit up, it will not be possible to have a bath or move from room to room. It is common for women who have an oxytocin induction to need/choose for an epidural to help them to cope with pain.

It is known that oxytocin could cause the uterus to contract too much which may affect the pattern of your baby's heartbeat. If this happens you could be asked to lie on your left hand side and the drip will be turned down or off to lessen the contractions. Sometimes another drug will be given to counteract the oxytocin and lessen the contractions.

⃠ Exceptions

Policies on induction vary from country to country and also from caregiver to caregiver. In some countries misoprostol is given before trying oxytocin.

Breaking the waters

In some countries caregivers will manually break your amniotic bag of water to attempt to induce labour. This is also known as an amniotomy. An amniotomy is generally only done to induce a second or subsequent birth. Your caregiver will insert an amniohook (a large crochet hook looking device with a small sharp end), and snag the amniotic membranes. By creating this tear in the bag, the amniotic fluid will begin to leak out.

The actual breaking of the bag of waters shouldn't be any more painful than any other vaginal exam. Quite soon after your water is broken you may begin to have contractions or you may just feel like your baby has dropped further in your pelvis. Some women need this pressure of the baby to slowly stimulate contractions.

If you were having contractions before your water was surgically ruptured, this is called augmenting labour.

Risks associated with breaking the water include:

- Fetal distress.
- Augmentation of induction with Oxytocin.
- Failure of labour to start.
- Increase in fetal malposition.
- Increases the possibility of a C-Section.
- Increase in pain sensation with labour.

INSOMNIA

Sleep during pregnancy could be disturbed for many reasons.

- It could be that your growing abdomen presses on your bladder, causing you to make frequent trips to the bathroom during the night.
- You may have heartburn, back pain or aching in your pelvis making it difficult to find a comfortable position to sleep in.
- You may even be kept awake by the fact that your baby seems to move more at night.
- Pregnancy can be a time of high anxiety with an endless flow of thoughts and speculations regarding labour and delivery, your baby's health and the future.
- Sometimes insomnia is caused by your body's reaction to the high levels of progesterone. This makes you feel as if you don't ever manage to achieve deep sleep and so you wake at every little sound or disturbance.

THERAPIES AND TIPS for insomnia

Golden Tip

Magnesium is helpful for treating insomnia. One of the many functions of magnesium is to help relax the muscles. Taking a minimum of 400mg and a maximum of 800mg magnesium an hour before bedtime can improve sleep due to its relaxing effect.

☯ Acupuncture

Acupuncture is a good therapy for treating insomnia.
☛My experience: I have excellent results in the practice when treating insomnia.

Bach Remedies

Both these Bach remedies work well for insomnia. Choose the one that is relative to your situation.

- White Chestnut for unwanted thoughts and mental arguments.
- Walnut for all new situations and changes.

Lifestyle

- Take a warm bath or shower before bedtime to help you relax.
- Make sure you have a good mattress that is neither too soft nor too hard. A futon for instance is far too hard to sleep on during pregnancy.
- Before retiring for the night, try some relaxation exercises you may have learned in your childbirth class.
- Ask your partner for a massage.
- Take a daytime nap but limit it to an hour and try to go to bed around the same time each evening.
- Get enough exercise but don't exercise too close to bedtime because you may be too wound up to sleep.
- Clear your mind by writing a journal before going to bed.
- Avoid caffeine.
- Make sure your bedroom is a comfortable temperature.

- Find a few comfortable positions for sleeping. Sleep on your side with a pillow between your legs. Support your abdomen and back with other pillows.
- Avoid watching television right up until bedtime. Exciting or traumatic programmes can keep your brain ticking over.

Nutrition

- It is very important not to eat too late or too much in the evening because digestion will disturb sleep.
- Magnesium is often deficient in pregnant women due to the fact that it works hand in hand with calcium, which is needed in large amounts during the development of the fetus. Although you tend to get a fair amount of calcium from your daily diet, unfortunately our magnesium reserves have been all but depleted so it is quite difficult to ingest enough magnesium during pregnancy. A lack of magnesium could be causing your insomnia – see Golden Tip.
- Bananas contain Tryptophan, a type of protein that the body converts into serotonin, known to relax and improve sleep but remember not to eat too much too late.

Meditation & Yoga

The practice of Meditation can be a very effective as well as an inexpensive way to help you deal with insomnia. Look into different kinds of meditation and choose the one you think might work best for you. The idea behind meditation is that it calms and relaxes you and this will help you to fall asleep

✳Aromatherapy

The following oils will help relax you and could therefore induce sleep: Rose, lavender and chamomile. Add any of these to a bath before bedtime or place a burner in your bedroom.

♣Phytotherapy/herbs

A cup of tea made with skullcap (Scutellaria lateriflora) soothes raw nerves and restores deep sleep.

Massage

Massage can help promote more restful sleep and help prevent pregnancy related insomnia, which is caused by high levels of progesterone.

When to consult your caregiver

If you are not sleeping at all and it is affecting you so badly that you are no longer able to function you need to tell your caregiver.

ITCHING

About twenty per cent of all pregnant women have some kind of generalized skin itchiness. Hormones and your stretching skin, especially over your growing belly, are probably to blame for your discomfort. Sometimes your liver has difficulty in processing the extra hormones and toxins during pregnancy, which can reflect in a slight allergic reaction of your skin. About two-thirds of all pregnant women will get slight itching or red and itchy palms and soles, a condition experts think is caused by an increase in oestrogen. This is not serious as long as the itching doesn't become severe. (see: "when to consult your caregiver".)

THERAPIES AND TIPS for itching

Lifestyle

- If you have a bath try a warm oatmeal bath. Some chemists sell them ready-made or you could just wrap a handful of oats in a muslin square and put it in your bath or hang it under the hot tap while running the bath. Also add a tablespoon of linseed oil to the bath.
- Apply chamomile lotion or a good after-sun crème (make sure that it contains only natural ingredients.)
- Try using Rescue Remedy crème.
- Drink more water.

♣ Phytotherapy/herbs

Milk Thistle improves liver function and has not been proven to be contra-indicated for pregnancy. Take 600mg per day.

✚ Homeopathy

- Chamomile D12 taken every two hours can help acute itching.
- Boldocynara drops help the liver to cope with the excess cleansing it has to do during pregnancy. Boldocynara is contraindicated in the presence of gallstones (obstruction of bile ducts), ulcerative colitis, Crohns disease, ileitis, stomach ulcers or hepatitis.

☯ Acupuncture

Sometimes acupuncture can help for itching.

☛My experience: I find that a session will help reduce itching for a day or so. I usually give women a point to which they can apply acupressure as homework, which normally helps the effect of my session to last a little longer.

When to consult your caregiver

In rare cases, severe itchiness in your third trimester can be a sign of a serious liver problem called obstetric cholestasis. In this case the itchiness is very extreme and widespread. It often includes itching of the hands and feet and may also be accompanied by nausea, vomiting, loss of appetite, fatigue and pale-coloured stools and jaundice (yellowing of the eye whites.) A blood test will assess your liver (especially bile) function. If the liver is affected, you may be given medication, but it may also be necessary to deliver your baby early.

L

LABOUR

During pregnancy the level of progesterone in your body is high. One of the important functions of progesterone is that it prevents your uterus from contracting. However, towards the end of pregnancy, the level of oestrogen increases in relation to the level of progesterone. At the same time your body is producing increased levels of oxytocin. The result of this hormonal cocktail is an increase in oxytocin receptors on the surface of your uterus, eventually resulting in enough to trigger the beginning of labour.

Prostaglandin production in your body is also increased during the last few weeks of pregnancy. Prostaglandin softens your cervix, allowing it to open when contractions begin. It also has a softening effect on your pelvic ligaments enabling your pelvis to open more effectively during labour.

As your baby descends into your pelvis towards the end of pregnancy (lightening or engaging), the presenting part of your baby begins to apply pressure to the internal part of your cervix. This pressure, when applied evenly, results in a reflex reaction that triggers your brain to release increased levels of oxytocin and if there are sufficient receptors on the uterus they react to this increase and contractions will start. As the contractions move down over your uterus, the pressure from them causes your baby's head to become more flexed (the chin tucked towards the chest) this is called Foetal Axis Pressure and allows your baby to descend even lower and apply greater pressure on your cervix, continually increasing the amount of oxytocin released.

Your uterus is a powerful muscle that tightens and relaxes rhythmically during labour, allowing the cervix to stretch open and then help push your baby through the birth canal.

Every woman's labour is different; but here are some signs, which could indicate that your labour has started

- Dull cramps similar to menstrual cramps starting in your lower back and moving to your abdomen that come at regular intervals for at least two hours, lasting a minimum or thirty to forty-five seconds and gradually increasing in intensity and length. These contractions could possibly be accompanied by bouts of diarrhoea and/or a pinkish or brownish (slimy!) discharge called "show".
- Fluid leaking or even gushing out of your vagina, this indicates that the amniotic sac has ruptured and is called, "waters breaking".

Additional information

Only a small percentage of women start labour with their waters breaking and sometimes the waters break but the contractions don't start. In this case you will need to be induced (remember to try the alternative route if your caregiver agrees, before being induced medically.) In most cases the waters usually break naturally during labour at approximately eight centimetres dilation.

Once your contractions have started

Your caregiver will probably have given you some guidelines about when to contact him or her once you think your contractions have begun or your waters have broken. If your contractions have stared, this is your first pregnancy and you are planning to give birth in a hospital, you should stay home for a while so that you can relax and remain unencumbered by the hospital routine and environment. Take a walk, catch a nap, enjoy a long shower, sip liquids (clear liquids only), eat a small snack, keep stress to a minimum and just try to relax and preserve your energy. Most caregivers recommend that during a first labour, the woman waits until contractions are five minutes apart, lasting around a minute per contraction for around two hours before coming to the hospital or birth centre or calling the

homebirth midwife. In subsequent pregnancies you may be advised to make contact sooner, since your labour can progress much more quickly.
You should contact your caregiver immediately if you notice any vaginal bleeding other than the pinkish 'show,' if you don't feel your baby move for an unusually long time, or if you have constant, severe pain rather than intermittent contractions.

Although the length of labour varies considerably, women experiencing their first full-term birth usually have the longest labours. About half will exceed twelve hours, and two in ten labours will last longer than twenty-four hours. Subsequent labours tend to be much shorter.

The Three Stages of Labour *generally* seen in a first birth

- The first stage begins with the onset of contractions and ends when the cervix is fully dilated (to ten centimetres.)
- The second stage is the pushing stage and involves the actually birth of the baby.
- The third stage entails delivery of the placenta and membranes or "afterbirth."

During a **first birth** the first and longest stage of labour has three phases; the *early*, or *latent*, phase; the *active* phase and the *transition* phase.

First Stage: Early (*latent*) Phase

During the early phase of labour, contractions are often widely spaced, perhaps ten minutes or more apart and feel like a tightening or pulling in your back or groin. They can vary considerably in frequency and intensity. At this point you may feel excited, sociable and talkative, or you may be a bit nervous. It is important for ultimate effectiveness of the hormones that you try remain calm, relaxed and focused right from the beginning of this early phase – this doesn't mean you can't be happy, excited and thrilled at the same time!
Support aids: walking, relaxation and breathing techniques.

First Stage: *Active* Phase

As you progress from the early to the active phase, your attention focuses completely on labour. Your contractions could be about 3 minutes apart, lasting about forty-five to sixty seconds, and are felt more centred in your abdomen or lower back. They also become stronger and more rhythmic, peaking and receding like waves. Your determination may waver during this phase of labour. Extra reassurance from your partner and birth assistant will help you to stay focused. Breathing exercises and other relaxation techniques also become more important as your cervix dilates to eight centimetres, nearly wide enough to allow for your baby to pass through.

Support aids: Shower or bath, massage, reflexology, acupuncture, acupressure, TENS machine, breathing exercises, positive encouragement and regularly changing your position.

First Stage: *Transition* Phase

Transition is the time when the cervix dilates the final centimetres. During transition, contractions come very close together and last sixty to ninety seconds. You may have little relief between them and their intensity may cause you to feel frightened and overwhelmed. While you may have enjoyed your partner's presence and physical touch throughout the earlier part of labour, transition may suddenly make you feel withdrawn, irritable, and short-tempered. You may develop chills, become nauseous or feel the urge to have a bowel movement. These positive, physical sensations reflect the descent of your baby into the birth canal and can become more intense as you enter the second stage of labour.

Support aids: Heating pads for your lower back, slight changes in position, making a (low-guttural) noise, shower or bath, positive encouragement, coaching and visualization techniques.

Second Stage: Pushing out your baby

When the widest part of the baby's head has settled into the birth canal your contractions may slow to four or five minutes apart and become less intense. Most women feel an urge to push and if you don't feel this urge your caregiver will encourage you to push when each contraction begins and will monitor the baby's "descent" on a regular basis.

Throughout the second stage of labour, which can last from fifteen minutes to two hours, your baby will continue to descend through the birth canal.

As your baby descends his/her pliable head will mould slightly to the contours of your birth canal. Once your baby's head slips under your pubic bone, birth is imminent.

Support aid: Acupressure, a hot face cloth against your perineum and your partner can help support your back or legs.

As the top of your baby's head appears, or "crowns," you may be told to pant, rather than continuing to push, so your baby's head can come out gently rather than bursting out. When your baby's head is through, your caregiver will check to ensure that the umbilical cord remains free of the baby's neck. With your next contraction your caregiver will help your baby's body to be born.

Try to ensure that your baby is placed on your tummy or chest (preferably skin-to-skin) as soon as possible to encourage mother-baby bonding. If possible many caregivers will give you a few (important) moments to first observe your baby before it is placed on you.

Within a few minutes of birth, your rapidly diminishing uterine contractions should cause the placenta to separate from the uterine wall. Generally, you can expect the placenta to be expelled quite rapidly. You may be given oxytocin to stimulate contractions while your uterus is massaged to help deliver the placenta and reduce bleeding at this stage.

The caregiver will examine the placenta and inspect your vagina for any tears or bruises. If you have torn or had an episiotomy the caregiver will stitch you. In the meantime you and your partner will hopefully be oblivious to these final details as you share the joy of your new newborn baby.

LEG CRAMPS

Leg cramps are a sudden tightening of muscles in your calves, feet or thighs, which can cause intense pain.

During pregnancy leg cramps are possibly caused by:

- Changes in blood circulation during pregnancy.
- The stress on your leg muscles from carrying the extra weight of pregnancy.
- The pressure of the growing baby on the nerves and blood vessels that go to your legs.
- A mineral imbalance or deficiency.
- Lack of fluids.

THERAPIES AND TIPS for leg cramps

Golden Tip

Magnesium has been proven to be beneficial in the treatment of leg cramps. Take a magnesium oxide supplement containing 400mg of magnesium in the evening. A magnesium supplement also containing calcium and potassium is preferable.

Nutrition

- Include potassium rich foods such as bananas, unpeeled potatoes, fish, dates, avocado, dried figs, melon, and beans (black, kidney, lima) into your diet to reduce leg cramps.
- Drink more water and include carrot and prune juices to your daily liquid intake.
- Reduce your intake of phosphorus-rich foods such as soft drinks, processed meats and snack foods.
- Drink nettle tea: four to five cups a day.

Lifestyle

- Avoid standing or sitting with your legs crossed for long periods of time.
- Stretch your calf muscles regularly during the day and several times before you go to bed.

- Rotate your ankles and wiggle your toes when you sit, eat dinner or watch television.
- Take a walk every day, unless your caregiver has advised you not to exercise.
- Avoid becoming over-tired.
- Lie down on your left side to improve circulation to and from your legs.
- Stay hydrated during the day by drinking water regularly.
- Try a warm bath before bed to relax your muscles.
- Rest when you are tired and elevate your legs when possible.
- Wear support stockings.
- Massage your legs with arnica oil daily to improve circulation.

If you get a leg cramp

- Straighten your leg.
- Flex your foot so that your toes point up towards your head.
- Walk around to stretch your calf.
- Avoid pointing your toes when you stretch your legs.
- Warming the muscle with a hot water bottle or heating pad may help relax the muscles.

M

MASSAGE DURING PREGNANCY

Many women suffer from aches and pains, stiffness and tension during pregnancy. Gentle massage can often help to relieve problems such as backache, insomnia, poor circulation, oedema and headaches. As well as relaxing and soothing away physical symptoms, massage can be a wonderful way of including your partner and children in your pregnancy.

When and how to massage

Although some schools recommend avoiding massage during the first three months of pregnancy, many women find gentle massage throughout their pregnancy to be very beneficial.

For a professional massage find a masseur/masseuse that is trained to massage pregnant women.

For massage at home stick to gentle relaxing massage avoiding too much pressure on the lower back until 38 weeks.

MATERNAL INSTINCT

Although most mothers feel an instant connection with their baby directly after birth, don't be surprised if your maternal instinct doesn't kick in right away. It's not unusual to feel a little ambivalent towards your newborn baby. For some women it may take a little time, but the feelings of love and protection will come.

How your baby might look directly after birth

Some babies are born with what is called a "cone head" because the baby's head has spent some time in the birth canal it could be long and pointy. The shape of your baby's head will slowly un-mould (take on their natural form.) Be patient, it could take a week or two.

Your baby's head, eyes and genitals are likely to be swollen or puffy in the first few days. The baby could be covered with body hair, especially if it is born early. This is called lanugo and disappears within a few weeks, if not sooner.

Early babies also may also have a layer of vernix, the cheesy white moisturizer that protects their skin inside the womb.

The baby's skin colour may not match the parents' at birth. It could be anything from pale to very red to purple. However, the natural pigmentation will slowly appear.

Enhancing Maternal Instinct

Bonding and maternal instinct is really a continuation of the relationship that began during pregnancy. Birth cements this bond and gives it reality. If you have had a natural birth in which all the natural hormones were present then from the moment your baby is born he/she will be awake, aware and ready to look into your face so that it can imprint your features into his "survival memory bank". A newborn has enormous, dilated pupils to enhance its "cute/lovable factor". Looking into your baby's face, smelling his or her special smell and touching this unique little being within the first moments of his or her life will help to trigger your maternal instinct.

Bonding and feeling your maternal instinct is not a now-or-never phenomenon. Bonding during the first moments after birth gives the parent-infant relationship a head start. However, immediate bonding after birth is not like instant glue that cements a parent-child relationship forever. Because of medical complications some mothers are temporarily separated from their babies after birth. And although epidemics of bonding blues have occurred in mothers who have had Caesarean births or who have had premature babies that need intensive care, as soon as mothers and babies are reunited, creating a strong mother-infant connection is often quickly established.

MID-PREGNANCY BLOOD PRESSURE DROP

During pregnancy your blood pressure will typically rise and fall. During the second trimester, maternal blood pressure usually falls below early pregnancy levels. This is known as the mid-pregnancy blood pressure drop. This drop in blood pressure could lead to dizziness or light-headedness. During the third trimester, blood pressure usually goes back up to the early pregnancy level.

MUCOUS PLUG

Throughout pregnancy a mucus plug blocks the opening of the cervix to prevent bacteria from entering into the uterus. Before labour, this mucus plug is expelled during the softening and ripening of the cervix in preparation for birth.

Somewhere in the last few days of pregnancy you may notice a pinkish mucous discharge, which is called the 'show' or 'bloody show,' as a sign that your mucous plug is being expelled. Remember though labour could be hours or even days away as the cervix gradually softens over time. If the mucous plug is lost weeks before your due date your body will generally make a new plug.

⃠ Exceptions

It is possible that you will loose some, or all, of your mucous plug a little early (anything up to two weeks) in second or subsequent pregnancies due to the fact that in subsequent pregnancies the cervix can ripen early and even open slightly in the last few weeks of pregnancy and so the plug becomes easily dislodged.

Sometimes the mucous plug is lost during labour and goes unnoticed.

N

A NATURAL THIRD STAGE OF LABOUR

An expectant or natural third stage involves letting nature take its course when the time comes for your placenta to be expelled. In an expectant or natural third stage the following protocols are followed:

- Your baby will placed on you as soon as it is born and you will hold your baby skin-to-skin. Some midwives like to allow you to observe your baby before placing it in your arms.
- You would be in an upright position – so not on your back with your legs in stirrups.
- The cord is left untouched and unclamped until it has stopped pulsing.
- When you feel contractions you will push and the placenta will be born.
- There should be no cord traction or fundal pressure and no drugs administered.

In some cases an expectant or natural third stage is contraindicated and a managed third stage would be considered the safest option. These are:

- If the mother has had any pain-relieving drugs during labour.
- If she has a history of postpartum haemorrhage.
- If her placenta had to be surgically removed in a previous birth.

- If she has had a multiple birth.
- If she has had drugs to stimulate or speed up labour.

THERAPIES AND TIPS to aid the birth of the placenta

Golden Tip

Acupuncture

- The use of acupuncture or acupressure is very effective in the release of the placenta. If your caregiver or doula does not use or know acupuncture then your partner could apply the following acupressure technique: He/she sits or stands directly behind you and applies very firm downward pressure on the top ridge of both shoulders (on the muscle between the curve of your neck and your actual shoulder) as you push.
- Standing (if possible) while blowing into a large empty bottle is sometimes very effective for releasing the placenta. By blowing into the bottle you will automatically put downward pressure on your pelvic floor, which could help to expel your placenta.

Homeopathy

Sabina 30c or Pulsatilla 30c: a single dose of either is taken to help expel the placenta.

NATURAL CHILDBIRTH

In many countries both pregnancy and childbirth have become a medicated and 'unnatural' event instead of being the natural process that it is. Although it feels as if this medical world has come to our rescue this is only so when there is a need for it. Normal pregnancy and childbirth has no need for this so-called assistance. A healthy pregnancy with both emotional and physical support enhances both the health of the baby, its long-term health and that of the mother.

Research has shown that babies born through the course of a natural, spontaneous labour experience their own peaks of oxytocin and endorphins, which makes them alert, ready to feed and bond. The mother experiences an enormous boost of oxytocin after natural childbirth enabling her to feel ready to bond and love her infant.

Natural Childbirth is made more possible when:

- The mother has the co-operation and encouragement of her partner.
- The mother wants her baby and fearlessly and lovingly welcomes its birth.
- The mother is healthy in mind and body.
- The mother is prepared in mind and body for the birth.
- The mother and her partner understand what is happening to her and her baby during the process of birth. The mother knows what the best way is for her to relax during labour when this is needed.
- The mother knows how to work with the forces of labour when this is needed.
- The mother has understanding, loving support and encouragement from those who attend her labour.

Additional information

The mother-infant relationship forms the elemental building block of all societies and cultures. If this relationship becomes contaminated with artificial hormones, painkillers, separation and pain, society will eventually suffer. The famous Obstetrician, Dr. Michel Odent, suggests that we are seeing these effects already in rising rates of ill health and social breakdown.

NAUSEA

Note that I don't call it morning sickness! Most women suffering from nausea during pregnancy have it all day or at various times

of the day and night. In my practice I have come across very few women that have pregnancy nausea ONLY in the morning.
No one knows what causes nausea during pregnancy but it's probably a combination of the many physical changes taking place in your body. These include:

- Rapidly increasing levels of the hormone *human chorionic gonadotrophin* (better known as HCG) during early pregnancy. No one knows why it contributes to nausea but the timing is right, nausea tends to peak around week 5, which is the same time that the levels of HCG peak too.
- A fluctuating blood sugar level is definitely the reason for many women.
- An enhanced sense of smell and sensitivity to odours definitely contributes to nausea. It is not uncommon for newly pregnant women to be suddenly overwhelmed by the smell of a steak frying two blocks away!
- Some women's gastrointestinal tracts are more sensitive to the changes of early pregnancy.
- Some women start a pregnancy already over-tired and stressed, which definitely increases their chances of becoming nauseous.

Nausea and how it affects your baby

Nausea and occasional vomiting won't threaten your baby's wellbeing as long as you're able to keep some food down and drink plenty of fluids. If you find that you're unable to eat a balanced diet, it is a good idea to take a multivitamin to make sure you're getting the nutrients you need. Hopefully you can find one that you can swallow and keep down, try powdered green food if you can't swallow tablets.
Some women even loose a little weight in the first trimester. This is not a problem as long as you're not starving yourself and are able to stay well hydrated. I have given some nutritional advice but you will most likely find that you have very specific foods that you can tolerate. It is a matter of trial and error; find out what works specifically for you and stick to that until you are able to switch back to eating a healthy balanced diet.

THERAPIES AND TIPS for nausea

Golden Tips

- Try an acupressure band called Sea Band. It is a soft cotton wristband that is available in chemists and is sold for nausea and travel sickness. You wear it so that a plastic button pushes against an acupressure point called Pericardium-6 Neiguan on the underside of your wrist. Instructions with a diagram are included when you buy the Sea Bands.
- The more dehydrated a woman becomes the worse her nausea gets so drink throughout the day even if you don't feel thirsty.
- Also eat soup as your basic food source. Soup often contains a good mixture of nutrients, is relatively easy to eat plus you get the benefit of extra liquid intake at the same time.
- Sniff a lemon! Many women find that sniffing a fresh lemon eases their nausea.
- If you able to, you should try sucking on an umeboshi "pill" or taking some umeboshi paste to alleviate your nausea - see Umeboshi.
- Increase the amount of protein in your diet – see Breakfast.

☯ Acupuncture

Acupuncture works very effectively for pregnancy nausea. You will need at least one to two treatments a week.

☛My experience: The most successfully treated ailment in my practice must be nausea! I do always combine my treatments with nutritional advice, a sea band and as homework I give women the following acupressure tip: Place two fingers, one on top of the other on your belly button and press firmly but gently for a minute when you are feeling nauseous.

Nutrition

- Try to avoid foods and smells that trigger your nausea and get someone else to do the cooking.
- Keep simple snacks, such as a yoghurt drink or a sandwich by your bed for nausea or hunger attacks at night.

- When you first wake up, eat some yoghurt or nibble a few crackers (preferably with cheese, meat or a nut paste) and then wait for ten minutes before getting out of bed.
- To keep your blood sugar level, eat small, frequent meals or snacks throughout the day so that your stomach is never empty. Always have something to snack on with you when you leave the house.
- Chicken soup is an excellent protein food and it is high in nutrients and liquids.
- Try drinking fluids primarily between meals.
- If you've been vomiting a lot, try sipping a non-fizzy sports drink that contains glucose, salt and potassium to replace lost electrolytes.
- Take your prenatal vitamin when you do eat to avoid it making you feel nauseous.
- Drinking elderflower cordial mixed with carbonated water can ease your nausea.
- Try chewing a few raw hazelnuts. You need to chew them for a long time, actually as long as possible, until they are totally pulverised and have become one with your saliva. It works for some!

High Protein and nausea

In my experience a high protein diet can drastically improve pregnancy nausea. Since many women will start cutting back food when they feel a little nauseated they start to experience highs and lows in their blood sugar. Anyone that has dealt with hypo or hyperglycemia knows that dramatic blood sugar swings can make you instantly nauseous.

Normally when we are nauseous we tend to want to eat simple carbohydrates, because they are bland. We avoid complex carbohydrates and foods rich in protein because they seem "heavy". Unfortunately, simple carbohydrates are quickly turned into glucose, which causes dramatic highs and lows in your blood sugar levels. Proteins combined with complex carbohydrates and high fibre foods process more slowly and help keep blood sugar levels more stable which in turn can help alleviate nausea.

Eat at least eighty to a hundred grams of protein a day.
It isn't easy finding and eating that much protein, especially if you have a pregnancy-induced aversion to meat, however, it is possible and very effective. Starting your day with a protein-rich breakfast (see the "Breakfast" chapter) really does help to get you going for the day and reduces nausea.
Many women report that on the days that that they manage to eat a good amount of protein they are hardly nauseous at all!

Protein foods:

- Fish
- Chicken, beef or turkey
- Soft (pasteurized) goats cheese
- Soybeans
- Baked beans
- Brown rice
- Lima Beans
- Organic live yoghurt
- Goat's milk
- Egg
- Nuts (raw not roasted)

☑ **Supplements**

- Vitamin B6 is given in hospitals to ease extreme nausea. Take 25 to 50mg daily.
- If you were very nauseous in a previous pregnancy there's some evidence that taking Milk Thistle as a supplement from three months prior to and throughout early pregnancy prevents nausea. Take the recommended dosage suggested by the product you buy.

♣ **Phytotherapy/herbs**:

- Try ginger to settle the stomach and help quell queasiness. See if you can find ginger ale made with real ginger and that doesn't contain too much sugar. A few studies found that taking powdered ginger root in capsules provided some relief otherwise make ginger tea and drink small cups of it throughout the day - also see "Ginger Tea".

- Drinking rooibos tea can settle the stomach.

Homeopathy

- **Nux vomica:** If you are nauseous, especially in the morning and after eating, you may respond to this remedy, especially if you are irritable, impatient and feel chilly. You may have the urge to vomit, often without success and you may have stomach cramps.
- **Pulsatilla:** This remedy can be helpful if your nausea is worse in the afternoon and evening. You may feel the need to drink something cool.
- **Sepia:** If you have gnawing, intermittent nausea with an empty feeling in your stomach. It is especially indicated if you are feeling irritable, sad and worn out. You feel worst in the morning before eating, but the nausea is not improved by eating.
- **Symphoricarpus Racemosa:** Is highly recommended if you are vomiting a lot.

Bach Remedies

Walnut assists in an adjustment to change.

When to consult your caregiver

If you are vomiting and not keeping down any foods or liquids you should contact your caregiver right away. You could be dehydrating and need hospitalisation.

NETTLE *(URTICA DIOCA)*

Nettle is one of the finest nourishing tonics known. The list of vitamins and minerals in this herb includes nearly every one known to be necessary for human health and growth.

Vitamins A, C, D and K, calcium, potassium, phosphorous, iron and sulphur are particularly abundant in nettles.

Some pregnant women alternate drinking nettle and raspberry brews for the last six weeks of pregnancy.

The benefits of drinking nettle infusion before and throughout pregnancy include:

- Aiding the kidneys. Since the kidneys must cleanse one and a half litres of extra blood for most of the pregnancy, nettle's ability to nourish and strengthen them is of major importance. Any accumulation of minerals in the kidneys, such as gravel or stones is gently loosened, dissolved and eliminated by the consistent use of nettle infusions (tea or tincture.)
- Easing leg cramps and other spasms.
- Diminishing pain during and after birth. The high calcium content, which is readily assimilated, helps diminish muscle pains in the uterus, in the legs, which are common after labour.
- Preventing haemorrhage after birth because nettle is a superb source of vitamin K and it increases the availability of haemoglobin.
- Fresh Nettle Juice, taken in teaspoon doses, can slow postpartum bleeding.
- Increasing the richness and amount of breast milk.

Making a nettle brew:

Pour a litre of boiling water over three to four tablespoons of dried nettle and let it steep for ten minutes before drinking.

Drink four to six cups a day for the last few weeks of pregnancy and in the first weeks after giving birth.

NUTRITION

Each time you choose something to eat, be it a meal, or a snack on the run, you are making a decision that influences both you and your baby because during pregnancy your nutrition not only fuels your body it also influences the growth and development of your baby.

Pregnancy is one of the most nutritionally demanding periods of a woman's life. Gestation involves rapid cell division and organ development. An adequate supply of nutrients is essential to support foetal growth. While caloric needs increase by only fifteen percent (300 cal/day), the requirements for some nutrients doubles during pregnancy. Your diet should constantly be providing your body with essential nutrients that both nourish your system and so automatically nourish that of your baby. Your nutrition also needs to help you stay healthy and aid you with the process of cleansing instead of burdening it with indigestible or excess food. An adequate nutritional intake will also help you to avoid possible complications during pregnancy.

For many women this requires some improvement in their current eating habits. The following information should help you to make wise food choices that could enhance both you and your baby's health.

Eat a wide variety of fresh foods and try to eat as many organic foods as possible

- Three to four servings of fruit per day.
- Three to four servings of vegetables per day.
- Four to six servings of whole grains, nuts, seeds and legumes per day.
- Three to four servings of animal protein per day – preferably organic lean meats, fish and eggs.
- Two servings of organic live dairy products or either goat's or sheep's cheese.
- Drink at least seven glasses of clean water daily.

Conscious eating

- Eat six small "meals" a day. Frequent eating is important to keep your blood sugar levels regular. As you get further on in your pregnancy you will find that you can't eat large amounts anyway due to the lack of space.
- Be creative and eat healthy snacks like vegetable sticks dipped in avocado salsa, smoked salmon with horse radish on a rice cracker, nut pastes instead of peanut butter, goat's yoghurt with berries, honey and nuts, a boiled egg with live yoghurt and chives dressing with a wheat-free cracker.

- Avoid gluten if possible. See "Optimum Nutrition to increase your chances for Natural Childbirth".

Flaxseed oil and Fish oil – sources of **Omega-3** fatty acids

There are three major types of omega 3 fatty acids that are ingested in foods and used by the body: alpha-linolenic acid (ALA), eicosapentaenoic acid (EPA), and docosahexaenoic acid (DHA). Once eaten, the body converts ALA to EPA and DHA, the two types of omega-3 fatty acids more readily used by the body. Omega-3 fatty acids and are essential for normal retinal, nervous system and brain development of your fetus. For you their benefits are that they will lift your mood and they work as "oil" for all joints to increase flexibility.

Eat fresh fish three times a week (avoid too much tuna due to the possible high levels of mercury) and use flaxseed oil (also known as linseed) sprinkled on salads.

Make sure you buy the flaxseed in small dark bottles and store it in a cool dark place. Don't keep an open bottle of flaxseed oil for longer than two weeks due to the fact that it oxidizes and becomes toxic. Some linseed products do contain vitamin E, which is an anti-oxidant (stops the flaxseed from oxidising) and then the product can be used for five to eight weeks.

To ensure you get enough Omega-3 during pregnancy take a supplement, 1000mg daily. Many pre-natal multivitamin formulas already contain Omega 3.

Complex Carbohydrates

Your calories should come from all three energy sources: complex carbohydrates, proteins and fats, but your preferable energy source should be complex carbohydrates. The body breaks these down more slowly than refined carbohydrates, thus releasing glucose (energy) into the blood over a longer period of time. If you restrict your carbohydrate intake during pregnancy you can put your fetus at risk. Without carbohydrates your body will burn proteins and fat for fuel. Two things happen physiologically (a body process) if your body burns protein and fat for fuel:

1. There may not be enough protein available for the developing brain and nervous system of the baby.
2. Burning fats can release ketones (an acid by-product of fat metabolism) that can be destructive to foetal brain cells and the delicate acid-base balance of the foetal system.
Therefore **low** complex carbohydrate diets can be dangerous in pregnancy.

Function of Complex Carbohydrates

- They are a source of fuel for the mother.
- They are high in fibre.
- They are high in B vitamins, which promote foetal cell division, aid in the digestion of nutrients and prevent anaemia.
- They are high in trace minerals such as zinc, selenium, chromium and magnesium.

Food sources of complex carbohydrates: Brown Rice, wild rice, bulgar, millet, oats, kasha, wheat, rice crackers, whole wheat pasta, whole grain cereals, rye, lentils, beans, fresh fruit and vegetables.

Potatoes are healthy carbohydrates when eaten in small amounts and always unpeeled but unfortunately most people eat potatoes in the form of greasy French fries or potato chips, and even baked potatoes are often topped with fats such as butter, sour cream, melted cheese and bacon bits. Take away the extra fat and deep-frying and potatoes are a very good source of vitamin C, vitamin B6, copper, potassium, manganese, and dietary fibre. Potatoes also contain a variety of phyto-nutrients that have antioxidant activity. Among these important health-promoting compounds are carotenoids, flavonoids, and caffeic acid, as well as unique tuber storage proteins, such as patatin, which exhibit activity against free radicals and newly identified blood pressure-lowering compounds called kukoamines.

Protein

Adequate protein is vital for the growth of your fetus. There are higher proportions of amino acids (what protein is made up of) in the foetal blood than there is in the maternal blood. It is essential for tissue repair and to make essential hormones and enzymes in the body.

Proteins are made up of amino acids (20 amino acids) and our bodies can manufacture all but eight. These eight are called essential amino acids and must be supplied by the food we eat. Animal products have all eight and are considered complete proteins. Vegetarian sources are lacking in the essential amino acids and are considered incomplete proteins unless they are combined properly.

Function of Protein

- Building blocks of all cells in the growing fetus.
- Essential for a healthy formation of the placenta.
- Vital to the development of brain cells.

Food sources of Protein – eat some protein every day

Eggs, fish, organic chicken and red meat, live organic yoghurt, soymilk, tofu, cheese, nuts, beans, lentils and seeds.

A vegetarian needs to combine a serving of beans/lentils with nuts, eggs or dairy to make up a complete protein meal.

Water

You should drink at least seven glasses daily plus one glass extra for each hour of light exercise. If you're not sure how much water you drink each day, fill a seven-glass container and finish it by the end of the day. Always take a bottle of water with you when you go out.

You should be eating enough fresh fruits and vegetables to provide a good additional balance of liquids. Juices can contribute to your fluid intake, but keep in mind that they can also provide a lot of extra sugars. Caffeinated beverages, such as coffee, colas, and teas don't count as part of your fluid intake because they are diuretics. They make you urinate more so you actually loose water. If you don't like the taste of water, try adding a wedge of lemon or lime, or a little juice for additional flavour.

Water plays many vital roles in a healthy pregnancy.

- Think of water as your body's transportation system, it carries nutrients through your blood to the baby.

- Water also helps prevent bladder infections, which are common during pregnancy. If you drink enough water, your urine will stay diluted, reducing your risk of infection.
- Water can also lessen the possibility of constipation.
- Although it may seem counterintuitive, the more water you drink during pregnancy, the less water your body will retain.
- Also, drinking enough water prevents dehydration. This is especially important in the third trimester when dehydration can actually cause contractions that can trigger preterm labour.

See "Vitamins and Minerals" for further information

※Additional information

Dr Brewer is a famous obstetrician has done research showing that if women who have had high blood pressure in a previous pregnancy eat a high protein diet, they do not suffer from high blood pressure in subsequent pregnancies. Although there is much proof of this diet working I also advise women to eat the high protein diet with a good amount of complex carbohydrates.

O

OMEGA-3 (AND ITS DERIVATIVE, DHA (DOCOSAHEXAENOIC ACID)

There are three major types of omega 3 fatty acids that are ingested in foods and used by the body: alpha-linolenic acid (ALA), eicosapentaenoic acid (EPA), and docosahexaenoic acid (DHA). Once eaten, the body converts ALA to EPA and DHA, the two types of omega-3 fatty acids more readily used by the body.

A developing fetus cannot make its own Omega-3 fatty acids. As the mother you must meet your baby's nutritional needs. Foetuses rely on a constant supply of Omega-3 and its derivative, DHA (docosahexaenoic acid) for the developing nervous system, brain and eyes during pregnancy and then after birth via breast milk. DHA is the building block of human brain tissue and is particularly abundant in the grey matter of the brain and the retina. The DHA content of your infant's brain triples during the first three months of life.

Low levels of DHA for mothers during pregnancy have recently been associated with depression, memory loss, dementia, post-natal depression and visual problems.

Unfortunately, DHA levels in the breast milk of most women are very low. Therefore, increasing DHA levels should be a primary goal for all pregnant and lactating women.

Research has shown that children who breastfeed score higher on I.Q. tests and have less incidence of allergies and ADHD than those fed formula, because during breastfeeding these fats continue to flow from your body into the body and brain of your child. Breastfeeding for at least a year is one of the best gifts you can give your baby as long as you maintain the fatty acid balance in your own body. Taking a supplement supplies the best source of Omega-3: 1000mg per day, starting before pregnancy if possible.

Checklist for foods that contain Omega-3: fatty fish; herring, mackerel, sardines, wild salmon, tuna and flaxseed oil, seaweed, walnuts, leafy green vegetables and crustaceans.

Anecdote

A colleague of mine keeps Icelandic horses. Last year when she was in Iceland looking to buy a new horse she was overwhelmed by the smell of raw fish at one of the paddocks. When she asked what it was that she could smell, the breeder laughed and said, 'Oh, we put vats of raw herring out for the pregnant mares, they eat tons of it when they are pregnant'.

Also see the **research** section in the appendix for more information on Omega-3 during pregnancy and lactation.

OPTIMUM NUTRITION TO INCREASE YOUR CHANCES FOR NATURAL CHILDBIRTH

Dr Gowri Motha, a famous obstetrician, has developed a special program to help women through their pregnancies, which equips them with the potential for a natural birth. In her wonderful book, *Gentle Birth Method,* she describes that working as an obstetrician in the UK she came to the conclusion that many births needing intervention were partly due to an obstruction in the pelvis caused by water retention (oedema.) This coupled with unfit, unprepared mothers and a pre-conceived fear of pain greatly limited any chance of gentle, natural childbirth. A part of her program is nutritional advice to help women avoid this "pelvic oedema" and to generally become healthier in their pregnancies.

The healthier and fitter you are during pregnancy the greater your chances are for a gentle, natural birth. In the following nutritional advice I have combined Gowri Motha's advice with my own. If you are interested to know more about Dr. Gowri Motha and her *Gentle Birth Method* I recommend you read her book *Gentle Birth Method.*

Remember that before reading through the foods that you will need to *restrict or cut out* you need to feel good about what you are doing. Don't forget why you are doing it and enjoy the fact that it will make you and your baby healthier and that you are increasing your chances of having a natural birth.

Foods that increase the possibility of pelvic oedema and excess weight gain

Wheat (bread, pasta, cookies, cakes, crackers, couscous, some cereals and spelt products)
Foods containing wheat are known to cause water retention (oedema.) The water retention congests the vaginal tissues and restricts the cervix from opening and widening.
Cut down on all wheat products during pregnancy and cut out wheat products completely in the last 6 weeks of pregnancy.

Alternatives to wheat

The following are grains that you can eat other than wheat: Barley, corn, millet, oats, rice, rye, quinoa, millet, sorghum and wild rice. Many health food stores sell bread and crackers made from these products. Alternatively they sell wheat-free flours so that you can bake your own bread, pancakes, cakes and crackers.
Potatoes are both wheat and gluten free but unfortunately, most people eat potatoes in the form of greasy French fries or potato chips, and even baked potatoes are often topped with fats such as butter, sour cream, melted cheese and bacon bits. This can make even baked potatoes a potential contributor to pelvic oedema. Take away the extra fat and deep-frying and potatoes are a very good source of vitamin

C, a good source of vitamin B6, copper, potassium, manganese, and dietary fiber. Potatoes also contain a variety of phyto-nutrients that have antioxidant activity. Among these important health-promoting compounds are carotenoids, flavonoids, and caffeic acid, as well as unique tuber storage proteins such as patatin, which exhibit activity against free radicals, and newly identified blood pressure-lowering compounds called kukoamines.

Sugar

The biochemical process in the body that releases energy from sugar for the body to use also releases free radicals that attack the muscles, tendons and ligaments in the body making them tough and non-elastic. During pregnancy and childbirth you need your pelvic ligaments to be extremely supple and flexible.

Alternatives to sugar

If you really can't do without something sweet, Stevia is a natural sweetener. It is very sweet and is derived from the leaves of a South American shrub. It is available in both powder and liquid forms from the health food store. Avoid any artificial sweeteners like Aspartame or Saccharin and watch out for hidden sugars in fizzy drinks, sugared cereals and fruit juices.

Fatty foods

In women any excess fats are stored in the hips, stomach and buttocks regions. These are exactly the areas that need to be fat-free to allow for supple movement during pregnancy and childbirth. It is very normal to gain a natural layer of fat as insulation and protection for your baby but any excess fat is detrimental. Check out the "Good Fats versus the Bad Fats" chapter.

Milk products

I generally advise women not to consume many milk products during pregnancy and that the products should be organic with a preference for live yoghurt or kefir. Milk products should be avoided completely if you know that you don't digest them well. Symptoms like stomach cramps, flatulence, skin rashes, breathing difficulties and diarrhoea are an indication that you could be slightly lactose intolerant, if this is the case cut out all cow's milk to avoid it creating tension and mucous in your intestines and abdomen.

Alternatives to milk

There are many alternatives to cow's milk: Goat's milk, soymilk, oat milk and rice milk. Try any of these to see which you prefer.

Caffeine

Caffeine is known to cause water retention (oedema.) Stop drinking all caffeinated drinks.

Foods that will increase health and flexibility during pregnancy and childbirth

Carbohydrates - your main source of energy

Although you need carbohydrates for energy avoid all refined carbohydrates, rather eat the following complex carbohydrates:

Brown rice

Rice is rich in carbohydrates it is an insoluble fibre, reduces the risk of bowel disorders and fights constipation. Rice is low in fat, contains some protein and plenty of B vitamins.

Oats

Oats contain carbohydrates, soluble and insoluble fibre, sodium, vitamins, minerals, fatty acids, amino acids and even more! Oats are what we call super foods. They benefit blood cholesterol, blood pressure, blood glucose metabolism, they provide energy & satiety, and promote gastrointestinal health.

Potatoes

Plain, unpeeled, boiled potatoes are healthy carbohydrates that contain high sources of vitamins and mineral. Avoid eating potatoes peeled, fried, as crisps and don't load them with fats like butter, sour cream and bacon bits.

Sweet potatoes (especially the orange ones) contain high amounts of Vitamin A and C. Yams, often confused with sweet potatoes, generally have rougher skin and are long and cylindrical with jutting out "toes". Yams contain high levels of calcium, potassium and folic acid.

Vegetables

Vegetables also contain carbohydrates. Steamed vegetables are the easiest to digest. If you eat raw vegetables make sure they are regular salad ingredients as raw vegetables can be difficult to digest during pregnancy because your gut is more sluggish due to hormones.

Whole grains

Choose whole grains such as rye, quinoa, millet, sorghum, barley, corn and millet.

Fresh fruit (3 helpings a day)

Fruits also contain carbohydrates. All fresh fruit is healthy but keep bananas, mangos and grapes to a minimum because of their high sugar content. Bananas are also mucous-producing and should not be eaten in the last month of pregnancy.

Protein

Adequate protein is vital for the growth of the fetus. It is essential for tissue repair and to make essential hormones and enzymes in the body. Eating a diet high in proteins can help to avoid high blood pressure and nausea during pregnancy.

Meat/Fish

Chicken and lean meats (preferably organic) are healthy during in pregnancy. Avoid eating any fat on meat.

Fish, especially fatty fish, contain Omega oils, which are essential for both mother and baby during pregnancy. They promote brain and nervous system development and lift the mother's mood. They work as "oil" for all joints to increase flexibility. Avoid eating too much tuna due to its high content of mercury.

Water

Drinking enough water is essential throughout pregnancy has many benefits plus it reduces the possibility of oedema (water retention.) Also refer to the chapter on Nutrition.

OVER DUE (GOING PAST YOUR DUE DATE)

Going "over due" or "post date" simply means that you don't give birth before or on your due date. There's nothing unusual about being overdue. In fact it's the norm. Statistics show that:

- Four percent of all women give birth on the due date.
- Five to ten percent of pregnancies last around 42 weeks.
- An average of first time pregnancies (primipara) last for two hundred and eighty-eight days (eight days past the due date.)
- Pregnancies of women having their second/third/fourth etc (multipara) baby last an average of two hundred and eighty-three days (three days past the due date.)

It can be frustrating to go past that date that you have been heading for since you knew you were pregnant but try to enjoy the time you have before your baby arrives.
Indulge yourself; soak in the bathtub, have a massage, spend an afternoon reading magazines or treat yourself to a sensational new hairstyle. Take time to pamper yourself now so that you'll be relaxed and rested when the time comes to give birth.

Spend some time with your partner. It may be some time before you can enjoy such luxuries as spontaneous sex or an uninterrupted meal again, so try to seize the moment. Also remember that sex can trigger the birth, semen contains prostaglandins which have an influence in readying your body for labour. You will also produce oxytocin if you have an orgasm and oxytocin is the hormone needed to stimulate contractions.

If you are pregnant with a second or third child enjoy this extra time you get to spend with your child/children before the new baby arrives.
Go to "Induction of Labour" for information and tips to try and get your labour started.

OXYTOCIN AND ITS ROLE IN LABOUR

Oxytocin is a hormone that is released during labour, it causes your uterine (womb) muscles to contract, which in turn causes your cervix to become thin and dilate (open.) During labour your body will continue to produce Oxytocin, which is triggered by the distension of your vagina, the pressure of your baby on the cervix, the distension of your pelvic floor muscles in the second stage of labour and the stretching of your perineum during crowning. Oxytocin also ensures the release of your placenta and is released when your newborn suckles on your breast.

In cases where uterine contractions are not sufficient to complete delivery, physicians usually administer oxytocin in a chemical form called Pitocin to stimulate uterine contractions.

Oxytocin release during labour is inhibited (suppressed) by the production of adrenaline, which in turn is triggered by loud noises, strangers coming in to your labour room/space, unfamiliar or hostile birth environments, interruptions and distractions, lack of privacy and acute embarrassment.

Adrenaline is also released by your body when you are expected to make important decisions or you are given disturbing news during labour.

On the question of "privacy" and labour, Michel Odent a famous obstetrician states; "The right place to give birth would be the right place to make love" (Odent, 1982.)

P

PAIN IN THE GROIN AND LOWER ABDOMEN

In the first few weeks of pregnancy every little twinge in the area of your uterus can be scary. Some pains are just natural, necessary symptoms of the changes that need to occur in that part of your body. You may feel a pulling pain in your groin or across the lower part of your abdomen or it can feel like sharp shooting pains on either side of the abdomen stretching down into the groin area. This sensation is due to the stretching of the ligaments in your pelvis that help keep your womb stable. The ligaments are being stretched during early pregnancy because the uterus is already growing. Unless you have a fever or are losing blood you should see these aches and pains as a positive sign.

⃠ Exceptions

This stretching pain often begins around week 7 in a first pregnancy but in a second or subsequent pregnancy you could feel it as early as 5 weeks.

Abdominal pain can also be caused by gas and bloating because of hormones that slow your digestion and the pressure of your growing uterus on your stomach and intestines. Constipation is another common cause of abdominal discomfort throughout pregnancy, thanks to hormones that slow the movement of food through your digestive tract and the pressure of your growing uterus on your rectum.

PAIN IN THE SIDE – OR PAIN IN THE RIBS

Sometimes women have odd aches and pains during pregnancy. One that I hear quite often is a pain in the side, just under the breasts, usually on the right but also sometimes on the left. This pain is dull, sometimes sharp and is difficult to locate exactly. Some women feel the pain specifically between their lower ribs. The pain generally starts around the 24th week of pregnancy but can be felt for the first time as late as 34 weeks.

Here are the possible reasons for this pain:

- The arrival the pain often seems to coincide with the "pushing" out of the lower ribs to allow for the growing uterus and the organs to fit underneath them. The reason most women have more pain on the right is that not only are ribs being forced "open" but the liver, which is located on the right and is rather large doesn't leave much room for manoeuvring. On the left, where you find the spleen and pancreas, there is a little more space.
- Sometimes the pains are caused by your baby kicking or punching you in that area.
- There are muscles between each rib called "intercostals" and if you are experiencing rib-pain you most likely have tight intercostals, at least in that area.

THERAPIES AND TIPS pain in the side

Lifestyle

- Try to make yourself as comfortable as possible by wearing lose fitting clothes and supporting yourself with cushions when lying down. The pain will likely subside when baby drops (into your pelvic cavity) in preparation for birth.
- There are some yoga postures and breath work you can do to ease the discomfort or you can try the following exercise: Stand facing a wall. With your feet 40cm (15inches) from the wall, stretch out your arms and cross them in front of your face. Then lean your crossed arms on the wall sliding

them up the wall above your head and stretching yourself up as far as possible. Hold the position for as long as it is comfortable. This lifts the diaphragm and rib cage up off the uterus and provides temporary relief.

- You might try getting a massage from someone who can gently get in between the ribs and help loosen those intercostals a little.
- Breathing exercises that expand the ribcage could be helpful.

◐ Chiropractic

Seeing a chiropractor can sometimes help if the pain is related to spine mal-alignment.

☯ Acupuncture

Sometimes acupuncture is helpful with reducing pain symptoms
☛My experience: I use both acupuncture and cupping to successfully reduce pain symptoms.

PAIN RELIEF/MANAGEMENT DURING LABOUR

As an expectant mother approaching your due date, you may start wondering/worrying about the pain that you will experience during labour.

Expectations regarding labour pain tend to be coloured by the past experience of your friends and family and sometimes by your own. However, the intensity of labour pain, the length of labour and each individual woman's response to the pain varies widely. Also the environment in which you give birth and the support you receive from your caregivers and companions will affect your reaction to pain and your ability to cope.

It is important to orientate yourself as to what pain management is available in the setting in which you plan to give birth. One thing is certain, the more you know about the process of giving birth and your options for managing the pain, the better your experience will be. In fact, education itself is a form of pain relief. It takes away the fear of childbirth and in doing so can minimize the pain when the time comes.

Options

Each pain management option has pros and cons.

- Relaxation, acupressure, acupuncture, massage and breathing techniques can help you to cope better with the pain but they won't take the actual pain away.
- Medication can make contractions less painful or even painless but any medication you take may affect your baby and possibly give you a sense of detachment.

The advantages of having a natural childbirth

If you want to be an active participant throughout labour and have minimal routine interventions in the birth process a natural, non-medicated approach to controlling labour pain will suit you best. Choosing this route is accepting that there will be pain and discomfort as part and parcel of giving birth but with the right preparation and support you could feel empowered and deeply satisfied by natural childbirth.

The pros for natural childbirth

- Natural childbirth techniques are not invasive, so there's little potential of harm or side effects for you or your baby.
- Many women have a strong sense of empowerment during labour and a feeling of accomplishment afterward. Despite having had to endure pain many women report that they would opt for natural childbirth a second time round.
- There's no loss of sensation or alertness. You'll be awake and active during labour and birth so you can aid the delivery process when it is time to push your baby out.
- Your partner will feel more involved as you work together to manage your pain.

- You won't need to be hooked up to an IV or monitoring machines so it's easier to move about, walk, take a shower or a bath and to use the toilet (instead of a bedpan.)
- You're less likely (than women who get epidurals) to need chemical Oxytocin (Pitocin) as stimulation, a vacuum extraction or forceps delivery or bladder catheterization.
- You are more alert when your baby is born so you can experience the first precious moments with your baby. It is the best start for your baby.

Natural pain management during labour

☯ Acupuncture and Shiatsu

Women who receive acupuncture during labour experience less pain and require less analgesic medication, according to a study in *The Clinical Journal of Pain* (2003;19:187–91.)
In many countries midwives are trained to give acupuncture during childbirth, if this is not the case in your situation, find an acupuncturist that specializes in acupuncture during childbirth.
If you don't like the idea of needles many acupuncturists will use acupressure during birth.

Reflexology

During labour, applying pressure or strokes to specific points on your feet is said to stimulate the pituitary gland to release hormones that benefit labour and reduce pain. As in any form of massage, reflexology encourages the body to release endorphins. Endorphins are natural pain killers and are needed in high quantities during childbirth

Massage

Massage can help you to focus on your breathing exercises during a contraction. Lower-back massage during a contraction can be a wonderful way to relieve pain as it works by releasing pain-killing endorphins. A foot massage can relax you and "pull" the energy out of your head and downward.

Some women find that they don't want to be touched others have a specific need for soft or hard massage during labour so although you could practice before labour, the comfortable massage pressure will be determined by you during labour.

Hypnosis

Hypnosis is a focused state of concentration that allows you to relax your body, guide your thoughts and control your breathing. Hypnosis doesn't stop the pain of contractions. It is simply a state of mind that may help you ride the wave of each contraction and trust in your body's ability to give birth. Self-hypnosis will aid you to let go of the fear of pain. There is a specialized childbirth self-hypnosis technique called HypnoBirthing where you learn self-hypnosis techniques. HypnoBirthing can help you to trust yourself and your body thereby allowing it to do what it is naturally able to do.

Breathing techniques

You can learn breathing techniques during pregnancy that you can use during labour. Good breathing techniques help lessen the pain due to the fact that your body relaxes.

Bradley Method

This method, developed by American obstetrician Robert Bradley in the late 1940s, embraces the idea that childbirth is a natural process and that, with the right preparation, most women can avoid pain medication and routine interventions during labour and birth. Proponents claim that nearly ninety percent of women who deliver vaginally using the Bradley method to do so without drugs. The program lasts 12 weeks, and is more intensive than other childbirth education classes. The Bradley philosophy says that it takes months to mentally, physically, and emotionally prepare for childbirth and parenting. It prides itself on addressing all aspects of natural childbirth, as well as many pregnancy and postpartum issues.

Lamaze

The primary goal of Lamaze is to increase a woman's confidence in her ability to give birth through education and support. Today's

Lamaze encourages women to trust birth, to actively work with their labours, and to choose caregivers and places of birth that promote, protect and support natural birth.

Warmth

Some women find warm water in a bath or shower - or even a sponge or footbath helps provide comfort and relief. Birthing pools, which you can rent for homebirths and are available in many hospitals, can provide some pain relief. A hot-pack, hot water bottle or simply warm towels on the lower back and even lower belly provide good pain relief.

You can provide your own hot-rice-sock to place on your lower back or feet.

To make a rice sock: Take a nice soft, clean sock and fill it three quarter full with white rice and tie it closed (tightly) with a knot. Place it in the microwave for two to three minutes. Check the temperature of the rice sock before placing it on your body.

Obstetric pulsar: TENS

A TENS (obstetric pulsar) machine works by "disturbing" pain messages from your body to your brain thereby reducing the pain. TENS also stimulates the release of endorphins - your body's' own natural pain-relieving hormones. The pain relief is administered by four electrode pads, which are placed on your lower back and are connected to the TENS machine. A TENS is most helpful in the earlier stages of labour. TENS machines can be hired or purchased.

Mobility

Sometimes simply being mobile will help you to cope with the pain. It will aid the baby's passage down the birth canal possibly making the birth shorter. Most women whose births I have attended are shocked to find what a positive difference it makes to be OFF their backs during contractions.

Medical pain management during labour

Drug pain relief

To choose the pain relief method or methods that are right for you, ask these following questions:

- What's involved in the method?
- How will it affect my birthing process and me?
- How will it affect my baby?
- How quickly will it work if I decide to use it?
- How long will the pain-relief last?
- Can I combine it with other methods of pain-relief?
- When during labour is the method available?
- Will I be able to feel enough to help push my baby out in the third stage of labour?

Gas and air (*entonox*)

Gas is a mixture of the anaesthetic gas, nitrous oxide and is helpful at the end of the first stage of labour.

Opioids: Pethidine and Stemetil (*prochlorperazine*)

Pethidine is the drug most commonly given during labour. It acts for 3-4 hours. The main problem with pethidine is that it may cross the placenta and could affect the baby so it needs to be given at the beginning to middle stages of dilation. In high doses it may depress the part of the baby's brain that controls breathing, so there may be a delay before natural breathing starts after birth. There is an antidote (*naloxone*) that can be given to the baby if pethidine delays the start of breathing.

Stemetil acts as a tranquillizer, and also treats nausea and vomiting. Some hospitals use Stemetil in combination with pethidine. Women who have the powerful combination of stemetil and pethidine often say they feel less aware of what is going on.

While opioids don't eliminate the pain they do change your perception of pain and make it more tolerable. All of the opioids have side effects such as dry mouth, urinary retention (inability to urinate), and decreased gastric motility (sluggish bowel.) Pethidine is excellent for mothers who are tense and unable to relax during labour. Giving Pethadine can often relax a woman enough for her to dilate more efficiently.

Epidural analgesia
Epidurals relieve labour pains by 'blocking' the nerves that run along the spine from the brain to the womb. Before an epidural is placed your back is first numbed and then the epidural is placed into your spinal fluid. There are many different types of epidural, but normally the main drawback is that it affects your bladder and you will not be able to move your legs. As a result you will have to remain in bed until the effect has worn off. There is also a risk that your blood pressure will fall making you feel dizzy and nauseous.
An epidural can slow your labour in which case you may need Pitocin, a chemical form of Oxytocin, to get your labour back on track.

It is important that you check out what options are available for you as the choices vary from hospital to hospital.

PALPITATIONS (IRREGULAR HEART BEAT)

Palpitations during pregnancy are due to the increased blood volume, which peaks at 28 to 32 weeks. The stroke volume of the heart increases under the influence of progesterone and so the heart can occasionally beat irregularly or with a strange fluttering sensation.

THERAPIES AND TIPS for palpitations

Nutrition
Although palpitations are a "symptom" of pregnancy you could help reduce palpitations by eating magnesium rich foods. Magnesium is important for nerve conduction, muscle contraction, blood vessel relaxation and tensing. It therefore has an influence on blood pressure and a normal heartbeat.

Magnesium is often lacking in food sources but can be found in very small amounts in the following foods: whole grain breads and cereals, rice, pasta, oatmeal, nuts, nuts, soybeans, kidney beans, baked beans, bananas, corn, artichokes, potatoes, sweet potatoes, watermelon, dried fruits, oranges, grapefruit, limes, avocado, yoghurt, meat, chicken, fish, eggs, dark green leafy vegetables, seaweed and dark chocolate!

☑ **Supplements**
Magnesium is often lacking in food sources due to hydroponic agriculture. Taking a supplement of 400 milligrams per day can sometimes help if you are suffering badly from palpitations.

☯ **Acupuncture**
Acupuncture can help relax you and therefore reduce palpitations.
☛My experience: A session once a week significantly helps reduce palpitations.

💣 **When to consult your caregiver**
If palpitations are paired with tiredness and paleness, being very aware of your heartbeat, breathlessness and dizziness you should contact your caregiver as you may be suffering from anaemia.

PELVIC FLOOR EXERCISES

The floor of the pelvis is made up of layers of muscle and other tissues. These layers stretch like a hammock from the coccyx to the pubic bone. Your pelvic floor supports the bladder, the womb (uterus) and the bowel. The urethra, the vagina and the rectum pass through the pelvic floor muscles. The pelvic floor muscles play an important role in bladder and bowel control and sexual sensation.
Pregnancy and childbirth put pressure on these muscles and you may find that you leak urine when you sneeze or cough - this is called 'stress incontinence'. You can tone these muscles so they maintain their strength - and regain it quicker after the birth - by doing regular 'invisible' exercises.

Identifying your pelvic floor

The first thing to do is to correctly identify the muscles that need to be exercised.

Sit or lie down comfortably with the muscles of your thighs, buttocks and abdomen relaxed.

Tighten the ring of muscle around your anus as if you are trying to control diarrhoea or wind. Relax it. Practice this movement several times until you are sure you are exercising the correct muscle. Try to gently but firmly tighten only that muscle and do not squeeze your buttocks.

When you are passing urine, try to stop the flow mid-stream and then restart it. Once you have identified this muscle do not stop you urine flow again as you may end up not emptying your bladder completely.

If you are unable to feel a definite squeeze and lift action of your pelvic floor muscles or are unable to even slow the stream of urine you should seek professional help to train your pelvic floor muscles to enable them to work correctly.

Doing pelvic floor exercises

Once you have identified the muscles exercise them by:

Tightening and drawing in the muscle around the anus, then the vagina and then the urethra and then lift them UP inside. Try and hold this contraction as you count to five then release and relax. You should have a definite feeling of 'letting go'.

Repeat ('squeeze and lift') and relax. It is important to rest for about ten seconds in between each contraction. If you find it easy to hold for a count of five, try to hold for longer - up to ten seconds.

Repeat this as many times as you are able up to a maximum of 8-10 squeezes.

Now do five to ten squeezes short and fast.

Do this whole exercise routine at least 4 times every day.

While doing the exercises:

- DO NOT hold your breath.
- DO NOT push down instead of squeezing and lifting up.
- DO NOT tighten your tummy, buttocks or thighs.

Do your exercises well - the quality is important. Fewer good exercises will be more beneficial than many half hearted ones.
It might be helpful to have four regular times during the day for doing the exercises. For example, after going to the toilet, after a meal, before going to sleep and before getting up in the morning.

PELVIC GIRDLE PAIN (PGP)

The pelvis consists of two iliac or 'hip' bones joined to a wedge shaped bone called the sacrum at the back. The two 'hip' bones are connected at the front by a stiff joint called the symphysis pubis. The joints between the sacrum and the 'hip' bones at the back are called sacro-iliac joints. All of these joints are stabilised by a dense network of ligaments, which means that under normal conditions, very little movement occurs.

These joints and pregnancy
In order to make your baby's passage through your pelvis at the time of birth as easy as possible, your body produces a hormone called relaxin that together with progesterone and oestrogen softens the ligaments in your pelvis. As a result, these joints tend to move more during and just after pregnancy.

What causes Pelvic Girdle Pain (PGP)?
It is thought that this softening, along with postural changes, muscle weakness and differences in the movement occurring between the left and right pelvic joints can cause too much stress on the joints, ligaments and muscles of the pelvis. Normally when you lie down, stand up or walk, your pelvis is in a 'locked' or stable position. Women who suffer from PGP are thought to perform these activities with a less stable or 'unlocked' pelvis. The result is inflammation or pain.
If you experience pain on or around your pubic bone at the front, you may be suffering from symphysis pain.
Pain at the back of the pelvis is known as Pelvic Girdle Pain (PGP) or sometimes referred to as Sacro-Iliac Joint (SIJ) pain. PGP is

often confused with or misdiagnosed as sciatica. Sciatica is caused by inflammation or compression of the sciatic nerve as it leaves the spine. This may be caused by a damaged disc or by pressure from surrounding joints or ligaments. Research shows that only two percent of women suffer from this during pregnancy. It is certainly not more likely to occur as a result of pregnancy. The majority of women who suffer from significant lower back or leg pain in pregnancy suffer from PGP.

Symptoms of PGP

The pain is often one sided and may be concentrated in the buttock area. It may appear to jump from side to side or be accompanied by a general back or symphysis pain. It can send shooting pains into your buttocks or down the back of your legs. If the pain is accompanied by pins and needles or numbness and extends further than your knee, it may be sciatica rather than PGP. You may also have pain in your hips. One or both of your legs may feel very weak and you may not be able to lift your legs, particularly when lying down.

PGP can begin as early as 8-12 weeks or as late as the last few days before delivery. If the pain comes on at the very end of pregnancy, it may be due to the baby's head 'engaging' or moving down into the pelvis. If this is the case, it is unusual to have pain after delivery. If you experience PGP in one pregnancy it is more likely to recur earlier in any subsequent pregnancy and without professional advice or treatment it may be more severe. Health professionals advise letting the symptoms from one pregnancy settle before trying for another baby.

PGP is not widely known or understood. You may have been told by your caregiver or physiotherapist that you have sciatica but it would be better for you to see a chiropractor or osteopath that has comprehensive experience in treating pregnant women to make sure of this diagosis.

THERAPIES AND TIPS for PGP

Lifestyle

The pain is usually felt when lying on your back, turning over in bed, walking and when standing up from a sitting position. It is often worse at night and the degree of night pain you may experience will probably be related to how active you are during the day. Separating your legs, especially when sitting in a slumped position or lying down can be painful. So the following tips could help:

- Move little and often because you may not feel the effects of a physically busy day until evening or after you have gone to bed.
- Rest regularly either by lying on your side or sitting upright with your back well supported.
- If you need to turn over in bed arch your lower back slightly, tighten your pelvic floor muscles and lower abdominal muscles and keep your knees together.
- Avoid lying on your back or sitting slumped, particularly with your legs straight (i.e. with your feet up on the sofa or in the bath.)
- Avoid heavy lifting or pushing (supermarket trolleys can be particularly painful.)
- When dressing, sit down to put on clothing such as your knickers or trousers. Pull the clothing over your feet and *then* stand up to pull them up. Don't try to put your legs into trousers, skirts or knickers whilst standing.
- Sometimes sleeping on a softer surface can help. Try placing a duvet under your sheet.
- Performing regular lower abdominal exercises can help to reduce the strain of the pregnancy on your back. To perform a safe and easy lower abdominal exercise: get down onto your hands and knees and level your back so that it is roughly flat (horizontal.) Breathe in and then as you breathe out, perform a pelvic floor exercise (pulling in your anus and vagina) and at the same time pull your belly button in and up. Hold this for 5-10 seconds without holding your breath and without

moving your back. Relax the muscles slowly at the end of the exercise.

- You can reduce the risk of developing back pain if you exercise regularly.
- Wear shoes that are comfortable for you. Some women will only be comfortable in flat shoes, however, other women need a bit of a heel to take the pressure off their back. Generally, if you have an arched lower back, high heels may increase this, whereas flat shoes tend to have the opposite effect.
- When standing, imagine that someone is making you taller by pulling a string attached to the top and back of your head. Tightening your pelvic floor muscles and your tummy muscles will help to support your back in this posture.
- Pelvic tilting can help to minimise the strain placed on your back by prolonged standing. Try this exercise: stand with your back against a wall. Position your feet a few centimetres away from the wall and allow your knees to bend very slightly. Slide your hand into the hollow of your back and tilt your pelvis backwards so that your back squashes your hand. Now tilt your pelvis the opposite way so that the pressure from your back is removed from your hand. Continue to tilt forwards and backwards in a rhythmical fashion. This exercise works best if you do it regularly.
- Get into a good sitting posture. When sitting, ensure that your back is well supported. Try placing a small towel rolled into a sausage shape in the hollow of your back, or ask your physiotherapist about a specialist lumbar roll (a round or D-shaped back support.) Sitting upright in a dining type chair will help your back and is better than sitting in a soft chair or sofa. If you have to sit for long periods, try to get up and walk around every twenty minutes.
- Try kneeling on your hands and knees. This is an excellent position for reducing pressure from the weight of your baby on your back. Try adopting this position regularly throughout the day.
- Try rounding your back up into a hump shape (tucking your tailbone underneath you) and then gently arching your back

in the opposite direction so that you stick your bottom out. Repeating this in a rocking motion can be very useful for back or pelvic pain.

- Getting out of bed. Roll onto your side with your knees together and bent, drop your feet over the edge of the bed and push yourself up sideways with your arms. Reverse the process when you lie down.
- Getting out of the bath. Roll onto your side in a sitting position and move onto your hands and knees. Stand up using the sides of the bath and perch on the edge of the bath. Holding firmly on to the sides of the bath behind you, arch your back and move one leg at a time over the bath sides. Always use a bath mat to prevent slipping.
- Wear a pelvic support belt.
- Gently exercise in water.

◐ Chiropractic

Find a chiropractor that works with pregnancy. Regular visits can prevent as well as treat PGP.

☯ Acupuncture

Acupuncture helps the pain associated with PGP.

☛My experience: I find PGP difficult to treat so I generally refer my clients to a chiropractor as well as treating them once a week.

◐ Physiotherapy

A physiotherapist can show you how to 'lock out' your pelvis during painful movements such as walking or standing up. She can also show you positions to make the delivery of your baby easier.

◐ Osteopathy

Osteopathy will help both during pregnancy and after childbirth if you are suffering from PGP.

Labour and PGP

With appropriate advice, it is rare for PGP to cause any problems in labour. If possible, avoid lying on your back to deliver your baby. Upright or kneeling positions protect the pelvic joints and are generally more comfortable. If you have to sit on the bed during labour, sitting as upright as possible makes separation of the legs easier. If your symptoms make it difficult for you to open your legs, it may be worth discussing with your caregiver what positions would be best for an assisted delivery should this prove necessary. In some cases, lying on your back with your hips and knees bent as far up as possible is actually a pain-free position. In this position, the pelvis is in its 'locked out' position whereas, in the traditional stirrups position your pelvis is unstable.

Post partum

PGP can linger after delivery and it is important that any treatment continues after pregnancy. Around fifty per cent of women can still experience pain at twelve weeks after delivery although it is usually much less severe than during the pregnancy. Very rarely women who have experienced PGP in a previous pregnancy have persistent pain beyond twelve weeks. Studies have shown that if PGP is differentiated from other forms of back pain and treated accordingly, women experience less pain after delivery.

PERINEAL MASSAGE

Perineal massage is the gentle stretching and massaging of the perineum (skin between the anus and vagina) during the last few weeks of pregnancy. This massage has been shown to reduce the incidence of episiotomy and perineal tears during childbirth. Like training muscles to perform at their best in an athletic event, conditioning the tissues around the vaginal opening with massage prepares the perineum to "perform" at birth. Midwives report that women who practice perineal massage in the last six weeks

Learn more about the Lakota (Sioux) culture at stjo.org/culture.

- folding brush
- hand salve
- Sm. ruler
- hair ties

Cancel
Augsburger
Monday

~~email / call Ting / Stephanie~~ Lesch

Dr Hall, Breeden, Bergstrom / Graham

OB open to twin vag. birth

454-9978

of pregnancy experience less of the burning sensation felt during crowning. Mothers with a more conditioned perineum are less likely to tear or need an episiotomy. An added value of perineal massage is that it familiarizes a woman with stretching sensations in this area so she will be able relax these muscles more easily during birth.

The technique

Clean your hands thoroughly and trim your thumbnails.

Sit in a warm comfortable place, spreading your legs apart. To become familiar with your perineal area use a mirror for the first few massages.

Use a massage oil without aroma added or use oil specifically made for perineal massage.

Insert both your thumbs (to about the first joint) inside your vagina facing backwards towards your anus. Using gentle but firm pressure, move the thumbs from the base of the vagina up the sides as if you were making a "U" and stretch the opening gently until you feel a slight burning or tingling sensation.

Hold this stretch until the tingling subsides and gently massage the lower part (the part closest to your anus) of the vaginal canal back and forth.

While massaging, hook your thumbs onto the sides of the vaginal canal and gently pull these tissues forward and outward, just as your baby's head will do during delivery.

Finally, massage the same area between your thumb and forefinger -(thumb on the inside and forefinger on the outside of the vagina.

Begin slowly and don't be too vigorous as this could cause bruising or swelling in these sensitive tissues. During the massage **avoid** pressure on the urethra (the tube that brings your urine down from the bladder to the outside) as this could induce irritation or infection.

You will find that your perineum will become more "elastic" and less sensitive each day. Remember to start slowly, never do the massage for too long and build up the intensity each day.

PHYSIOLOGY OF PREGNANCY

From within your uterus your baby is the first to initiate a biological relationship with you as its mother. Signals from your fetus initiate the production of human chorionic gonadotrophin (hCG) via the corpus luteum. This hormone communicates the fact that there is a new element in your body, which triggers your body's mechanism of adaptation. Your fetus literally modifies your physiological activities. It needs to occupy its own space inside you. The response of your body to this process is one of physiological disorder characterised by change and adaptation.

There are changes in your taste, smell, weight, sleeping and waking patterns, as well as changes in behaviour and emotions. Eating habits change and your immune system momentarily lowers its defences because of the initial increase in cortisol, which facilitates the process of the embryo implanting into the endometrium.

All of these changes in your body at the beginning of a pregnancy can cause certain natural symptoms like nausea, fatigue, sensitive breasts, mood swings, abdominal cramps, excess urination, constipation etc.

The hormones

Increasing rates of oestrogen will increase the size of your breasts and together with relaxin they soften all the mucosa in your body and making it more flexible. Relaxin also increases elasticity in the venous system, which plays an important role in the formation of the placenta. Oestrogen also 'softens' your emotions, readying you to accept the new growing fetus.

A sudden increased production of oestrogen at the end of pregnancy can cause the following pregnancy symptoms: An increase in vaginal discharge, a blocked nose, sensitive breasts and a magnification of your emotions.

Increasing rates of progesterone slow down the activity of smooth muscle in your body in order for it to contain and nurture your fetus. Your body could suffer 'side effects' or symptoms due to the fact that the progesterone slows down all smooth muscle activity. Some of these symptoms are: Constipation, heartburn, gas, burping, indigestion, haemorrhoids, insomnia, pelvic and pubic pain, lower backache and breathlessness.

At the end of pregnancy a new hormone called oxytocin appears which also stimulates the production of prolactin. Oxytocin prepares you for birth; it coaches the uterus to contract and it stimulates a proactive attitude in you. Oxytocin is often called the nurturing and love hormone. Prolactin prepares you for breastfeeding and nurturing. It is also an important hormone for foetal metabolism. After delivery, hormone levels rapidly decrease, and their fall may contribute to postpartum blues and postpartum depression.

A natural rhythm

It is important to be aware of the natural physiology of your body during pregnancy. This will help you to understand whether you are experiencing potentially debilitating symptoms or whether they are just the natural reactions of your body to the enormous changes it needs to go through during pregnancy. There is a fine balance between recognising a debilitating symptom and a natural symptom of pregnancy. If you would like to determine whether a symptom is having an impact on your health you can try to establish if there is a natural rhythm present. A natural rhythm simply means that you have some good days and some bad days but not consistent pain/vomiting/insomnia etc. and that you are able to function normally in your day-to-day life. Also check to see if your "symptoms" correspond with your particular gestational period. For example: if you are having regular Braxton Hicks but you are only 18 weeks pregnant then that is not normal.

PLACENTA PRAEVIA

Placenta Praevia means that the placenta is partly or fully covering the cervix (opening) of your womb. If you have an ultrasound scan in early pregnancy and the placenta seems to be near, or even covering, the cervix, don't be too alarmed. In the majority of cases, as the womb grows, the placenta continues to grow away from the cervix. If this is the case you have the same chance of having a normal vaginal delivery as anyone else. Occasionally the placenta does not move from the cervix in which case you will need to have a Caesarean section.

PLACENTA

The placenta is particular to pregnancy. It is an entire organ with the term "placenta" originating from the Latin word for "flat cake".
The primary function of the placenta in all species is to promote a selective transport of nutrients, oxygen and waste products between mother and fetus.

POSITIONS FOR LABOUR

Why not labour lying flat in bed
When you consider the direction that your baby has to go in order to come through your birthing canal, lying down really doesn't make much sense. Your baby needs to descend (come down) so if you are more upright, gravity helps you to manoeuvre the baby's head down onto your cervix (neck of the womb), which in turn will help your cervix to dilate efficiently. Often women that have not been lying down during labour find that when they do lie down, even for just a few minutes while having an internal examination for example, it can be very uncomfortable and makes the contractions feel much more painful. Research has shown that women who remain mobile during labour have shorter labours and need fewer drugs for pain relief than those who take to their beds. Having said all that it is important to try and keep in touch with what you need or want during labour, as there could always be a moment when you want to lie down on your side (preferably the left) to rest a little.

Best positions for labour

When your labour starts, you'll probably feel quite restless and excited. You'll want to be moving around and keeping busy. Just take care that you don't get over-tired before your labour is properly underway. Try to relax and rest between each contraction. If the contractions don't get closer together or stronger you might want to walk or sit in an upright position to see if you can get your baby's head to press more on the pelvic floor. It might help to get things going.

As your contractions get stronger, you'll need to concentrate more on each one, focusing on what is happening to your body and your baby, and practicing your breathing and relaxation exercises. Now is the time for you to choose various positions that help you cope with your contractions.

Try to change your position every twenty to forty minutes.

Various birthing positions:

- While standing, lean onto a work surface, the back of a chair or sofa.
- Put your arms round your partner's neck or waist and lean/hang on him/her.
- Lean onto the bed - if you are in the delivery room the beds have handy height-adjustment possibilities especially for your comfort - or a windowsill.
- If you are at home you may discover a table or kitchen surface that is just the right height to lean on during a contraction.
- Kneel on a large cushion or pillow on the floor and lean forwards with your head resting on your arms, on the seat of a chair.
- Sit astride a chair, resting on a pillow placed across the back and top.
- Sit on the toilet, leaning forwards, or sit astride facing backwards, leaning onto the cistern.
- Go onto all fours with pillows under your knees or kneel on a bed.
- Kneel on one leg, the other bent with your foot flat on the floor.
- Squat, with your partner supporting you from behind.

- Walk between contractions and stop to lean during each contraction.
- Use a long pole (a long window cleaning mop.) Place the pole upright and hold it quite high up with both hands while "hanging" onto it with a pulling down motion.
- Hang one or two cloths/sarongs attached to strong hooks in the ceiling (if you have beams you can throw the cloths over the beams.) Make a knot in the lower end and use them to "hang" onto during a contraction. The action of pulling and hanging creates an opening, downward movement in your pelvis and helps you to relax you entire lower abdomen.
- Standing and rocking your hips backwards and forwards or in a circle will help your baby to move through your pelvis.

Changing position

Changing positions throughout labour can help to make your contractions more efficient. Allow your labour assistants to help you move into a new position every forty-five minutes. Their job is to keep you mobile and make you comfortable wherever you choose to be.

When you are in very strong labour, you will probably find that you don't want to move around a great deal. You'll need all your strength simply to cope with each contraction as it comes along. Don't worry, you will naturally find the position that suits you best.

If you get really tired and a bed seems like the best place to be, lie down on your left hand side, rather than propped up on your back. Lying on your left side is a good position for your baby because he/she gets more oxygen that way, and it can move into the birthing canal in this position. Once you feel rested you could try to change your position again.

Positions for backache labour

If you have backache in between as well as during contractions, your baby might be in a posterior position. You'll find labour very hard to cope with unless you get the weight of the baby off your spine.

The following could help you if you have backache during labour:

- Get onto your hands and knees with pillows under them to keep comfortable – or kneel on a bed or couch.
- Remain upright as much as possible.
- Avoid lying on a bed for any length of time.
- Avoid leaning back between contractions if you are sitting on a chair or bed, slumping forward is better.
- Walk up and down stairs between contractions, doing stairs two at a time. If you don't have stairs then make the same climbing movement by using a low bench onto which you can step up and down.
- Get into a knee-to-chest position on hands and knees (your belly is in the way but get your knees as close to your chest as they will go) and stay there for at least fifteen minutes at a time, or until baby moves more off your spine. You can move into a normal kneeling position during each contraction if needs be. Be sure to have lots of pillows on hand so you can stay in this position comfortably and for as long as possible.
- Ask your partner or caregiver to massage your lower back or place a hot water bottle on your lower back.
- Rock your pelvis during contractions to help your baby turn as it passes through the pelvis.

Positions for pushing Your baby will find it easier to be born if you are in an upright position because you will be able to bear down more efficiently and gravity will help too. The combination of the muscular action of the womb, your pushing efforts and gravity is a powerful one.

If the caregiver prefers you to give birth on the bed, kneel on the mattress and lean against a large pile of pillows placed at the top end. Or while kneeling on the bed put your arms round your partner's neck as he stands next to the bed so your caregiver has good access to your emerging baby. You could also try squatting on the bed supported by your partner from behind. Some hospitals have a birthing stool, which allows you to sit while pushing and gives your caregiver easy access to you and your baby.

Both the squatting position and being on hands and knees have been shown to increase the outlet through the pelvis compared to lying in a supine position.

Birthing stools

A birthing stool helps you to keep upright while you're pushing. They've been used for centuries in all parts of the world. Some research shows that they tend to lead to the mother losing more blood, however, other experts think the apparently increased blood loss is simply due to the fact that its easier to collect and measure the blood when the woman is sitting on a stool.

If you have an epidural

You'll have to stay in bed as the epidural will have made you completely numb from the waist downwards - your legs will be numb too. A good position could be with you on your side, sufficient pillows in the small of your back to keep you there with your partner holding your top leg up (opening your pelvis to allow your baby to pass more easily) with each contraction.

PRE-ECLAMPSIA

Pre-eclampsia is also known as pregnancy induced hypertension (high blood pressure.) It is something that only ever happens in pregnancy and it tends to occur after 26 weeks. It is diagnosed by a combination of signs and symptoms:

- Blood pressure that suddenly rises and stays high.
- Swelling of lower legs, ankles and feet.
- Upper abdominal pain mainly occurring on the right side.
- Visual disturbance such as flashing lights, blurred vision or spots before your eyes.
- Signs of protein in your urine.
- Headaches.
- Sudden weight gain.

Modern medicine does not know the cause of pre-eclampsia. Pre-eclampsia can range from mild to severe and although it cannot be cured, it can be managed.

You are more at risk of getting pre-eclampsia if you:

- Are under twenty or over thirty-five.
- Have a BMI of 30 or more.
- Have one of the following chronic medical problems: chronic high blood pressure, lupus, diabetes or kidney problems.
- Are carrying twins or multiples.
- Have a family history of pre-eclampsia, particularly if it occurred in your mother or a sister.
- Have had it before.
- Had your last baby ten years ago or more.

What will your caregiver do in the case of pre-eclampsia?

Treatment for mild pre-eclampsia may include bed rest at home or in hospital and careful, daily monitoring of you and your baby. Blood tests, urine tests and scans will be used to monitor you and your baby's growth and wellbeing. If you are under 36 weeks pregnant the aim will be to prolong your pregnancy as long as possible, to give your baby the best chance to develop and grow. Medication may be needed to lower your blood pressure if it gets too high. Magnesium Sulphate is often given. A large research study published in 2002 found that if mothers with pre-eclampsia are given magnesium sulphate, it roughly halves the risk of developing full-blown eclampsia.

If your blood pressure cannot be controlled, your obstetrician may suggest that you have your labour induced or that your baby is delivered by a Caesarean.

HELLP Syndrome

Pre-eclampsia is a serious condition. In rare cases it can lead to complications such as HELLP, a syndrome that can sometimes develop before the pre-eclampsia has been diagnosed. Symptoms of HELLP syndrome include headaches, nausea and pain in your upper abdomen. HELLP Syndrome is diagnosed by checking your blood for elevated liver enzymes and low platelets.

PREMATURE LABOUR

Premature labour is when labour begins prior to the 37th week of gestation.

PROBIOTICS – INTESTINAL FLORA

Probiotics are organisms that contribute to the health and balance of the intestinal tract. Probiotics are also referred to as the "friendly", "beneficial" or "good" intestinal flora. When ingested, intestinal flora acts to maintain a healthy intestinal tract to help fight illness and disease.

The gut is actually home to billions of bacteria, good and bad. When the bad bacteria become the majority, they cause a variety of upsets like irregular bowel movements, fungal infections such as thrush (yeast), low immunity, exhaustion, bloating and re-occurring infections (often bladder or sinuses during pregnancy.)

Because of the effect of progesterone on the mucosa during pregnancy your intestinal flora could struggle to stay healthy especially if you have needed to take antibiotics.

Antibiotics kill all bacteria, also the good bacteria, so it is essential to take **Pro**biotics after taking a course of antibiotics to help re-establish the natural balance of the good bacteria in the intestine.

Probiotics taken during pregnancy will ensure that the beneficial flora will "colonize" in both your intestines and your birth canal. When your baby passes through a healthy vagina (instead of an infected one) he or she becomes "inoculated" with helpful bacteria and yeast. An amazing phenomenon then occurs, colostrum and breastmilk, rich in essential sugars, encourage the growth of the beneficial flora in your baby. Reproducing rapidly, they set an "inner ecosystem" into place in the baby's own gut.

Our inner ecosystem is largely responsible for helping us resist infections. Without one, our babies are susceptible to a number of inherited infections like Group B Strep and candidiasis (thrush).

You'll know your baby's inner ecosystem is not forming well if he or she is colicky. In which case you can give your baby a specially formulated Probiotic for newborn babies to support his/her microflora development.

Fermented foods like yogurt, kefir, miso, and tempeh are known as "Probiotic foods". Eating these foods and taking Probiotics as a supplement helps re-colonize the intestines with beneficial flora/ bacteria and thereby keep the bad bacteria from multiplying.
Take the recommended dosage suggested by the product you buy.

PRODUCTS

THE NETHERLANDS

VITALS

www.vitals.nl

"Green Food" plus enzymes - Essential Food
Probiotics – Natren – Trenev Trio (for baby – Lifestart)
Liquid Iron – Elementair Ijzer
Liquid Zinc – Elementair Zinc
Omega-3 - High DHA and EPA/DHA
Psyllium husks – Psylliumvezels

ORTHICA

www.orthica.nl

Enzymes – Enzym Complex
Omega 3 – Fish EPA Forte
Probiotics – Orthiflor
Magnesium 400mg
Pregnancy Multivitamin - Prena-Fem (contains Omega 3)
L.Lysine 500mg

DR VOGEL

www.i-drogist.nl

To assist kidney function: Nephrosolid by Dr Vogel.
Colds and flu: Influasan, Echinaforce
Bladder infection: Solidago Complex
Breech presentation: Pulsatilla
Candida: Molkosan
Digestion: Boldocynara
Aneamia: ferrum phos d6

www.vita4all.nl

New Chapter: Perfect Pre-natal

www.vsm.nl

For itching – Cardiflor salve

THE USA

MINAMI NUTRITION

www.minami-nutrition.com

Omega 3: Eskimo MorEpa

NOW

www.nowfoods.com

Omega 3 1000mg

NATREN

www.natren.com

Probiotics

ENZYMATIC THERAPY

www.enzy.com

Omega 3: Eskimo-3 Fish Oil

Probiotics: Acidophillus Pearls

JARROW FORMULAS

www.jarrow.com

Pregnancy Multivitamin: Preg-Natal + DHA

Omega 3: EPA-DHA Balance

www.drugstore.com

Tucks Hemorrhoidal Pads with Witch Hazel – Parke-Davis

www.evitamins.com

Liquid minerals

Iron tonic: Floradix - Flora

Magnesium 400mg – Now

Magnesium: Natural Calm, Raspberry Lemon – Natural Vitality

Liquid Vitamin B6 – Carlson Labs

www.baselinenutritionals.com

Digestive Enzymes

www.enzymedica.com
Digestive Enzymes

UNITED KINGDOM

www.zitawest.com
Pregnancy Multivitamin: Vital-Essence
Omega 3: Vital DHA
Perineum massage oil

www.nealsyardremedies.com
Homeopathy
Herbs
Aromatherapy
Flower Remedies
Organic Body Products for Mother and Baby

www.synergy-health.co.uk
Digestive Enzymes

www.juiceland.co.uk
Enzymes & Green Food & Omega oils: Beyond Greens - Udo's Choice
Probiotics: Udo's Choice super 8 Probiotic
Digestive Enzymes: Udo's Choice Enzyme Blend

www.worldwideshoppingmall.co.uk
Omega 3: MorEpa – Minami Nutrition

www.goodnessdirect.co.uk
Vitamin B6: Higher Nature

www.simplysupplements.net
Omega 3
Cranberry 5000mg

www.nutritioncentre.co.uk

Nature's Plus Source of Life Prenatal – Multi vitamin
Viridian: Tri-Blend Probiotic Powder
Viridian: Pregnancy Complex
New Chapter: Perfect Pre-natal

SOUTH AFRICA

www.viridian-nutrition.com
Viridian: Tri-Blend Probiotic Powder
Viridian: Pregnancy Complex

www.probiota.co.za
Probiotics

www.medicoherbs.co.za
Milk Thistle

www.phyto-force.co.za
Milk Thistle
Witch Hazel

www.yourlifesource.com (click on South Africa)
Barley Green

www.florahealth.com
Udo's Choice – beyond greens
Udo's Choice – Probiotic Blends
Udo's Choice – Oil Blends

WELEDA

Weleda products:
Pregnancy body oil
Perineum Massage oil
Rhinodoron Nasal Spray
Salt Toothpaste
Blackthorn Elixir (contains a little sugar!)

The Netherlands
www.weleda.nl

USA
www.weleda.com

UNITED KINGDOM
www.weleda.co.uk

SOUTH AFRICA
www.weleda.co.za

All countries
Floradix – Flora – for sale in most drugstores, health food stores and chemists

Nature's Sunshine Candida
Homeopathic remedy for Candida
http://lactinv.com/yeast_treatment.htm#ns_candida

PROGESTERONE

Progesterone affects almost every aspect of pregnancy. It relaxes smooth muscle and decreases prostaglandin formation, which is so that your uterus is less likely to contract and cause a miscarriage. All your abdominal organs also become more "flexible" from progesterone, which is necessary for when they get pushed aside by your enlarged uterus in late pregnancy. Progesterone increases your body temperature and your breathing rate and it causes your blood vessels to dilate making it possible for them to carry more blood.
The following smooth muscle is also affected by the high levels of progesterone during pregnancy:

- Your lower oesophageal sphincter, which can result in increased heartburn and acid reflux especially in the later stages of your pregnancy.
- Your anal sphincter, which could result in haemorrhoids.
- Your colon, which could result in constipation.
- Progesterone also softens cartilage and is therefore responsible for the commonly occurring hip and pubic bone pain.
- Progesterone can also cause tenderness in your breasts early on in pregnancy and a bloated feeling, which you may experience throughout pregnancy.

PTYALISM

Some pregnant women (one in every thousand) develop a very strange symptom called ptyalism. This is an excessive flow of saliva. So much extra saliva is made that it is impossible to keep swallowing it and most women need to carry a cup around to constantly spit the excess saliva into. Some women also have an excess production of thick sticky saliva-like mucous that tends to "dribble" down from the sinuses into the back of their throat causing a very bad taste and nausea. Strangely, although there is an excess of salvia (whether it is foamy or sticky), many women find that they actually get a very dry feeling in the back of their throats, which causes a retching reaction.

Most women find that the symptoms are reduced by the end of the first trimester. But like nausea, the condition may persist throughout pregnancy for some women. In the rare case that ptyalism does stay all through pregnancy the symptoms tend to disappear after delivery of the baby.

THERAPIES AND TIPS for ptyalism

Nutrition

- Cut out sugars, they induce saliva more than any other food. Sugar also leaves a bad aftertaste that can make you feel nauseated.

- Foods that contain wheat or flour (bread, crackers, grain bars, granola, etc.) tend to make the saliva production increase. This is because the digestion of carbohydrates begins in the mouth.
- Foods that contain wheat and gluten often stick to your tongue even after having swallowed, indicating to your mouth that you are still eating, which produces even more saliva. If you can't see yourself cutting out grains then make sure you thoroughly clean your mouth afterward either by brushing your teeth or scraping your tongue. (This is the only time I agree with tongue scraping!)
- Eat foods with a naturally salty flavour like seaweed, anchovies, capers, dill pickles and soy sauce and use natural unrefined sea salt. Salt naturally absorbs water so it will keep your mouth comfortably dry. You need to make sure you don't eat unrefined salt or salty processed foods like crisps because these could increase blood pressure and won't help reduce your saliva production. Try sucking on an umeboshi "pill" for its salty taste.
- High protein foods like chicken, fish, lean beef and eggs will help with both excessive saliva production and nausea.
- If you are vegetarian, celery seems to work quite well. Just make sure to keep munching it at regular intervals throughout the day.
- Make sure you drink enough water because your body is making so much extra saliva, which you are tend to be spitting out, that you are essentially losing a lot of fluid.
- If you can find umeboshi plum lozenges you can suck these to minimize the saliva production.

Lifestyle

- Using a neutral tasting toothpaste could help since most toothpaste uses a sugar free sweetener which will leave a bad aftertaste in your mouth. Try naturally salty toothpaste.
- Try to keep your tongue clean. Any food morsels left in the mouth keeps your body producing more saliva.

- Gargle with unrefined sea salt water. 2:1 salt to water. It is said to stop the excess saliva production for at least 20-30 minutes. Please don't swallow this mixture.
- Try "rinsing" out your sinuses with warm salt water to reduse the sticky saliva production.
- Try to discover if there is an emotional link to your ptyalism, I find in my practice that ptyalism is often linked to emotional stress.

PUBIC PAIN

Pubic pain is also known as pubic symphysis pain. The pregnancy hormones progesterone and relaxin soften and relax the symphysis ligaments. This allows your pelvis to become a lot more 'elastic' so that the pelvic bones have the ability to stretch and open more easily to make way for both the growth and the birth of your baby. Where the pelvic bones come together at the front (your pubic bone) they do not quite touch; there is a small gap between them connected by fibro-cartilaginous tissue reinforced by several ligaments. This area is called the Pubic Symphysis. For some women, either because of excessive levels of hormones, extra sensitivity to hormones, or a pelvis that is out of alignment, this area is either unstable or there is extra pressure on the joint causing pain. Symphysis pubis pain can range from being an annoying twinge to a debilitating pain. The discomfort is usually felt low, in the middle at the front, just below the pubic hairline. Some women will experience pain or discomfort in the symphysis during their pregnancy, in labour and even after the birth if the symphysis joint is very loosened. This can be felt as an ache, sharp pain, 'clicking' sensation or a shooting pain into the clitoris. Often movement will aggravate the pain because it is the job of the symphysis pubis joint to hold your pelvis steady when using your legs, and if the ligaments have softened or have stretched too much it can't work properly and strain is put on your other pelvic joints, causing pain. Sometimes the position of your baby will affect the level of discomfort, for instance when your baby's head engages late in pregnancy.

THERAPIES AND TIPS for pubic pain

Golden Tip

There are different schools of chiropractic technique. Some adjust with quick sudden movements, while others adjust only with gentle, almost imperceptible movements. A chiropractor will aim to realign the pelvis, the back, and all affected areas through the use of manual adjustments. Many women with pubis symphysis pain anecdotally report the greatest improvement from chiropractic treatments. Find a chiropractor that works with pregnant women.

Lifestyle

- You need to get as much bed rest as possible.
- You should not be lifting anything at all.
- You need to take stairs both up and down facing backwards.
- Make sure you keep your knees together when getting out of bed, a car, when standing up from a sitting position and keep your knees tightly together when you roll over in bed - Some women also find it helpful to have their partners stabilize their hips and hold them 'together' when rolling over in bed.
- In some countries they advise women to lie in a hammock for a few hours a day. This literally pushes the joint together for a few hours taking the strain off the ligaments.
- Support your back with a sturdy pillow while sitting.
- Wearing a pelvic support belt is recommended.

NOTE: In the rare case that the joint has become inflamed an ice pack is often recommended to reduce the pain. I would advise **against** excessive cooling of the pelvic region during pregnancy.

Obstetric Physiotherapist

An Obstetric Physiotherapist can supply a pelvic support garment to wear such as a Fem Brace or Tubigrip Bandage, and crutches if walking is difficult. They will also give you gentle exercises to help strengthen the muscles supporting the pelvis and general advice about posture and which activities you should avoid.

◐ Osteopath

Osteopaths work with realigning the bones, ligaments; soft tissues and fascia of the body. Osteopaths are trained in traditional medicine as well as the musculoskeletal system, but they tend to place more emphasis on preventive medicine, in looking at the body as an interconnected system, and they will sometimes combine the use of osteopathic manipulation and other 'non-traditional' therapies.

Polarity Therapy

You can have someone do this therapy on you at home. While lying on your side, your partner sits behind you (they will have to lean over you so they will need to shift up close to your back) and places four fingertips of his/her **right hand** on the middle of your pubic bone and the **left hand** rests flat on your sacrum (the whole area just on and above your tailbone or coccyx.) The hands should remain still on these two places until warmth or a tingling can be felt equally in both your partner's hands. The idea is that he/she creates a circulation of energy from the front to the back of your body. By doing this there is an improvement in the polarity (positive and negative energy poles) that exists naturally in the body and this in turn can help relieve pain.

☯ Acupuncture and Shiatsu

Acupuncture does not resolve pelvic misalignment, but it has been used successfully to treat the pain. Always try to find and acupuncturist who is well trained and experienced in working with pregnant women.

☛My experience: I find that acupuncture works well for symphysis pain. The point used is on the pubic bone. I give this same point as acupressure homework.

Acupressure Point

Whenever you are feeling pain on your pubic bone, place your thumbs (one on top of the other) on the central area of your pubic bone and press with even pressure for about ten to twenty seconds, do this at least once or twice a day. It could hurt at first but it will actually feel a lot better once you have done it. Its even better if you can get someone else like your partner to do it because they will exert a little more pressure than you will let yourself do. Never go over your pain threshold! Let your partner know when he/she should ease up a little.

✚ Homeopathy

Some women report improvement in pain with the use of the homeopathic remedy, Kali Carb, 30c. However, homeopathy is very much based on an individual's personal circumstances, personality, and needs and you might need an individual consultation to know what remedy would work best for you.

♣ Phytotherapy/herbs

Teasel (*Dipsacus Japonicus*) tincture, fifteen drops taken three times a day has helped many women with pubic symphysis pain. This herb is also used during pregnancy to prevent habitual miscarriages.

Movement/Strengthening Therapies

Several women have reported that movement and strengthening therapies like the Alexander Technique and Pilates have helped them with postpartum pubic symphysis pain.

Giving birth with pubic/symphysis pain

You might need to discuss delivery options and positions with your caregiver if your symptoms are extreme. Here are standard pieces of advice:

- Don't pull your knees back too far during pushing. This puts a great deal of strain on the pubic symphysis joint. Be sure to let your caregiver, nurses, doula, or labour coach know that you are not able to do this!
- Don't put your legs on your attendant's hips as a support during pushing. Again, this strains the pubic symphysis joint.
- Avoid stirrups at all costs!

- Standing, kneeling, and all fours are the best positions for the second stage of delivery.

R

RED RASPBERRY LEAF TEA (RUBUS SPP.)

Brewed as a tea or as an infusion, raspberry leaf is the best known, the most widely used and the safest of all uterine and pregnancy tonic herbs. It contains fragrine, an alkaloid, which gives tone to the muscles of the pelvic region, including the uterus itself.
The rich concentration of vitamin C, the presence of vitamin E, vitamins A and B and the easily assimilated calcium, iron, phosphorous and potassium indicate that raspberry leaves are also powerful in their nutrient content.

The benefits of drinking a raspberry leaf brew throughout pregnancy include:

- Reducing pain during labour and after birth, by toning the muscles used during labour and delivery. It does not, however, counter the pain of dilation.
- Raspberry leaf works to encourage the uterus to let go and function without tension. It does not strengthen contractions, but does allow the contracting uterus to work more effectively providing the possibility of a safe and speedy birth.

Drink four cups a day from 36 weeks of pregnancy to prepare your uterus for birth.

BREAKFAST (also see "Breakfast" chapter)

Oats With Live Yoghurt And Grated Apple

(you can substitute with a grated pear or some berries if you are allergic to apples)

1 serving

Ingredients:

½ cup of rolled oats

1½ to 2 cups of organic live yoghurt

1 apple (pear or berries can substitute apple if you are allergic to apple)

Sesame, sunflower and pumpkin seeds to taste

Preparation:

Place the rolled oats into a breakfast bowl, add the organic live yoghurt, mix well and leave for 5 to 10 minutes to allow the oats to soften. Now grate the apple (with skin) into the bowl, mix again, sprinkle with seeds and eat.

Pumpkin Seed And Apricot Muesli

Serves: 2

Ingredients:

50gr (2oz) rolled oats

1 tablespoon of sultanas or raisins

1 tablespoon pumpkin seeds

1 tablespoon chopped almonds

25gr (1oz) organic dried apricots

2 tablespoons of apple juice

2 small apples

Soya or goat's milk or organic live yoghurt – goat's or cow's

Preparation:

Place the oats, sultanas or raisins, seeds, almonds and dried apricots in a bowl with the fruit juice.

Grate the apples into the mix, top with the milk or yoghurt and serve.

Apple "Pancakes" – High Protein, Grain-free Breakfast

(recommended for nausea and high blood pressure)

Ingredients:

Organic apples

Eggs - as many eggs as apples

Butter for frying

Cinnamon

Preparation:

Peel and core apples
Grate apples
Mix the apples, eggs and cinnamon
Melt butter in a pan
Drop as you would pancakes (small pancakes work better so you can brown them on both sides)
Brown slowly and serve

LUNCH

Pitta Rounds Stuffed With Sweet Roasted Vegetables

Servings: 4

Ingredients:

1 large Portobello mushroom (6 oz.) cap thickly sliced
1 bunch fresh asparagus, about 1 lb. trimmed, cut into 2-inch lengths
1 red and 1 yellow bell pepper, seeded, cut into 1-1/2 inch chunks
3 tablespoons Roasted Red Pepper or Sun Dried Tomato dressing
Salt and freshly ground black pepper
4 whole-wheat pita bread rounds, cut in half crosswise
8 romaine lettuce leaves

Preparation:

Heat oven to 425°F. In a shallow roasting pan lined with parchment paper, toss together mushroom, asparagus, bell peppers and 1 tablespoon of the dressing. Sprinkle salt and pepper over vegetables and toss again. Roast 12 to 14 minutes or until vegetables are crisp-tender. Transfer vegetables to a bowl and chill in refrigerator 5 minutes. Open pita pocket halves; line with lettuce leaves. Add the remaining 2 tablespoons dressing to roasted vegetables, tossing well. Spoon mixture into lettuce-lined pita pockets.

Barbeque Broccoli Sandwich

2 servings

Ingredients:

1½ cups (3 ounces) extra-firm light silken tofu
1 tablespoon chopped flat-leaf parsley
¾ tablespoon lemon juice
1½ tablespoons of water
1½ teaspoons sea salt
1½ tablespoons olive oil
½ cup thinly sliced red onion
1½ cups of chopped broccoli florets
A pinch of freshly ground black pepper
2 tablespoons maple-barbeque sauce
Cornbread or wholegrain bread roll

Maple-barbeque sauce:

4 tablespoons of pure maple syrup
2 tablespoons Dijon mustard, or other strong mustard
Juice of 1 medium lemon (about 2 tablespoons)
1 clove of garlic, crushed
1 teaspoon of ground black pepper
½ teaspoon dried thyme leaves, crushed
5 tablespoons olive oil added slowly at the end to bind the sauce

Preparation:

Combine tofu, parsley, lemon juice, water and one-quarter teaspoon of salt in a blender container or food processor. Blend until smooth; set aside. Heat a large non-stick skillet over medium-high heat. Add oil, then onion; cook 4 minutes, stirring occasionally. Add broccoli, remaining one-quarter teaspoon salt, and pepper; cook 4 minutes, stirring occasionally. Add barbeque sauce; continue cooking 2 minutes or until thickened. Spoon the broccoli mixture evenly onto the bread. Add tofu dressing and serve.

Cool Cucumber Salad

Ingredients:

1 large cucumber, peeled and thinly sliced
2 tablespoons olive oil
1 tablespoon of sesame oil
2 tablespoons organic apple cider vinegar
1 teaspoon of honey (buy honey from the health food store)
½ teaspoon sea salt
1 tablespoon chopped fresh coriander
Pepper, to taste
Sesame seeds to garnish

Preparation:

Place the cucumber slices in a medium bowl, set aside. In a small bowl combine remaining ingredients. Add the dressing to the cucumber, toss well. Cover and refrigerate for up to 2 hours.
Serve

Crunchy Broccoli Salad

Ingredients:

3 cups broccoli florets
1 onions, chopped
2 cups sliced mushrooms
½ cup toasted sliced almonds
¼ cup unsalted roasted sunflower seeds
3 tablespoon toasted sesame seeds
2 cups of rice noodles, soaked in boiling water

Dressing:

1 clove garlic, chopped
½ cup vegetable oil
3 tablespoon of rice vinegar
2 tablespoon of sodium-reduced soy sauce

1 tablespoon of honey
1 teaspoon of sesame oil
½ teaspoon freshly ground black pepper
Pinch of sea salt

Preparation:

Steam the broccoli for 2 to 3 minutes, or until tender-crisp. Drain and rinse under cold water until chilled. Drain and place in a large bowl.

Add mushrooms, onions, sunflower seeds, almonds, and sesame seeds to broccoli and mix well. Place the rice noodles on top.

In a small bowl, combine garlic, vegetable oil, vinegar, soy sauce, honey, sesame oil, pepper and salt. Pour dressing over broccoli salad and mix well.

DINNER

Yoghurt Marinated Chicken

Serves 4

Ingredients:

½ cup low-fat live organic yogurt
1 clove chopped garlic
¼ tablespoon minced gingerroot
1 tablespoon freshly squeezed lemon juice
½ tablespoon vegetable oil
1 Teaspoon paprika powder
¼ teaspoon chilli powder
½ teaspoon crumbled dried rosemary
Freshly ground black pepper
¼ teaspoon turmeric
4 boneless skinless organic chicken breasts (about 750g)

Preparation:

In a large bowl, combine yoghurt, garlic, ginger, lemon juice, oil, paprika, chilli powder, rosemary, pepper and turmeric; whisk until smooth. Add chicken, turning to coat all over. Cover and refrigerate for 24 hours.

Preheat oven to 350° F.

Place chicken in single layer in baking pan, reserving marinade. Bake in preheated oven for 20 – 25 minutes or until no longer pink inside.
Spoon additional marinade over the chicken halfway through baking.
Serve with couscous or brown rice

Chicken Vegetable And Rice Soup

Ingredients:

½ cup dried navy beans
2 tablespoons olive oil
One 4pound organic chicken, cut into serving pieces
1 Teaspoon salt
½ teaspoon freshly ground black pepper
1 cup chopped yellow onions
½ cup chopped carrots
½ cup chopped celery
1 tablespoon minced garlic
½ cup chopped zucchini
½ cup chopped yellow squash
2 quarts chicken stock (check that it doesn't contain MSG)
½ cup seeded and chopped plum tomatoes
4 sprigs fresh parsley
3 bay leaves
¼ teaspoon cayenne
6 tablespoons of uncooked brown rice
½ cup chopped green onions (green and white parts)
1 tablespoon minced fresh thyme
¼ cup chopped fresh flat-leaf parsley
1 cup torn spinach leaves

Preparation:

Put the beans into a bowl and add enough water to cover by 2 inches. Soak for 8 hours, then drain.
(For a quick soak, bring the beans and water to a boil over high heat and cook for 2 minutes, then remove from heat and allow to stand for 1 hour. Drain.)
Heat the oil in a large heavy pot over medium-high heat. In batches, cook the chicken, seasoning with the salt and pepper and turning

once, until evenly brown, about 10 minutes. Transfer the chicken to a platter. Pour off all but 2 tablespoons of the fat from the pot.

Add the onions, carrots, and celery. Cook, stirring often, until softened, about 3 minutes. Add the garlic and stir until fragrant, about 1 minute. Stir in the zucchini and yellow squash and cook for 1 minute. Add the stock, drained beans, tomatoes, parsley, bay leaves, and cayenne. Return the chicken to the pot. Bring to a boil over high heat. Reduce the heat to medium-low and simmer, uncovered, until the beans are almost tender, about 1 hour.

Using a long-handled slotted spoon or tongs, carefully transfer the chicken pieces to a plate. Cool slightly, then remove the meat from the bones, discarding the skin and bones.

Return the chicken meat and any accumulated juices to the pot. Add the rice, green onions, thyme, parsley, and spinach and simmer until the rice and beans are tender, about 15 minutes. Discard the bay leaves.

Ladle into warm bowls and serve hot.

Makes 12 servings! I make one big batch and freeze small portions that can be defrosted during labour and after birth.

Broccoli Chilli And Garlic Pasta

Serves 2

Ingredients:

1 broccoli head
2 cloves garlic, chopped
A dash of olive oil
Whole wheat or spelt pasta
Chillies to taste, sliced

Preparation:

Cut the broccoli head into florets and the stem into bite sized pieces and steam for about 3 minutes or until 'al dente'. Save the water from the steamer. While you are boiling the pasta in the broccoli water, fry the sliced chilli (preferably fresh) in olive oil in a pan or wok for about 2 minutes then add 2 cloves of coarsely chopped garlic and fry for another minute taking care not to brown the garlic. Add the strained broccoli and keep turning until heated through. Hopefully the pasta is cooked about now. Combine in the ingredients in the pan to ensure that the pasta is coated in the tasty oil and serve immediately.

Curried Lentil Soup

Serves 4

Ingredients:

1 carton (8 ounces) organic live yoghurt
2 teaspoons olive oil
1 large white onion, chopped
2 large carrots, thinly sliced
¾ cup red lentils
2 teaspoons curry powder, preferably Madras curry powder
1 teaspoon freshly ground coriander seeds
1 teaspoon freshly ground cumin seeds
4 ¼ cups fruity red wine such as merlot
4 ¼ cups low-salt chicken or vegetable stock (MSG free)
Sea salt to taste
¼ cup chopped cilantro (fresh coriander)

Preparation:

Place a strainer over a bowl; line with a clean kitchen towel. Place yogurt in the strainer to drain and thicken while you prepare the soup.

Heat a large saucepan over medium-high heat. Add oil, then onion; cook 5 minutes stirring occasionally. Stir in carrots, lentils, spices and curry powder; cook 1 minute. Stir in the stock, wine, and salt; cover and bring to a boil over high heat. Reduce heat and simmer uncovered 20 to 40 minutes or until lentils and vegetables are tender. Ladle into soup bowls; top with thickened yogurt and chopped cilantro.

Peppers With Lentils And Goat's Cheese

Serves 4

Ingredients:

225g (8oz) Split red lentils
Sea salt and pepper to taste
4 red or green peppers

2 onions, chopped
175g celery stalks, chopped
Olive oil
170g (6oz) fresh soft goat's cheese
10 black olives, halved and pitted
Basil sprigs, to garnish

Preparation:

Cook the lentils in boiling salted water for 15 to 20 minutes until tender. Drain. Meanwhile halve the peppers lengthwise and remove the core and seeds. Grill the pepper halves in the oven for 10 minutes, turning occasionally, until the skin is slightly browned and the flesh softened. Finely chop the onions and celery. Heat the olive oil in a saucepan and sauté the onions and celery for 2 minutes. Stir in the lentils; stir in the goat's cheese and then spoon the mixture evenly into the pepper halves. Grill under moderate heat for 2 minutes until the filling is golden. Garnish with basil sprigs and serve hot, with a tomato and rucola salad.

Cauliflower With Saffron, Pinenuts And Raisins

Serves 2

Ingredients:

1 medium cauliflower
3 Tablespoons olive oil
1 large onion, thinly sliced
Pinch of saffron, infused in - 4 tbsp boiling water
3 tablespoons of pine nuts, lightly toasted
75g raisins, soaked in warm water
Sea salt & black pepper

Preparation:

Put the cauliflower florets in a pan of boiling water. Bring back to the boil and blanch for 1 min then drain. Heat the olive oil in a heavy saucepan then add the onion and a pinch of sea salt. Cook on a low heat, stirring regularly, then drain the onion and keep the oil. In the saucepan reheat the oil and add the florets and the smallest leaves from the cauliflower. Fry until the cauliflower begins to colour, then add the onion, saffron water, pine nuts and drained raisins. Cook for 5 minutes until the water has evaporated then season and serve.

Grilled Butternut Squash

Serves 2

Ingredients:

1 butternut squash
Olive oil
Coriander & cumin (seeds ground in a mortar & pestle)
Salt & pepper

Preparation:

Cut 1 butternut squash in half (there is no need to peel}. Sprinkle the olive oil, crushed coriander, salt and pepper onto the squash. Preheat the oven to 350°F before placing in oven.

Bake the squash until soft; then simply scoop the squash out of the skin, add a little organic butter and serve with brown rice.

Pan Grilled Citrus Salmon With Cole Slaw

Serves 4

Ingredients:

½ large (or 1 small) pink or red grapefruit
2 tablespoons hoi sin sauce
2 teaspoons dark sesame oil
4 skinless salmon fillets
¾ teaspoon salt
2 cups (6 ounces) mange tout, cut lengthwise into thin strips
1 cup sliced cabbage
½ cup sliced radishes
2 teaspoons sesame seeds, toasted

Preparation:

Peel and coarsely chop grapefruit, saving juices. Measure juices, squeezing the chopped grapefruit a little more if needed to measure 2 tablespoons juice. Combine the 2 tablespoons grapefruit juice, hoi sin sauce and sesame oil. Transfer 2 tablespoons of the mixture to a large bowl. Brush remaining mixture over salmon fillets; sprinkle with ½ teaspoon sea salt. Heat a ridged grill pan over medium heat until hot. Add salmon; cook 3 to 4 minutes per side or until salmon is opaque and firm to the touch.

Meanwhile, add mange tout, cabbage, reserved chopped grapefruit and remaining ¼ teaspoon of sea salt to the bowl with reserved hoi sin sauce mixture; toss well. Arrange on four serving plates; top with salmon and sprinkle with sesame seeds.

Honey And Mustard Roasted Chicken

Serves 2

Ingredients:

½ lb. potatoes cut into wedges
1 lb. chicken
3 medium carrots, sliced
1 tablespoons olive oil
1 tablespoons honey
1 tablespoons mustard
½ teaspoon rosemary
1 clove of garlic
Sea salt and pepper to taste

Preparation:

Preheat oven to 425° F. In a shallow pan, toss potatoes and carrots with oil, salt and pepper. Peel the garlic and nestle the garlic amongst the vegetables and scatter the rosemary on top. Arrange the chicken pieces among the vegetables and bake uncovered for 30 minutes. Stir together the mustard and honey, and spread over chicken. Stir vegetables, return chicken to the oven and bake 10-20 minutes, until chicken is cooked and vegetables are tender.

Portuguese Bean Soup With Sweet Potatoes

Serves 4

Ingredients:

2 teaspoons olive oil
1 cup coarsely chopped white onion
3 cups reduced-sodium chicken stock
1 cup diced (one-half inch pieces) unpeeled sweet potato
3 teaspoons chilli garlic sauce
1 clove of garlic, chopped
1 can (14.5 ounces) diced tomatoes, undrained
1 can of cannelloni beans
4 cups sliced Swiss chard or pakchoi

4 teaspoons balsamic vinegar (optional)

Preparation:

Heat a large saucepan over medium-high heat. Add oil, then onion; cook three minutes, stirring occasionally. Add stock, sweet potato, garlic and chilli sauce; bring to a boil over high heat. Reduce heat; simmer uncovered five minutes. Stir in tomatoes and beans; return to a simmer. Stir in Swiss chard or pakchoi. Simmer until sweet potatoes and greens are tender. Stir in vinegar, if desired, and ladle into four serving bowls.

Whole Zucchni (Courgette) Stuffed With Quinoa

Serves 4

Ingredients:

1 cup Quinoa (pronounced KEEN-wa, a grain from the Andes.)
2 cups low-salt chicken stock
1 cup frozen baby Lima beans
2 large zucchini squash (about 1½ pounds)
1½ teaspoons olive oil
1 clove of garlic, chopped
Splash of Tabasco sauce
1 small tin of tomato puree
Sea salt
3 tablespoons chopped cilantro (coriander)
¼ cup toasted pumpkin seeds or sunflower seeds (optional)

Preparation:

Combine quinoa and stock in a medium saucepan. Bring to a boil over high heat. Reduce heat; simmer gently for 10 minutes. Stir in lima beans; continue to simmer 5 to 6 minutes or until liquid is absorbed. Meanwhile, cut zucchini lengthwise in half. Cut out and discard the seeds. Using a sharp paring knife, cut out flesh leaving a 1/3-inch-thick shell. Save the flesh and chop, set aside. Place hollowed halves on a baking tray in the oven and grill for 5 to 10 minutes until they are cooked al dente.

Heat a large skillet over medium-high heat. Add oil, fry up the garlic for 1 minute then add chopped zucchini flesh; stir-fry 2 minutes.

Add tomato puree and Tabasco sauce; simmer 3 minutes or until zucchini is tender. Stir ½ cup of salsa mixture into quinoa mixture. Arrange cooked zucchini halves on four serving plates; sprinkle with sea salt. Spoon the remaining salsa mixture into the zucchini halves. Spoon quinoa mixture onto and around the zucchini; top with cilantro. Sprinkle 1 tablespoon of pumpkin or sunflower seeds over each serving.

Spelt Or Wholewheat Pasta With Cauliflower, Walnuts And Feta

Serves 2

Ingredients

1 head cauliflower
1 medium onion
4 cloves garlic
250g spelt or whole-wheat pasta
Olive oil
Sea salt & pepper
1 pinch dried chilli
White wine vinegar
½ lemon
50g toasted walnuts
50g feta cheese
Parsley, chopped

Preparation:

Put a large pot of water on to boil. Cut the cauliflower into small florets. Peel the onion and slice it very thin. Peel and finely chop the garlic. Put the pasta on to cook. Next sauté the cauliflower in olive oil in a large sauté pan and when it begins to soften, season with salt and pepper and add the sliced onion and a pinch of dried chilli. Sauté over medium to high heat until the cauliflower and onions are brown and tender. Add the garlic and remove from the heat, tossing so the garlic does not burn. Add a splash of wine vinegar, the juice of ½ lemon and the toasted walnuts. Taste and adjust the seasoning. When the pasta is done, drain and add to the cauliflower, adding enough olive oil to coat the pasta thoroughly, toss together. Sprinkle with chopped parsley.

Umeboshi And Rice Salad With Pickled Ginger And Sugar Snap Peas

Ingredients

2 cups Japanese rice or other short-grain rice such as Arborio
3 cups water
3 tablespoons seasoned rice vinegar
1/2 cup umeboshi
1/3 cup drained pickled ginger (preferably amazu shoga)
1/4 pound sugar snap peas or snow peas

Preparation

Rinse the rice in a bowl using several changes of cold water until water is almost clear and drain in a colander. Let rice stand, uncovered, in colander at least 30 minutes.

In a 3-quart saucepan bring the rice in 3 cups of water to boil over high heat and then boil, covered, 2 minutes. Reduce heat to moderate and boil rice, covered, 5 minutes more. Reduce heat to low and cook rice, covered, until liquid is absorbed, 10 to 15 minutes. Let rice stand, covered, 10 minutes and spread it out onto in a large shallow baking pan. Sprinkle rice with vinegar and toss with a wooden spoon to cool slightly.

Pit umeboshi and coarsely chop umeboshi and ginger. In a bowl stir together rice, umeboshi, and ginger and cool to room temperature. Salad may be prepared up to this point 4 hours ahead and kept, covered, at cool room temperature. Have ready a bowl of ice and cold water. In a saucepan of boiling water cook peas until bright green, about 30 seconds, and transfer to ice water to stop cooking. Drain peas and cut crosswise into thin strips. Peas may be cooked 1 day ahead and chilled in a sealable plastic bag.

Just before serving, stir peas into salad and season with salt.

DESSERT

Fruit Salad With Yoghurt & Honey Dressing

Serves 2

Ingredients:

1 cup live organic yoghurt
2 tablespoons honey
½ teaspoon ground cinnamon
2 large oranges, peeled, sliced
½ large pineapple, peeled, cored, sliced, and cut into wedges
1 apple, cored and chopped
1 ripe pear, cored and sliced into wedges
1 kiwifruit, peeled and sliced

Preparation:

In a small bowl, combine the yoghurt, honey and cinnamon. Stir well to blend ingredients

Arrange fruit on plates and drizzle the honey-yoghurt dressing on top.

Triple Berry Smoothie Desssert

Serves 4

Ingredients:

2 cups mixed frozen berries such as blueberries, raspberries and strawberries
2 cups unsweetened apple juice
2 cups raspberry or strawberry sorbet

Preparation:

Combine berries and juice in blender container. Cover and blend at high speed 30 seconds. Add sorbet; blend for another 30 seconds.

Cooking Without by Barbara Cousins is a cookbook that has recipes, which are free from: Gluten, sugar, dairy, yeast and saturated fat.

RESTLESS LEGS (RLS)

Restless leg syndrome begins as a strange feeling in your legs while sitting or lying down that seems to get worse until you stand up and move around. Deep inside your legs you can feel burning, creeping, and crawling sensations that are hard to describe. These vague symptoms describe something called restless legs syndrome (RLS.) You'll usually notice symptoms when you're at rest, especially right before you fall asleep or when sitting still for long periods. Most of the time, you'll feel it in your legs, but some women experience it in their arms as well. Moving your limbs brings immediate relief, but unfortunately, it is only temporary. As soon as you sit or lie down again, the sensations return. Your restless legs may even be waking you up once you're asleep.

The following best describes RLS:

- An irritating sensation in your legs that gives you an overwhelming urge to walk around and move them.
- Symptoms occur or worsen when you are lying down, sitting, resting or relaxing for long periods of time.
- Symptoms improve when you move your legs around.
- Symptoms are worse in the evening and throughout the night.
- The sensations feel like insects crawling just under the skin.
- Little involuntary movements of your toes, feet or legs may be visible when you are sitting still.

There are a number of theories about why some women experience RLS during pregnancy. Iron deficiency, magnesium deficiency, hormonal changes and circulatory changes are all possible culprits.

THERAPIES AND TIPS for RLS

Golden Tip

Magnesium (oxide) 400mg to 800mg taken at the end of the day has been proven to improve RLS by seventy five percent, especially helping women who found that they weren't sleeping due to restless legs.

☑ **Supplements**
Iron will help to relieve RLS in women who are iron-deficient. Liquid chlorophyll is an excellent supplement during pregnancy. If you can't find liquid chlorophyll then you could take any "green food" supplement like spirulina or barley grass. (See Anaemia for more information on iron deficiency.)
Take the recommended dosage of the product you buy.

Nutrition

- It is important to avoid caffeine, not only does it reduce your body's ability to absorb iron but because it is a stimulant it can make you generally more restless.
- Eat plenty of foods that are high in iron. Be sure to eat foods that contain Vitamin C to aid the absorption of iron.

Foods that contain vitamin C are: Red peppers, pineapple, citrus fruits, strawberries, peas, broccoli, kiwi, potatoes, pawpaw, Brussels sprouts, cauliflower, tomatoes, apples, dried apricots and asparagus.
Foods that are high in iron include: Red meat, chicken, turkey, fish, beans, leafy green vegetables, dried fruits such as raisins, prunes and apricots, prune juice, cereal and other foods made from whole grains.

Lifestyle
Some women find it helpful to have a massage or practice relaxation techniques.

ROUTINE ANTENATAL CHECK-UPS

You will usually have a monthly antenatal check-up during your pregnancy until around week 28 when the visits will become

fortnightly and then from around week 36 they will become weekly visits.
The routine antenatal tests most likely to be carried out by your caregiver will include:

- A basic all round physical including your blood pressure and fundal height.
- In some countries: weighing and measuring of the mother occurs. Her height and sometimes even shoe size are measured to give a global guide to the size of her pelvis.
- In some countries: examination of breasts and nipples are done.
- A urine test is done to screen for a possible urinary tract infection and to check for any appearance of protein in the urine (proteinuria.) In most countries your caregiver will check your urine for glucose and protein at each visit.
- A blood test is done to establish your blood group, possible anaemia, immunity to rubella and toxoplasmosis. Syphilis, hepatitis and HIV testing are also offered in most countries.

At a routine visit your caregiver will check your blood pressure and measure the growth of your uterus by checking the height of your fundus. The fundus is the medical term for the upper portion of the uterus. Fundal height is generally measured using a tape measure and measuring from the top of your pubic bone to the top of your fundus. Fundal height is measured in centimetres and should closely match your baby's gestational age. So, for example, if you're 24 weeks pregnant, your fundal height should be around twenty-four centimetres. Fundal height can vary from person to person and it is not an exact measurement. It does however give your caregiver a good indication as to how your baby is growing as she can compare it the measurement to your previous visit. Some caregivers "measure" fundal height by palpation (feeling).
As you approach late pregnancy, fundal height will become less accurate. Please remember that fundal height is only one factor in assessing foetal development.
At a routine visit the baby's heartbeat will also be monitored.

At around 30 weeks your caregiver will check your blood again for possible anaemia.

Rhesus Factor: If you're Rh- (negative) there's the possibility that your baby will have a blood group that is incompatible with yours, and this could cause problems. If the blood of anyone who's Rh- comes into contact with Rh+ blood, it will react to it as 'foreign' and will develop antibodies to the Rh+.

In some countries anti-D injections are given routinely to every pregnant woman who is Rhesus negative at about 28 weeks (and in many cases also at 34 weeks) in an effort to prevent the 0.2% of women who may develop antibodies during late pregnancy for no apparent reason. Sometimes Anti-D immunoglobulin is given by injection to Rhesus negative women within seventy-two hours after a vaginal bleeding event during pregnancy or after the birth of their baby (if their baby's cord blood test shows the baby to be Rhesus positive.) The aim of giving the injection is to prevent antibodies forming, just in case some of the baby's blood has passed into the mother's system.

Around 34 weeks your caregiver will determine if your baby is lying in a head-down position.

In some countries, during the last few visits, your caregiver may do an internal exam to check for thinning (effacement) and opening (dilatation) of your cervix (the opening to your uterus.)

S

SAFE PLACE - VISUALIZATION

For some women visualizing that you are retreating to a "safe place" is a wonderful tool for managing contractions during labour. It is a mental distraction technique that reduces the amount of pain the brain registers. It helps to deeply relax you within seconds aiding the body to work more efficiently during labour.
To begin your visualization, try to imagine a place where you could feel truly relaxed, unhurried and safe. It may be a beautiful white beach, a cool garden or a lovely, intimate room. Whatever or wherever it is it needs to be a place that you will want to keep coming back to.
Take a deep breath and say, 'I am going to my safe place now'. Sometimes it helps to imagine a staircase or a path that leads you to your safe place. Begin to count from one to five and slowly move into that special/safe place in your mind. Spend a few minutes there feeling, smelling, seeing and hearing to familiarize yourself with this place. If, for instance, you chose a beach then try *hear* the waves, *smell* and *taste* the salty sea mist, *feel* the warmth of the sand between your toes. The more details you can build up of your safe place the better. Feel your body relaxing as you begin to feel the soothing qualities of your secret retreat.

In the last few weeks of pregnancy revisit your safe place again and again. Saying in your mind each time before you go there, 'I am going to my safe place now', or choose some trigger words that will conjure up your safe place in a few seconds. If you like you can share

these with your partner or doula so that they can say them to you during labour to help you to retreat to your safe place.
By going to your safe place many times before your labour begins it will take literally seconds for your mind to transport you to this familiar place during labour by simply saying the words, 'I am going to my safe place now', or by saying or hearing your trigger words. The feeling of peace and calm that you are able to create by doing this will balance your hormones and activate your parasympathetic nervous system, assisting a more efficient opening of your cervix

Additional information
Visualization may not be a suitable technique if you feel that "stepping outside your body" will not help you to open and relax during labour.

SCIATICA

The sciatic nerve is a large nerve which comes from your lower back and travels down the back of your legs and then branches out to your feet. It allows you to feel sensations and move muscles in your legs. Sciatica is when inflammation or pressure from the back causes the sciatic nerve to become painful. Sometimes, the function of the nerve can become impaired resulting in weakness or pins and needles. Sciatica can be present with or without backache and can send pain down the back of your leg.
Pregnancy related changes could cause pelvic pain and backache and occasionally sciatica. The majority of women who think they have sciatica during pregnancy actually have a condition known as Pelvic Girdle Pain.
In younger people, sciatica is often caused by damage to a disc leading to inflammation around the nerve or direct pressure from a prolapsed or 'slipped' disc. In older people, it may be due to compression from a ligament or bone. Neither of these situations occur more frequently in pregnancy and the chances are that if you do have sciatica during pregnancy it would have come on whether you were pregnant or not.
(See Pelvic Girdle Pain for more information)

SCREENING AND DIAGNOSTICS

There is a range of different screening and diagnostics tests that give you a better idea of your baby's health during pregnancy.

Ultrasound scan
The first is an ultrasound scan. In normal situations the first ultrasound scan will be done between 11 to 14 weeks to determine exactly how far into your pregnancy you are or to check if you may be carrying twins. Between 11 and 14 weeks an ultrasound scan called a nuchal fold scan can be made to measure the clear ("translucent") space in the tissue at the back of your developing baby's neck. This measurement can help your healthcare practitioner assess your baby's risk for Down Syndrome (DS) and other chromosomal abnormalities.
Another ultrasound scan will be made around 20 weeks to check the internal organs, length of limbs, possibly the sex of your baby and to locate the position of your placenta.

Blood test
Multiple Marker is a blood test and a screening, which measures the levels of the hormones Estriol and Human Chorionic Gonadotropin (hCG), as well as Alpha-fetoprotein (AFP), in your blood. The results of the Multiple Marker test comes back in one to two weeks. If a fetus has Down Syndrome, hCG levels are often higher than normal, Estriol levels and AFP often are lower than normal. Remember this is an estimate and if the results raise concerns your caregiver will do any of the following tests:

Chorionic Villus Sampling (CVS)
CVS is done around 11 to 12 weeks and is a test that gives a complete picture of the genetic makeup of the developing fetus. This procedure involves taking a sample of the chorion, a membrane surrounding the fetus, either via the vagina and cervix, or through a needle inserted through the abdominal wall. The examination of this sample can help in detecting disorders like Tay-Sachs, sickle-cell anaemia, most types of cystic fibrosis, the Thalassaemias, and Down

Syndrome. CVS is not risk free and carries a two percent risk is of causing a miscarriage.

Amniocentesis

Amniocentesis is done between 15 to 20 weeks and is helpful in diagnosing birth defects such as neural tube defect (NTD), including anencephaly (failure of brain formation), Down Syndrome (DS) and spina bifida (open spine.) A small sample of the amniotic fluid in which the baby lies is drawn off through a needle. The test measures the amount of foetal protein both in the mother's blood as well as in the amniotic fluid. An amniocentesis is usually advised for women over thirty-five, women who have had three or more miscarriages, if the Multiple Marker has come back with concerning results or if either parent or a sibling has a known chromosomal abnormality or a hereditary disease. The risk of miscarriage as a result of amniocentesis is about one in every hundred.

SENSE OF SMELL

Your sense of smell is far more acute during pregnancy, especially in the first trimester. Smells that you previously never noticed or seemed pleasant to you may now bring on extreme nausea and even a gag reflex. Theory has it that a heightened sense of smell helps a pregnant woman identify foods and substances that may be harmful for her baby.

SHOW

During pregnancy, a thick plug of mucus seals the opening of the cervix to prevent bacteria and other germs from entering the uterus. As your body prepares for labour, the cervix begins to thin out and relax, and the mucous plug is dislodged. When this happens, you may notice a thick or stringy discharge that may be tinged with blood. This is known as the bloody show.

SKIN TAGS AND SKIN CHANGES

Some pregnant women develop strange growths called skin tags. These are small to medium polyps (wart-like protrusions) that occur anywhere where skin rubs up against skin or clothing. You might get them in the folds of the neck or along your bra line. Some women get them on their eyelids. These skin tags disappear after birth and if they don't they are easily removed by a dermatologist.

Chloasma

Chloasma is the so-called mask of pregnancy (hyperpigmentation). Women with darker complexions are more prone to this condition than women with lighter skin. The effects of chloasma may even become more pronounced with each pregnancy.

Dark patches can show up around your upper lip, nose, cheekbones, and forehead, sometimes in the shape of a mask (as in Zorro). They may also appear on your cheeks or along your jaw line. You may develop dark patches on your forearms and other parts of your body that are exposed to the sun.

You may find that your more pigmented skin such as your nipples, freckles, scars, and the skin around your genitals become darker during pregnancy.

These changes are caused by hormonal changes during pregnancy, which stimulate a temporary increase in your body's production of melanin, the natural substance that gives colour to hair, skin and eyes. The areas of increased pigmentation will probably fade within a few months after the birth of your baby and your skin should return to its normal shade, although in some women the changes never completely disappear.

If you do have chloasma you need to protect yourself from the sun. This is crucial because exposure to the sun's ultraviolet (UV) rays intensifies pigment changes. Use a broad-spectrum sunblock (a formula that protects against both UVA and UVB rays) with SPF 30 or higher *every day*, whether it's sunny or not, and reapply often during the course of the day if you're outside.

Linea nigra
Before pregnancy, there is already a line called the linea alba running from your belly button to your pubic bone. You probably didn't notice it though, because it was the same color as the rest of your skin. The same increased production of melanin that causes facial patches is responsible for darkening this line on your belly and then it is called linea nigra. It generally fades back to its pre-pregnant color several months after you give birth.

SPOTTING

Many women experience spotting around one week to ten days of pregnancy, and to any woman during her pregnancy this is very scary. What you are actually experiencing is "implantation spotting". This is when the embryo burrows into the wall of your womb and it can cause a small amount of dark brown discharge. If the blood is red, or you have any cramps, do seek medical advice immediately.

STRESS

All stress does not have to be bad. When managed properly, stress can provide us with the drive to meet new challenges. A pregnant woman (or anyone else) who feels she is coping well with stress; in other words functioning well at home and work, taking good care of herself and feeling energized, rather than drained, probably does not face health risks from the stress she is encountering.
However, when physical or emotional stress builds up to uncomfortable levels, it can be harmful for you and your baby. In the short term, a high level of stress can cause fatigue, sleeplessness, anxiety, poor appetite or overeating, headaches and backaches. When a high level of stress continues for a long period, it may contribute to potentially serious health problems, such as lowered resistance to infectious diseases, high blood pressure and heart disease. Studies also suggest that high levels of stress may affect your baby and increase the risk

of preterm labour and low birth weight. Babies that have difficulty in feeding and "cry-babies" are also thought to be partly due to high stress levels during pregnancy.

THERAPIES AND TIPS for stress

Lifestyle

- Having a good support network, which can include your partner, extended family and friends to help you with daily tasks or give you emotional support, could help reduce your stress. Some studies suggest that having good support actually may reduce the risk of preterm labour and low birth weight.
- A number of stress reduction techniques have been used successfully in pregnancy. These include biofeedback, meditation, guided mental imagery and yoga. Unless you have practiced these techniques previously, you may need instruction from an expert.
- Childbirth education classes teach relaxation techniques and help reduce anxiety by educating you about what is happening to your body and what to expect during labour.
- Allow sufficient time to relax each day, even if you have a busy, stressful day you can de-stress your body and mind by taking small relaxing breaks at regular intervals.
- Practice relaxation breathing on a regular basis, not only can it help to reduce stress levels but it is good practice for your birth. Put one hand on your abdomen and practice breathing all the way into your abdomen so that your hand rises and falls while you breathe. Once you've mastered that try breathing deeply and pausing slightly before you exhale. Then as you exhale slowly count to four. After five minutes you'll find that your breathing gradually slows down, your body starts to relax and your mind begins to feel calmer.
- Monitor your muscles. Learn to recognize tension in your body's major muscle groups and try to stretch and relax them a few times a day.
- Listen to relaxing music.
- If you feel your pulse racing, try to consciously slow it down by deep, slow breathing. Close your eyes for a minute and

imagine yourself in your favourite restful place, maybe on the beach, by a stream or on a mountaintop. Just a few minutes of this conscious attention to your racing pulse can create enough relaxation to undo the damage of a stressful hour!

- Exercising during pregnancy helps to reduce stress, improves your overall health and fitness, it gives you a much needed-energy boost and can help to ward off pregnancy-related complaints. Of course, you'll want to ensure that your exercise is pregnancy-friendly. That means avoiding high-risk activities that could result in injury or a lack of oxygen to your baby. The best exercise would be walking, stationary cycling, swimming and yoga.

☯ Acupuncture

Acupuncture is an excellent support therapy to help you cope with excess stress.

☛My experience: If there is one thing that I feel my treatments can provide for women during pregnancy then it must be to support them in coping with stress.

Massage

Massage tends to soothe and relax the nervous system by releasing endorphins into your body.

Bach Remedies

- Rescue Remedy: is an excellent Bach Flower Remedy to help deal with stress.
- Walnut: is my favourite Bach for when the cause of stress stems from struggling to adjust to a new situation or change in your life.
- Impatiens: addresses metal stresses and tensions. It calms feelings of impatience and irritability. It slows the tendency to move to quickly without care or forethought.

Dosage: Ten drops in bottle of water, sipped as often as needed or in acute situations take four drops (undiluted) under the tongue.

Nutrition

- Avoid stimulants like caffeine. Too much caffeine can lead to poor concentration; sleep disturbances and increased levels of cortisol, the stress hormone.
- Make sure you eat small amounts of healthy food, often and don't skip meals. When we don't eat enough food, or don't eat healthy enough food (too little protein and healthy carbohydrates, too much sugar etc.) we can experience blood sugar fluctuations. These fluctuations can lead to mood swings, fatigue, poor concentration and feelings of stress.
- Eat foods that release their fuel slowly, such as fresh vegetables, fruits, nuts, oranges, apples, apple juice, oatcakes, pumpernickel, porridge, whole grains and pulses, to keep the blood sugar balanced. Avoid fast release carbohydrates which send the blood sugar up, giving you an initial burst of energy but then leaving you feeling even more tired (very similar to the reaction to stress itself); glucose, sugar, honey, watermelon, raisins, bananas, white bread and pastries.

☑ Supplements

Vitamin B is the "stress" vitamin and you can take a Vitamin B complex as stress support.

Reflexology

Reflexology is a wonderful way to induce relaxation and restore balance.

✳ Aromatherapy

Aromatherapy oils that can be beneficial are chamomile, lavender, mandarin, sandalwood, and rose. Diffuse some calming vapours around the room by placing a few drops of oil on a light bulb ring or in an essential oil heater, or add a few drops to tissue and place it on a hot water radiator. Add a few drops of oil to the bath.

♣ Phytotherapy/herbs

Herbs that help to combat stress are lime flowers, lavender, chamomile and hops. They help by relaxing both the mind and muscles and can be drunk in the form of tea.

Drink 4 to 5 cups of tea containing one or more of the above herbs per day.

When to consult your caregiver

If you feel unable to cope with the levels of stress in your daily life you need to talk to your caregiver about seeking professional support.

STRETCH MARKS

Genetics appear to play a role in whether or not you are predisposed to getting stretch marks. This means that if your mother got stretch marks during pregnancy you may be more likely to get them yourself. However, there are some things you can do to limit intensity of stretch marks.

THERAPIES AND TIPS for stretch marks

Lifestyle

Overall good health and skin condition will go a long way toward putting the odds in your favour. Use a body scrub a few times a weeks to increase blood circulation to your skin and even though it hasn't been proven to work it is worth keeping your skin liberally and effectively moisturized throughout your pregnancy. Use vitamin E oil if you already have stretch marks. Vitamin E reduces scaring.

Nutrition

- One reason for pregnancy-related stretch marks is uncontrolled weight gain. So, control your weight gain by eating a healthy diet and exercising during pregnancy. Walking and stretching are also highly recommended during pregnancy. With these precautions, weight gain will follow the normal pattern and your skin will not be subjected to abrupt stretches.

- Drink plenty of water because a well-hydrated and healthy skin is more able to stretch.
- Eat more of the following foods that contain zinc: beans and lentils, yeast, nuts, seeds and wholegrain cereals. Pumpkin seeds provide one of the most concentrated vegetarian food sources of zinc.

☑ Supplements

A lack of zinc can cause stretch marks. Take a multivitamin that contains zinc or take a zinc supplement containing 15mg per day.

Additional information

The good news is that although stretch marks are often bright red and noticeable during the pregnancy, they usually slowly change to pink and then silvery and pale as time passes.

Laser therapy, topical medications and dermabrasion, alone or in combination have all been shown to be effective in diminishing the appearance of stretch marks if you are still unhappy with how they look a year after giving birth.

STRIPPING THE MEMBRANES (SWEEPING THE MEMBRANES)

Stripping of the membranes causes an increase in the activity of prostaglandins as well as causing mechanical dilation of the cervix, which also releases prostaglandins, in the hope that it causes contractions to start. Membrane sweeping involves your caregiver placing one or two fingers just inside your cervix and making a circular, sweeping movement to separate the membranes from the cervix. Some women find that stripping the membranes can cause discomfort and others don't feel very much. In most countries the membranes are stripped to induce labour when there are no medical indications and only once a woman has gone past her due date by one week.

SUPPLEMENTS

Even though you should be able to get most of your nutrients, vitamins and minerals needed for a healthy pregnancy from a healthy balanced diet, unfortunately not many of us have the time or the resources to eat a perfectly healthy, balanced diet. Besides that it is not always possible to find foods that still contain all their organic nutrients. A combination of a diet that is as healthy as possible and a supplement especially meant for pregnancy is often advisable.

A pregnancy multi-vitamin supplement should contain at least the following:

Vitamin A
The supplement should contain low doses of Vitamin A (not more than 5mg) in a beta-carotene form. Excessive levels of Vitamin A are associated with birth defects.

Vitamin B
The B vitamins are known as the stress vitamins. All the B vitamins are essential as they play important roles in the conversion of carbohydrates to fats, stress management, nerve tissue damage repair, building of amino acids, immunity, prevention of anaemia and much more.

Vitamin B6 especially helps to fight nausea in pregnancy and is required for the metabolism of lipids, carbohydrates and proteins. Vitamin B6 is also needed for the conversion of essential fatty acids into prostaglandins (chemical messengers.)

Folic Acid is the most famous B Vitamin involved in pregnancy. It has been proven to be dramatically effective in reducing neural tube defects like Spina Bifida.

Folic acid is necessary for DNA synthesis, and therefore critical in the development of all tissues, particularly the nervous system. Oral contraceptives may deplete folic acid levels.

There isn't a recommended length of time before conception that women should start taking folic acid supplements. The important thing is for women to make sure that they consume adequate amounts of folate – the natural form of folic acid – from the foods they eat, and take a daily folic acid supplement (400mcg) – from before they conceive until the twelfth week of pregnancy. It's a good idea for women of childbearing age to follow this advice if there's a possibility of an unplanned pregnancy.

B12 is essential for vegans and vegetarians during pregnancy. It is needed for the production of red blood cells for both mother and baby. B12 is found mainly in animal products.

If you take a B12 supplement you should do so sublingually. This literally means "under the tongue" but the supplement is usually a lozenge that dissolves in your mouth. This is much more effective than swallowing a tablet due to the fact that many pregnant mothers have trouble in absorbing B12 because of the enormous change to all mucous membranes during pregnancy.

Vitamin B deficiency check: cracks and sores on the corner of your mouth, fatigue and inability to cope with normal levels of stress.

Vitamin C is essential for collagen synthesis, as well as amino acid and thyroid hormone production; it also aids iron and calcium absorption.

Vitamin C deficiency check: frequent colds, low resistance, tiredness, easy bruising and bad skin.

Vitamin D is important in the absorption of calcium and phosphorous and for bone and tooth development of your fetus.

Vitamin E is important for red blood cell growth, proper immune function and is an essential antioxidant.

Vitamin E deficiency check: dry skin, tingling or loss of sensation in the arms, hands, legs or feet.

Calcium

Calcium is essential in the development of bones and teeth and in the functioning of muscles and nerves. During pregnancy large amounts of calcium are needed for the development of your baby. This means that the need for calcium increases hugely for the mother.
Calcium deficiency check: cramps (although this is usually in combination with a magnesium deficiency), muscle fatigue.

Vitamin D (fish oil, see essential fatty acids) and Magnesium are necessary to absorb Calcium so make sure you get all three.

Magnesium

Magnesium plays an important role in energy production and is important in the functioning of muscles and nerve impulses. Most magnesium activity occurs between cells and can activate a number of metabolisms in the body (ovulation, digestion, liver function etc.) Magnesium supports the absorption of other minerals and because it works hand in hand with calcium it is often deficient during and after pregnancy, this can cause muscle fatigue, insomnia, cramps, restless legs and depression.
Magnesium deficiency check: muscle cramps; especially at night, muscle twitching and restless legs, exhaustion, insomnia and depression.

Iron

Your iron requirement increases during pregnancy; extra blood volume – yours and your baby's – means you need more iron to make the extra haemoglobin. As in most situations during pregnancy the placenta favours the requirements of your baby and so you could end up with a deficiency if you don't make up for it.
You need at least 30mg per day for the last six months of pregnancy, which is double the amount that you would need when you are not pregnant.

Iron deficiency check: restless legs, pale, very white eye whites, dizziness & exhaustion.

Zinc

Is very important for general growth and plays an important role in the immune system. It is needed for enzyme production; brain nerve formation and it also lessens the chance of stretch marks because it ensures elasticity of the skin. For a man it is essential for fertility and it is often deficient in women who suffer from depression.
Zinc deficiency check: stretch marks and non-elastic skin, flaky or patchy skin, depression.

If the following is not included in your pregnancy multi then they should be taken separately:

Omega-3 (often also called DHA, EPA, Essential Fatty Acids or Fish Oil)

There are three major types of omega 3 fatty acids that are ingested in foods and used by the body: alpha-linolenic acid (ALA), eicosapentaenoic acid (EPA), and docosahexaenoic acid (DHA). Once eaten, the body converts ALA to EPA and DHA, the two types of omega-3 fatty acids more readily used by the body.
A developing fetus cannot make its own Omega-3 fatty acids. As the mother you must meet your baby's' nutritional needs. Your fetus relies on a constant supply of Omega-3 from you for his/her developing nervous system, brain and eyes during pregnancy and then after birth via breast milk. DHA (a derivative of Omega-3) is the building block of human brain tissue and is particularly abundant in the grey matter of the brain and the retina. The DHA content of your infant's brain triples during the first three months of life.
Low levels of DHA have recently been associated with depression, memory loss, dementia, post-natal depression and visual problems in pregnant and post-partum mothers.

Unfortunately, DHA levels in the breast milk of most women are very low. Therefore, increasing DHA levels should be a primary goal for all pregnant and lactating women.

Research has shown that children who breastfeed score higher on I.Q. tests and have less incidence of allergies than those fed formula, because specific fats that are found in mother's milk are important for proper brain and immune system development. Those fats continue to flow from your body into the body and brain of your child during breastfeeding. Breastfeeding for at least a year is one of the best gifts you can give your baby as long as you maintain the Omega-3 balance in your own body.

Taking a supplement supplies the best source of Omega-3: around 1000mg per day. Start taking an Omega supplement before pregnancy if possible.

Intestinal Flora (Probiotic)

Intestinal flora produce the digestive enzyme lactase, give general support to digestion as a whole, guard against toxins forming and gas formation in the gut, lower the acid level in the gut, produce anti-bodies for the immune system, produce folic acid, vitamin B12, vitamin K and see to the synthesis of niacin, biotin, folic acid and B6, ensure that nutrients are absorbed in the small intestine and they have a positive influence hormonal balance.

So as you can see a correct balance in the intestinal bacterial flora is essential for good overall health. Taking capsules of these 'friendly' bacteria (Probiotic) will help re-establish and maintain a favourable intestinal flora especially during and after pregnancy when the delicate balance of the intestinal flora can easily be tipped.

If you suffer from any of the following you would be well off taking Probiotics: bloating, flatulence, bad digestion, re-occurring infections, Candida, thrush and athlete's foot.

SWIMMING DURING PREGNANCY

Swimming is great exercise because it uses all the large muscle groups and although it is a low-impact sport it provides good cardiovascular (aerobic) benefits. Any type of aerobic exercise helps increase your

body's ability to process and use oxygen, which is important for you and your baby. Swimming also improves circulation, increases muscle tone and strength and builds endurance while allowing you to feel weightless.
If you swim you will feel less fatigued, sleep better and be able to cope better with any of pregnancy's physical and emotional challenges.
Swimming is one of the safest forms of exercise. If you swam regularly before pregnancy you should be able to continue without much modification. If you didn't swim or exercise at all you should still be able to swim but you'll need to start slowly and don't over exert yourself.

Because you are exercising in water, it can be easy to forget to stay well hydrated. A good guideline is to drink one cup (eight ounces) before you start swimming, one cup for every twenty minutes of exercise, and one cup after you get out of the pool. In hot and/or humid weather you'll need to drink more.

Best strokes for pregnancy

The breaststroke is probably your best bet while pregnant since it requires no rotation of the torso (as does the front crawl) and requires less exertion. While pregnancy forces the spine and shoulders to round forward and the pelvis to tilt out of alignment, the breaststroke gently strengthens the muscles and counteracts that tendency.
Another good stroke is the backstroke. Because the water reduces the effects of gravity on your body, you can lie on your back to do the backstroke without risking the impaired blood flow, which occurs out of wale.

Additional information

Swimming in a cool outdoor pool in warm weather is perfectly fine but avoid extreme temperature changes like going from a sauna to a freezing plunge pool.
Swimming in a chlorinated pool shouldn't be a problem as long as the chemicals are appropriately monitored.

T

TENS MACHINE (TRANSCUTANEOUS ELECTRICAL NERVE STIMULATION)

A TENS machine is used for pain management and is therefore often used during labour. The machine is a small box about the size of a small radio with wires leading out of it connected to four plaster-like pads. It gives out little pulses of electrical energy via the wires and through the pads, which are stuck onto the lower back of the mother. The pulses distort pain signals sent from the womb and cervix to the brain and also stimulate the body to release endorphins.

TENS machines are thought to work in two ways

When the machine is set on a high pulse rate (90-130 Hz) it triggers the 'pain gate' to close. This is thought to block a pain nerve pathway to the brain. This is the normal method of use.

When the machine is set on a low pulse rate (2-5 Hz) it stimulates the body to make its own pain easing chemicals called endorphins. These act a bit like morphine to block pain signals.

The pads are elongated and the 1st pair should be placed on your lower back on either side of the spine between Thoracic 10 and Thoracic 12 with the second pair placed each side of the spine from the second sacral foramen to the forth sacral foramen.

Tips
It takes around an hour for your body to start producing endorphins, so if you decide to use a TENS machine, you should start using it earlier on in your labour. If you do want to try the TENS it may be worth first trying massage and then the TENS on your lower back to discover what you feel is more effective.

Benefits of using a TENS

- A TENS is portable and so it doesn't stop you from being mobile.
- It is non-invasive and entirely under your control.
- It is easy to use.
- It can be used for as long as you feel comfortable using it.
- It has no known side effects.

When not to use a TENS

- If you have a pace-maker.
- In water (bath or birthing bath) or under the shower.
- On wounds.

There are various types and brands of machine. *Always follow the manufacturers instructions supplied with the machine.*

THIRST

During pregnancy, your metabolic rate increases so you will need to urinate more frequently. This increases the amount of water you will need to drink. Drinking more also helps your kidneys rid your body of the extra waste products produced by the baby. Your body is also conserving water, preparing for added blood volume and for the increased demands of pregnancy. Increased thirst is a necessary adaptation by your body, which encourages you to drink more, and can be very normal.
Even if you are not thirsty you should drink throughout the day.
An extra benefit of drinking enough water is that it will help you avoid constipation and urinary tract infections.

When to consult your caregiver

When thirst is excessive and you are also experiencing fatigue and frequent urination you should contact your caregiver as you could have pregnancy diabetes.

TIREDNESS

One of the 'normal' symptoms of the first trimester is extreme tiredness. This tiredness can often be a problem because most women haven't told friends or colleagues that they are pregnant yet and it becomes hard to explain why you keep nodding off at work and dinner parties! It is a strange phenomenon for many women to feel their bodies taking total charge and nothing they can do relieves that exhaustion other than loads of sleep. Most women will begin to feel less tired around 16 weeks. Unfortunately tiredness often returns in the last trimester when it is again time to slow down and prepare for birth and baby.

Here are some of the reasons you are so tired

- High levels of progesterone can have a sedative effect.
- You metabolic rate increases to accommodate the developing fetus.
- Your body will put the development of the fetus first sometimes leaving little energy for you.
- Many women wake up more often to urinate, which disturbs their sleep.
- Progesterone sometimes induces insomnia meaning you don't get enough sleep.
- Nausea can increase tiredness especially if you are waking from nausea at night.
- Anaemia can sometimes be the cause of tiredness.

The most important way to combat tiredness is to give in to it! Try to slow down, sleep/nap as much as possible and don't be shy about asking your partner or a friend who knows you are pregnant to help out with housework and chores.

If you have insomnia, anaemia or are spending most of the night going up and down to the toilet, go to those particular chapters for advice.

TRIMESTER

Pregnancy is divided into trimesters.

- The first trimester is up to the end of week 13.
- The second trimester is week 14 up to the end of week 27.
- The third trimester is week 28 up till birth.

Pregnancy is counted from the first day of your last menstruation and generally lasts anything from 38 to 42 weeks.

Your due date will be calculated at 40 weeks.

TRAVEL

Travelling is perfectly safe for most pregnant women. Just remember a few things to help make your travelling more comfortable and safe:

- Try to do the majority of your travelling in the second trimester, you will tend to be more comfortable and in general the risk of miscarriage and preterm labour is lower.
- Avoid excessive flying. Although there are no hard and fast rules, there are records showing that flight attendants flying an average of seventy-four hours per month have high miscarriage rates.
- Talk to your caregiver before flying if you are more than 36 weeks pregnant and remember that all airlines have policies regarding pregnancy and flying. So check with your particular airline before booking a flight. Most airlines allow pregnant

women to travel up to the eighth month. After that, flying is usually only allowed with permission from your caregiver.

- When flying, fasten the safety belt under your abdomen across the tops of your thighs.
- Flex and extend your ankles regularly to prevent swelling and clotting.
- Make comfort arrangements; try to get seats with more legroom and plan to walk in the aisles
- Avoid travel to countries that would require immunization or malaria medication. Talk to your practitioner for more information on immunizations.
- No matter how you are travelling, take healthy snacks with you. Snacking on long airplane flights or long car trips can help ensure that you're well nourished. It is also a good idea to have snacks with you just in case you get stuck in traffic or at the airport. This can help ease common discomforts of pregnancy like morning sickness and low blood sugar.
- Take stretch breaks whether you're in a car or in an airplane, getting up to move around at least every other hour is a must.
- Always carry a copy of your current prenatal record and your insurance card with you. While you don't anticipate problems, it is always a possibility that you may need to see someone in a foreign country if you need assistance. You can get your prenatal record from your caregiver by simply asking.
- Keep drinking; you need a lot of fluids during pregnancy. Travelling makes it very easy to become dehydrated. Be sure that you always carry a water bottle with you.
- Dress appropriately for the trip. Wear comfortable clothes and wearing layers will give you more ease in staying cool or warm as you can take off or add layers as you need them.

Staying well in a foreign country

- Wash your hands well before eating.
- Drink only bottled water.
- Don't buy ready made food from market stalls.
- Peel all fruit.

- Don't have any ice in your drinks.
- Stay out of direct sunlight for long periods.
- Try not to over-heat.

TRUE OR FALSE LABOUR

You often hear about women who have been told that they were not really in labour when they thought they were and that they are experiencing something called false labour. True labour starts with the latent (early) phase during which the cervix is being thinned out before it can begin to dilate. With a second or third birth this phase sometimes goes unnoticed or is very short. In a first birth however this phase can take quite long and sometimes it actually stops after a few hours and only continues much later (sometimes as long a 24hrs later!) Some women also experience very strong pre-labour also known as Braxton Hicks, which they confuse with true labour.

Additional information
Some women experience a whole night of regular contractions when their baby is engaging. This could be weeks before the actual birth and is generally not very painful but can be very uncomfortable and confusing.

If this is your first labour and you are in doubt as to whether you are truly in labour here are some guidelines:

FALSE LABOUR

The contractions:
Are usually irregular and short.
Do not get closer together.
Do not get stronger.
Walking does not make them stronger.

Lying down may make them go away.
Are usually felt only in your groin or locally in your vagina.

TRUE LABOUR

The contractions:

May be irregular at first.
Become regular and longer.
Get stronger.
Walking makes them stronger.
Lying down does not make them go away.
Usually start in your back and radiate to the front.

U

THE UMBILICAL CORD

The umbilical cord is a narrow, tube-like structure that connects your developing baby to the placenta. The umbilical cord begins to form about five weeks after conception. It becomes progressively longer until about 28 weeks of pregnancy. As it gets longer, the cord generally twists around its self and becomes slightly coiled. There are three blood vessels inside the umbilical cord, two arteries and one vein. The vein carries oxygen-rich blood and nutrients from the placenta to your baby, while the two arteries transport waste from your baby back to the placenta, where the waste is transferred to your blood and disposed of by your kidneys.

UMEBOSHI PLUM

The first record of Umeboshi being used for medicinal purposes is in the tenth century, when it was reportedly used to treat Emperor Murakami. Throughout history this sour fruit, which has a zesty palate-cleansing flavour and fast-acting medicinal effects, has been used as a cure for vomiting, intestinal worms, fevers, coughs and colds. Many Japanese regularly eat one pickled Umeboshi plum every morning, washed down with copious cups of green tea. In fact there is quite a lot of scientific evidence to support the benefits of eating Umeboshi. The sour alkaline taste stimulates the secretion of saliva and gastric juices, activating the digestive system. The citric acid in the dried fruit also increases metabolism and more importantly assists the absorption of calcium in the intestine. The pyric acid in Ume fruit enhances liver function, for counteracting nausea, it is used for coughs and colds, as a sterilizer and antibacterial agent with sore throats, it kills bacteria and can be taken after you think you may have eaten "bad" food to prevent food-poisoning.

You can buy Umeboshi plums pickled, as Ume balls/pills or as Umeboshi paste. They are used grated on top of Japanese salads and the pickled juice from the plums is used in salad dressing.
Umeboshi plums and purée are lively and versatile seasonings that add a pleasant tartness to salad dressings, cooked vegetables, and sauces. They are also commonly served in Japan as a condiment with rice, or tucked inside a rice ball wrapped with nori (sea-weed.)

Pregnant women often desire an alkaline food such as lemon, grapefruit, or sauerkraut. This craving is because the blood has a tendency to become more acidic during pregnancy. By eating the craved foods you instinctively try to alkalize your blood.
If however, you eat foods that create more acidity (white bread, sugars, milk, meats), your blood will generally stay very acidic and you may start to experience nausea, tiredness, heartburn and constipation as a result.
A good way to prevent all these symptoms is to avoid the acid foods and to start each day with a large cup of Umeboshi tea, **or** a whole Umeboshi plum **or** a quarter teaspoon of Umeboshi paste.
The abrupt, tart, tangy, salty taste jolts your eyes open, shakes your stomach awake, sandpapers off any staleness from your taste buds, and gets the day off to an unforgettable start!

V

VAGINAL DISCHARGE – ALSO SEE CANDIDA

Vaginal discharge **without** itching, burning or a strong unpleasant smell is very normal during pregnancy. This is due to a combination of a few things; the build up of mucous that occurs in the cervix to create a plug in order to shield your developing baby from infections and the high levels of oestrogen and progesterone which make the mucous membranes softer and wetter.

Additional information

During the last few weeks of pregnancy you will notice that your vaginal discharge increases. This is a normal reaction to the increase of oestrogen at the end of pregnancy.

Tips that could help avoid skin irritation from excess discharge

- Wear natural cotton panty-liners if possible.
- Make sure your underwear is cotton – avoid nylon and polyester (especially pantyhose.)

When it becomes more than just discharge

If your discharge is yellowish and or there is burning or itching it means that there is an imbalance between the friendly and unfriendly bacteria in your vagina. This could make you more prone to thrush. Thrush is a yeast infection and is also known as Candida.

THERAPIES AND TIPS for vaginal discharge

Lifestyle

- Always wipe front to back after going to the toilet.
- Try to air your vagina as much as possible - sleep without wearing underwear for instance.
- Keep the area as dry as possible because Candida thrives in warm, moist areas.
- Don't douche or wash out your vagina with soap or consumer products made for douching.
- Avoid using vaginal deodorants and powders. (These should be avoided during pregnancy anyway.)

☑ Supplements

Probiotics will restore the good flora in the intestine and by doing this it eliminates the Candida, which resides in all mucous membranes especially in the intestine. Probiotics are widely recommended for the treatment of Candida as they establish large healthy populations of friendly bacteria that compete with and eliminate the yeast fungus.

Nutrition

Eat a diet high in grains, vegetables and protein and avoid eating processed foods, sugar and alcohol. You may also want to reduce the amount of simple carbohydrates in your diet (white flour products, white pasta and potatoes. Candida is a yeast-form and thrives on sugars and glucose in the body.
Eat live yoghurt, which contains Probiotics.

Warning!

Don't apply live yoghurt locally either inserted on a tampon or smeared on and in the vagina. Leaving yoghurt in the vagina for a few hours could result in the formation of Listeriosis. Listeria is a bacterium that can cross the placenta, which could result in a miscarriage.

♣ Phytotherapy/herbs
Use a tea tree spray locally twice a day.
Make a sitz bath with 200ml warm water and ten tablespoons of apple cider vinegar or a douche with one cup of warm water and two teaspoons of apple cider vinegar.

✤ Tissue salts
Kali Muriaticum: is a tissue salt that is known as a blood conditioner. It is used to treat any thick white or yellow mucous excretions in the body.

When to consult your caregiver:
If your discharge is yellowish and or there is burning or itching it means that there is an imbalance between the friendly and unfriendly bacteria in your vagina. This could make you more prone to thrush or Candida. If you suspect that you have thrush or Candida you need to tell your caregiver.

VARICOSE VEINS

Varicose veins are swollen veins that may bulge near the surface of the skin. These blue or purple veins are most likely to show up in your legs, though you may also get them in your vulva or elsewhere.
You may never have had varicose veins until pregnancy. As your uterus grows, it puts pressure on the large vein on the right side of your body (the inferior vena cava), which in turn increases pressure in the leg veins. Veins are the blood vessels that return blood from your extremities to your heart, so the blood in your leg veins is already working against gravity.

The amount of blood in your body increases when you're pregnant, adding to the burden on your veins plus your progesterone levels rise, causing the walls of your blood vessels to relax.

You're more likely to get varicose veins if other members of your family have had them. They're much more common in women than men, and if you have them, they tend to get worse with each successive pregnancy and as you get older. Being overweight, carrying twins or other multiples and standing for long periods can also make you more susceptible.

The good news is that varicose veins tend to improve after you give birth, particularly if you didn't have any before you got pregnant.

THERAPIES AND TIPS for varicose veins

Lifestyle

- Exercise daily even just a brisk walk around the block can help your circulation.
- Elevate your feet and legs whenever possible using a stool or box to rest your legs on when you're sitting and keep your feet elevated on a pillow when you're lying down.
- Don't cross your legs or ankles when sitting.
- Don't sit or stand for long periods without taking breaks to move around.
- Sleep on your left side with your feet on a pillow and wedge a pillow behind your back to keep yourself tilted to the left. Since the inferior vena cava is on the right side, lying on your left side helps to keep the weight of the uterus off the vein.
- Wear special support prescription-strength hose, known as graduated-compression stockings. They are available from medical supply stores and pharmacies. These stockings are twice as thick as normal pantyhose and are tight at the ankle getting looser as they go up the leg, making it easier for blood to flow back up toward your heart. As a result, they help prevent swelling and may keep your varicose veins from getting worse. Put them on before getting out of bed in the morning, while you're still lying down, to prevent blood from pooling in your legs, and keep them on all day. These support hose may be bothersome, especially in hot weather, but bad varicose veins can be even more uncomfortable.
- Swimming is good gentle exercise to help improve circulation to your legs.

- An abdominal support belt can sometimes help to lessen the pressure in your groin and thereby improve the pressure in your legs.
- Avoid excessive weight gain.

✳Aromatherapy

Use this aromatherapy blend on your varicose veins
Geranium - fifteen drops
Cypress – five drops
Diluted in two tablespoons vegetable oil base.
Stroke the legs very gently, working upwards from ankle to thigh. The geranium will encourage the circulation of blood and cypress has an astringent effect upon the whole venous system.
Foot baths also help, especially if you place a dozen or so small, round pebbles in the bottom of the footbath and rub your feet gently back and forth over them. Add two drops each of geranium and cypress essential oil to the footbath.

Yoga

There are several yoga postures that are particularly good for varicose veins. Ask your yoga teacher to show you these.

Nutrition

Eat foods containing vitamin C, this helps keeps your veins healthy and elastic: citrus fruits (oranges, tangerines, grapefruit and lemons), blackcurrants, strawberries, papaya, broccoli, kiwi fruit, bell peppers, tomatoes and green leafy vegetables.

☑ Supplements

Taking vitamin C (acid-free 1000mg per day) & vitamin E (400Iu per day) can improve blood circulation and strengthen the walls of the veins and capillaries.

☯ **Acupuncture**

☛My experience: If started early I find that acupuncture is excellent in reducing the pain sometimes experienced from varicose veins.

VEGETARIANISM

Well-planned vegetarian diets support good nutritional status and health. However, ensuring nutritional adequacy as a vegetarian becomes more challenging when nutrient needs are higher during pregnancy.

Types of Vegetarian Eating

Today, people may identify themselves as vegetarian, or primarily vegetarian, although they eat some fish or chicken, milk products, eggs and animal by-products like butter. However, vegans avoid all foods of animal origin.

Women who eat fish and some animal products usually get enough nutrients but there is a high risk of nutrient inadequacy in pregnant women who are vegan.

Looking at nutrients of vegetarians and vegans during pregnancy

Iron

The best source of iron comes from red meat (such as beef, veal and lamb), with lesser amounts in chicken, fish, pork, ham and eggs. Shellfish are quite high in iron content. These are known as "haem" sources of iron and are readily absorbed by the body (up to 25%.)

Vegetarians have to get their iron from plant foods (or "non-haem" sources of iron), which are not as readily absorbed into the body (up to 10%.) These include breads, grains, cereals, dark green leafy vegetables (spinach, broccoli and parsley), potatoes, dried fruits, beans (baked, green, kidney, black), peanuts, sunflower seeds and tofu. However, their absorption can be increased by up to 4 times if they are eaten with foods or drinks rich in vitamin C.

Excess calcium in milk products (or calcium supplements) and tannic acid in tea and coffee can inhibit iron absorption.

Calcium
There is no evidence of poor calcium status among vegetarians.

Vitamin D
Vitamin D is commonly found in fluid milk, margarines and fatty fish such as salmon. Vegans may be at risk of inadequate vitamin D intake.

Vitamin B_{12}: Vegans and vegetarians are at high risk of inadequate intake of vitamin B_{12}, which is available only from animal sources (contrary to popular belief, seaweed is not a good source of vitamin B_{12}.)
All pregnant women that are vegan or vegetarian should consume a sublingual (absorbed in the mouth) supplement of at least 1 µg (0.74 mmol) vitamin B_{12} per day.
The homeopathic remedy, Nux Vormica D6 improves the absorption of B12.

Zinc: In general, zinc status among vegetarians is good. Vegetarian sources of zinc:
Nuts, legumes, whole grains, milk and egg yolk.
Take a zinc supplement either in liquid form or as a tablet 15mg a day.

In general vegetarians should aim to eat the following foods to ensure an adequate intake of protein:

- Nuts and seeds such as almonds, cashews, Brasil and peanuts –make sure your peanuts come from a health food store- sesame, sunflower and pumpkin seeds.
- Pulses such as chickpeas, lentils, and beans.
- Yoghurt and goat's cheese.
- Free-range organic eggs.
- Soya products.

VITAMINS AND MINERALS

Vitamins

Vitamins are substances found in plants and animals that are required for life-sustaining processes in the human body. They cannot be manufactured by the body and must be obtained through diet or supplements.
The following vitamins are important during pregnancy:

Vitamin A & Beta Carotene

Although liver and liver products, such as paté and liver sausage, are good sources of iron, they can also contain very high concentrations of vitamin A. If taken in excess, this vitamin can build up in your liver and cause serious harm to a growing baby.
As a result, the Department of Health advises all pregnant women to avoid liver and liver products. You should also be aware that some vitamin supplements are high in this vitamin, so always choose a specially prepared pregnancy supplement.
However, the form of vitamin A derived from green, orange, and yellow fruit and vegetables - known as carotene - has very positive health benefits.

Food sources

Red/yellow/orange peppers, mango, carrots, sweet potatoes, apricots, tomatoes and watercress.

Thiamin/B1

Raises your energy level and regulates the nervous system.

Food sources

Whole grain, fortified cereals, wheat germ, eggs, rice, pasta, berries, nuts, legumes and pork.

Riboflavin/B2

Maintains energy levels, is good for eyesight and healthy skin.

Food sources

Meats, poultry, fish, dairy products, fortified cereals and eggs.

Niacin/B3
Promotes healthy skin, nerves and aids digestion.
Food sources
High-protein foods, fortified cereals and breads, meats, fish, milk, eggs and peanuts.

Pyridoxine/B6
Helps form red blood cells and it is known to help with morning sickness.
Food sources
Chicken, fish, liver, pork, eggs, soybeans, carrots, cabbage, cantaloupe, peas, spinach, wheat germ, sunflower seeds, bananas, beans, broccoli, brown rice, oats, bran, peanuts and walnuts

Folic Acid/Folate
Helps support the placenta, and prevents spina bifida and other neural tube defects. As well as taking a supplement, you can also increase the amount of folic acid in your diet.
As it does with many vitamins, cooking can easily destroy folic acid. Try steaming or stir-frying vegetables that have high levels of folic acid, or cook them in the minimum amount of water.
Food sources
Oranges, orange juice, strawberries, green leafy vegetables, spinach, beets, broccoli, cauliflower, Brussels sprouts, iceberg lettuce, peas, pasta, beans, nuts, parsnips and cereals fortified with folate (check the nutritional information chart on the packaging of your cereal.)

Vitamin C
Vitamin C is an antioxidant that protects tissues from damage and it helps your body absorb and effectively use iron (essential during pregnancy) and other nutrients from your food. Vitamin C helps to fight infections and a deficiency in Vitamin C is linked to gestational diabetes.
Food sources
Good sources include citrus fruits (oranges, tangerines, grapefruit and lemons), blackcurrants, strawberries, papaya, broccoli, kiwi fruit, bell peppers, tomatoes and green leafy vegetables.

Herbs include dandelion leaves, nettles, elderberries, rosehips, cayenne, violet leaves and alfalfa.

Vitamin D

This is sometimes referred to as the 'sunshine vitamin' because it is made when the skin is exposed to sunlight. The major biologic function of vitamin D is to maintain normal blood levels of calcium and phosphorus. Vitamin D aids in the absorption of calcium, helping to form and maintain strong bones. Recently, research also suggests vitamin D may provide protection from osteoporosis, hypertension, cancer, and several autoimmune diseases.

Pregnant and breastfeeding women with dark skin or those who always cover their skin (due to their belief), are at particular risk of a vitamin D deficiency and may require a supplement.

Food/other sources

Fatty fish and sunshine (Vitamin D is also milk but that is generally because it has been added by the manufacturer).

Vitamin E

Helps body form and use red blood cells. Vitamin E prevents a chemical reaction called oxidation, which can sometimes result in harmful effects in your body. It is also important for the proper function of nerves and muscles.

A deficiency in Vitamin E is rare.

Food sources

Vitamin E is found in various foods including vegetable oils (corn, cottonseed, soybean, safflower), wheat germ, whole-grain cereals, nuts, seeds, olives, avocados, and green leafy vegetables. Cooking and storage may destroy some of the vitamin E found in food. Herbs include alfalfa, rosehips, raspberry leaf, and dandelion.

Vitamin K

Vitamin K is necessary for the formation of thrombin, a chemical critical to blood clotting. In the presence of certain intestinal bacteria, our bodies can make this fat-soluble vitamin. Insufficient vitamin K can contribute to postpartum haemorrhaging.

Food sources kale, green tea, leafy greens such as turnip greens and spinach, broccoli, lettuce, cabbage, watercress, asparagus, oats, nettle, dandelion, green peas and whole wheat.

Minerals

Minerals are inorganic substances. This means they're found in the rocks and soil and therefore in ground water.

Vegetables absorb mineral goodness as they grow, while animals and humans digest it through their diet.

Minerals can be divided into two groups - those that are needed in minute quantities, called trace minerals, and those that are needed in larger quantities, called the major minerals.

The major minerals - include calcium, magnesium, sodium, potassium and phosphorus.

Trace minerals - include iron, zinc, iodine, selenium and copper.

Calcium

Calcium is essential for the development of your baby's bones. There is also some research indicating that adequate calcium may help prevent high blood pressure during pregnancy and possibly premature birth. Calcium is particularly important during pregnancy because your baby will draw on the calcium stores in your bones, for his or her own growth and development inside the womb. Pregnant and breastfeeding women should aim and have at least 900 to 1200 milligrams of calcium each day (or 3 to 4 servings of calcium rich foods.) Pregnant and breastfeeding women under the age of 20 need at least 1200 milligrams (or 4 servings) because their body is still building bone density for later life.

Women carrying twins need to have at least 1200 to 1500 mgs of calcium per day during pregnancy (or 4 to 5 servings of calcium rich foods.) This is also recommended for women who breastfeed twins. Your caregiver may prescribe calcium supplements to help you keep up with the calcium your body needs during this time.

Food sources

Dairy foods tend to contain the highest amounts of calcium. However many dairy products are contaminated with toxins due to the high amount of medication that most dairy-cows receive and many people are allergic or intolerant to dairy, plus there is controversy about the body's ability to assimilate calcium from pasteurized, homogenized milk so don't be lulled into thinking you are getting enough calcium if you are eating a lot of milk products.

Turnip greens, mustard greens, tofu, cabbage, green leafy vegetables, canned sardines and tuna (they are usually canned with the fine bones), cod, whole grains, apple syrup.

Vitamin D (fish oil, see essential fatty acids) and Magnesium are necessary to absorb Calcium so make sure you get all three.

Some commercially prepared foods have added calcium. For example, there are now some brands of orange juices, cereals and tofu with added calcium.

Magnesium

Magnesium is needed during pregnancy for the baby's and mother's tissue growth. Magnesium helps maintain normal muscle and nerve function, keeps heart rhythm steady, supports a healthy immune system, and keeps bones strong. Magnesium is also a mineral component passed to the baby through breast milk. Low magnesium levels may be linked to leg cramps, restless legs, insomnia and fluid retention during pregnancy.

Food sources

Magnesium is often lacking in food sources due to hydroponic agriculture and the fact that magnesium resources have almost been entirely depleted in the earth's soil.

If you suffer from any of the symptoms mentioned it is necessary to take a magnesium supplement. Take 400mg in the evening.

Food sources include whole grain breads and cereals, rice, pasta, oatmeal, wheat germ, nuts, peanut butter, soybeans, kidney beans, baked beans, bran, bananas, corn, artichokes, potatoes, sweet potatoes, watermelon, dried fruits, oranges, grapefruit, limes, avocado, yoghurt, meats, chicken, fish, eggs, dark green leafy vegetables such as spinach, broccoli, seaweed and chocolate!

Phosphorus
Phosphorus is essential for the overall formation of cells, bones and teeth and it maintains acid-alkaline balance for both you and your baby during pregnancy.

Food sources
Phosphorus is part of all cells, therefore is abundantly present in all natural foods. The richest sources are in live yoghurt, meat, fish, chicken, eggs, legumes, breads, rice, pasta, tofu, seeds, beans, fruits and vegetables. Phosphorus is also a common food additive.

Iron
Having an adequate iron intake helps to prevent the depletion of the oxygen carrying red blood cells called haemoglobin. If you don't have enough haemoglobin you develop anaemia. Adequate haemoglobin helps to support the health of the pregnancy, supply the baby with oxygen during pregnancy to grow and develop as well as reducing the chances of the baby becoming distressed during labour. It also allows you to tolerate a normal blood loss at the birth.
Adequate haemoglobin levels also help to establish and produce breast milk for the baby and assist in recovery after the birth. In the last three months of the pregnancy, your unborn baby will start to store iron in their liver (increasing your iron needs at this time.) This is nature's way of providing iron stores for the first 6 months of the baby's life, before they need to start solid foods.

Blood tests for iron levels and haemoglobin are routinely performed twice during pregnancy. A few women will also be tested after the birth if their blood loss was significant.
Food sources. The best source of iron comes from red meat (such as beef, veal and lamb), with lesser amounts in chicken, fish, pork, ham and eggs. Shellfish are quite high in iron content. These are known as 'haem' sources of iron and are readily absorbed by the body (up to 25%.)

Plant foods (or non-haem sources of iron) are not as readily absorbed into the body (up to 10%.) These include breads, grains, cereals, dark

green leafy vegetables (spinach, broccoli and parsley), potatoes, dried fruits, beans (baked, green, kidney, black), peanuts, sunflower seeds and tofu. However, their absorption can be increased by up to 4 times if they are eaten with foods or drinks rich in vitamin C.
When 'haem' and 'non-haem' foods are eaten together (especially with fruit and vegetables with vitamin C), they interact with each other to maximise the body's ability to absorb the iron they contain. For example, having baked beans with tomato and ham on toast will increase the iron you absorb from all these food when compared to eating them separately.

Excess calcium in milk products (or calcium supplements) and tannic acid in tea and coffee can inhibit iron absorption.

Potassium
Potassium maintains fluid and electrolyte balance, cell integrity, muscle contractions and nerve impulse transmission in the body.
Food sources
Potassium is found in most fresh fruits, vegetables, meats, chicken, fish, dairy foods, breads and cereals. Sources that are especially rich include tomatoes, oranges, carrots, potatoes, artichokes, bananas, grapefruit, avocado, cod, green beans, chocolate, molasses and live yoghurt. Processed foods tend to contain less potassium (and more salt.)

Zinc
Zinc is vital for conception and reproduction. During adolescence it helps with the healthy development of the sexual organs and contributes to adequate sperm counts in adult men. During pregnancy your new baby needs zinc for cell division and tissue growth. They will use this mineral to utilise protein from their mother for growth and development.
Some research has indicated that adequate zinc may be protective against a prolonged labour, premature labour, going past the due date (reducing the need for induction), depression and high blood pressure.

Some caregivers will recommend a zinc supplement during pregnancy if the woman's diet lacks zinc-rich foods. A few women will take zinc (usually as zinc gluconate) to boost their immune system for illnesses such as herpes outbreaks, the common cold and to prevent or treat post-natal depression. Pregnant and breastfeeding women need about 4-6 mg of extra zinc per day. There appears to be no adverse affects from sensible supplementing, up to 50 mg per day. A liquid zinc supplement has proven to show quicker results. Take the dosage indicated on the package.

Food sources. The richest sources of zinc are in meat, fish, oysters, shellfish, prawns (or shrimps), crab, turkey, chicken and ham. Zinc is also present in live yoghurt, ricotta, beans (green, kidney, baked), peanut butter, nuts, tofu, lentils, eggs, breads, cereals, pasta, rice, wheat germ, bran, onions, ginger and sunflower seeds.

W

WATER BIRTH

The use of warm-water pools for labour and childbirth is a relatively recent phenomenon in Western culture. During the 1960s, Russian researcher Igor Charkovsky undertook considerable research into the safety and benefits of waterbirth in the Soviet Union. In the late 1960s, French obstetrician, Frederick Leboyer developed the practice of immersing newborn infants in warm water to help ease the transition from the womb to the outside world and to mitigate the effects of any possible birth trauma.

Another French obstetrician, Michel Odent, took Leboyer's work further and used the warm-water birth pool for pain relief for the mother, and as a way to normalize the birth process. When some women refused to get out of the water to give birth, Odent started researching the benefits for the baby of being born under water and the potential problems in such births. By the late 1990s, thousands of women had given birth at Odent's birth centre at Pithiviers, France and the notion of water birth had spread to many other western countries.

Considerable research has been undertaken into the safety of water birth. Two of the most prolific researchers have been Michel Odent and the American obstetrician Michael Rosenthal. Dianne Garland, a midwife in the UK, has focused on gathering research through the National Health system, and has published a book called, *Water birth: An Attitude to Care*. In the US, Barbara Harper, a nurse and childbirth educator, has explored water birth throughout the world, and chronicled the history and current use of water birth in dozens of countries in her book, *Gentle Birth Choices*. Harper has compiled an extensive bibliography of research on the subject, which can be seen at the website for Waterbirth International.

The advantages of water birth for the mother

The warm water is relaxing and eases labour by reducing the amount of adrenaline produced by the mother. The water also stimulates the release of endorphins. The elasticity of the perineum is increased helping to ensure easier birth with fewer lacerations and tears.

With increased buoyancy in the water you can change your position easily. In most cases, water births are shorter and less painful reducing the need for analgesics. Specially designed birth pools are large enough to accommodate a labour support person such as the father, or a doula, and some are equipped with waterbed style heaters to maintain optimum water temperature. However, a roomy standard tub is also sufficient for those planning a home birth on a tight budget.

The great majority of women who have experienced water birth say that they would never want to have a baby any other way.

The advantages of water birth for the baby

Birth can be a strenuous experience for the baby as well. Water eases the transition from the birth canal to the outside world, because the warm liquid resembles the familiar intra-uterine environment, and softens light, colours and noises.

Additional information

There are some concerns with regard to water births, though most objections are because the idea is still unusual. There is a minute risk that the baby can aspirate water if it is raised to the surface after the birth and then re-immersed. However, midwives and obstetricians are well aware of this risk and once the baby is brought to the surface the baby is placed straight on the woman's chest and not re-immersed in the water. There is normally no threat that the newborn will inhale water during the birth process since its trigger to breathe oxygen is not present until it makes contact with the air.

WEIGHT

Dieting during pregnancy is hazardous to you and your developing baby. Many weight-loss regimes are likely to leave you low on iron, folic acid, and many other important vitamins and minerals. Remember, a normal amount of weight gain is one of the most positive signs of a healthy pregnancy. Women who eat well and gain a normal amount of weight at a slow steady pace are more likely to have healthy babies. Weight gain during pregnancy should be gradual with the most weight being gained in the first and last trimester.

Consider the following:
If you are a normal weight before pregnancy you should gain from 25 to 35 pounds (14 to 18kg) during pregnancy.
If you are overweight before pregnancy you should gain from 15 to 25 pounds (8 to 14kg) during pregnancy.
If you are underweight before pregnancy you should gain from 28 to 40 pounds (15 to 20kg) during pregnancy (depending on your pre-pregnancy weight.)
If you have a multiple pregnancy (twins, triplets or more): See your health care provider. You will need to gain more weight during pregnancy depending on the number of babies you are carrying.

These are estimated amounts of the weight gained purely due to the pregnancy:
Baby = 7-8 pounds (3-4kg)
Placenta = 1-2 pounds (around 0.91kg)
Amniotic fluid = 2 pounds (0.91kg)
Uterus = 2 pounds (0.91kg)
Maternal breast tissue = 2 pounds (0.91kg)
Maternal blood = 4 pounds (1.82kg)
Fluids in maternal tissue = 4 pounds (1.82kg)
Maternal fat and nutrient stores = 7 pounds (3.18kg)

Overweight mothers

The following are potential problems if a mother becomes **overwieght**:

- Gestational diabetes.
- Backaches.
- Leg pain.
- Increased fatigue.
- Varicose veins and haemorrhoids.
- Increased risk of Caesarean delivery.
- Increased risk of assisted delivery (forceps, vacuum extraction.)
- Increased risk of high blood pressure.

Underweight mothers

Underweight mothers are at risk of giving birth prematurely to a baby with possible malnutrition. Underweight mothers often suffer from vitamin and mineral deficiencies, which could lead to malformation in the baby.

Y

YOGA DURING PREGNANCY

Doing prenatal yoga can be a wonderful way to put time aside for yourself during pregnancy. It is a great tool for becoming better acquainted with your body and it helps to strengthen and stretch muscles, release tension and maintain good posture. Prenatal yoga also teaches you to relax on command and keep a positive outlook while clearing the mind of the stresses associated with pregnancy.
Practicing yoga during pregnancy can also help relieve back pain, nausea, improve sleep, ease heartburn and increase stamina.
An added benefit is that the breathing techniques practiced in a yoga class are good preparation for labour.

REFRENCES

Zita West, *Natural Pregnancy and Acupuncture in Pregnancy and Childbirth*

Giovanni Maciocia, *Obstetrics and Gyneacology*

Verena Smidt, *Physiology in Pregnancy and Childbirth*

Dr. Gowri Motha, *Gentle Birth Method*

Michel Odent, *Primal Health*

Herbal for the Childbearing Year, Susun S. Weed

Bailliere's Midwives Dictionary

Grantly Dick-Read *Childbirth Without Fear*

Elizabeth Davis *Heart and Hands*

Robert Bruce Newman *Calm Birth*

Mothering Magazine www.mothering.com

Your Pregnancy Week by Week, Lesley Regan

Arms, Suzanne. *Immaculate Deception II: Myth, Magic & Birth*. Rev. Edition. Celestial Arts, 1997.

Balaskas, Janet. *Active Birth. The New Approach to Giving Birth Naturally.* The Harvard Common Press, 1992.

Goer, Henci. *The Thinking Woman's Guide to a Better Birth*. Perigee Books, 1999.

Gaskin, Ina May. *Ina May's Guide to Childbirth*. Bantam Dell, 2003.

Harper, Barbara. *Gentle Birth Choices*. Healing Arts Press, 1994.

Noble, Elizabeth. *Essential Exercise for the Childbearing Year. A Guide to Health & Comfort Before and After Your Baby is Born*. New Life Images, 4th Edition, 2003.

Odent, Michael. *Birth Reborn*. Second Edition. Birth Works Press, 1994.

Scott, Pauline. *Sit Up and Take Notice! Positioning Yourself for a Better Birth*. Great Scott Publications, 2003.

Sears, William & Sears, Martha. *The Birth Book. Everything You Need to Know to Have a Safe and Satisfying Birth*. Little, Brown and Company, 1994.

Simkin, Penny. *The Birth Partner. Everything You Need to Know to Help a Woman Through Childbirth*. Second Edition. The Harvard Common Press, 2001.

Simkin, Penny & Ancheta, Ruth. *The Labour Progress Handbook*. Blackwell Science Ltd, 2000.

"Easier Births Using Reflexology." By Gabriella Bering Liisberg, "Tidsskrift for Jordemodre", No. 3, 1989.

http://www.fdz.dk/english/research/reports.htm. Siu-lan, Li and Cai-xia, Shu, "Galactogogue Effect of Foot Reflexology in 217 Parturient Women," (19)96 Beijing International Reflexology Conference (Report), p. 14

Odent M. 1982, *Birth Reborn*, BBC Documentary video.

Haire D. 1994, 'Obstetric drugs and procedures: their effects on mother and baby', paper presented at the Future Birth Conference, Australia.

Lagercrantz H. & Slotkin T. 1986, 'The "stress" of being born', *Scientific American*, April, pp. 92–102.

Newton N. 1971, The trebly sensuous woman', *Psychology Today*, vol. 98, pp. 68–71.

Newton N. 1978, 'The role of the oxytocin reflexes in three interpersonal reproductive acts: coitus, birth and breastfeeding', *Clinical Psychoneuroendocrinology in Reproduction*, proceedings of the Serono Symposia, Academic Press, vol. 22, pp. 411–418.

Robertson A. 1994, *Empowering Women --- teaching active birth*, ACE Graphics, PO Box 173, Sevenoaks Kent UK TN14 5ZT.

Wagner M. 1994, *Pursuing the Birth Machine --- the search for appropriate birth technology*, ACE Graphics ibid.

Whittlestone W. 1982, 'Obstetric practice and lactation: the inhibitory effects of large doses of oxytocin', unpublished manuscript, available from ACE Graphics ibid.

Liu, C. CF, et al. ÒIncrease in plasma phasonalipid DHA and EFAs as a reflection of their intake and mode of administration,Ó Pediatr. Res., 1987: 22: 292-6.

Liebman, Bonnie, ÒBaby Formula: Missing Key Fats?~ Nutrition Action Healthletter, p. 8-9, (October 1990.

Holman, Ralph T., Johnson, Susan, Ogburn, Paul, ÒDeficiency of essential fatty acids and membrane fluidity during pregnancy and lactation,Ó Biochemistry, Proc. Natl. Acad. Sci. USA, Vol. 88: 4835-4839, June 1991.

Innis, Sheila M., and Kuhnlein, Harriet V., ÒLong-chain n-3 fatty adds in breast milk of Inuit women consuming traditional foods,Ó Early Human Development, Elsevier Scientific Publishers Ireland Ltd., 18: 185-189, 1988.

Bjerve K.S., Thoereson, ÒLinseed oil and cod liver oil induce rapid growth in a seven-year-old girl with a N-3 fatty acid deficient,Ó JPEN, J. Parenter, Enteral Nutr., Sept.-Oct., 12(5): 521-5, 1988.

Holman, Ralph, et al., op. cit.

Simopoulos, Artemis, M.D., Nutrition Today, March/April 1988 & May/June 1988.

Price, Weston, Nutrition and Physical Degeneration, La Mesa, California: Price-Pottenger Nutrition Foundation, 1954.

Pottenger, Elaine, and Robert Pottenger, Jr., eds. PottengerÕs Cats: A Study in Nutrition (edited writings of Francis Pottenger), La Mesa, California: The Price-Pottenger Nutrition Foundation, 1983.

Schauss, Alexander G., M.D., Crime, Diet & Delinquency, California: Parker House, 1981.

Jensen, Bernard, and Anderson, Mark, Empty Harvest, New York: Avery, 1990.

Budwig, Dr. Johanna, Flax Oil as a True Aid against Arthritis, Heart Infarction, Cancer and Other Diseases, Vancouver, Canada: Apple Publishing, 1992.

Schmid, Ronald F., M.D., Traditional Foods Are Your Best Medicine, New York: Ballantine, 1987.

RESEARCH DATA

ACUPUNCTURE

ACUPUNCTURE TREATMENT DURING LABOUR – A RANDOMISED CONTROLLED TRIAL

Agneta Ramnerö, , Ulf Hanson,, Mona Kihlgren

Objective To investigate acupuncture treatment during labour with regard to pain intensity, degree of relaxation and outcome of the delivery.

Design Randomised controlled trial.

Setting Delivery ward at a tertiary care centre hospital in Sweden.

Population Ninety parturients who delivered during the period April 12, 1999 and June 4, 2000.

Methods Forty-six parturients were randomised to receive acupuncture treatment during labour as a compliment, or an alternative, to conventional analgesia.

Main outcome measures Assessments of pain intensity and degree of relaxation during labour, together with evaluation of delivery outcome.

Results Acupuncture treatment during labour significantly reduced the need of epidural analgesia (12%*vs* 22%, relative risk [RR] 0.52, 95% confidence interval [CI] 0.30 to 0.92.) Parturients who received acupuncture assessed a significantly better degree of relaxation compared with the control group (mean difference -0.93, 95% CI -1.66 to -0.20.) No negative effects of acupuncture given during labour were found in relation to delivery outcome.

Conclusions: The results suggest that acupuncture could be a good alternative or complement to those parturients who seek an alternative to pharmacological analgesia in childbirth. Further trials with a larger number of patients are required to clarify if the main effect of acupuncture during labour is analgesic or relaxing.

Sacral acupuncture for pain relief in labour: initial clinical experience in Nigerian women.

Sacral acupuncture was used for pain relief during labour in 30 pregnant Nigerian women. It produced clinically adequate analgesia in 19 women (63.3%.) 6 women in this group (31.6%) reported that they had experienced no pain whatsoever throughout the period of labour and delivery (average duration - 8 hours.) 11 women (36.7%) had no pain relief and required pethidine injection when sacral acupuncture proved ineffective. 24 women (80%), including 5 who did not obtain relief, indicated their wish to have sacral acupuncture during their next confinement. 2 women (6.7%) objected to needling, 3 considered acupuncture useless while another 2 did not believe in it. The patients' cardio-respiratory functions and uterine contractions were not adversely affected. There were no untoward effects on the mothers or their neonates. The procedure was technically simple, the equipment light and cheap. The needles did not interfere with nursing or obstetric manouvres. The procedure was however time consuming. The results were inconsistent and unpredictable. Despite these limitations, the simplicity, cheapness and absence of physiological complications associated with the procedure, make it a worthwhile medical armament for pain relief in the Nigerian environment, with limited resources and specialized manpower.

Women who receive acupuncture during labour may experience less pain and require less analgesic medication, according to a new study in *The Clinical Journal of Pain* (2003;19:187–91.) A large majority of women receiving acupuncture treatments during labour said they would want it again if they were to give birth again.

In the new study, 200 pregnant women were randomly assigned to receive acupuncture treatments during labour or no acupuncture. Specific acupuncture points were chosen by the midwife based on the woman's needs during labour. The needles were left in for about 20 minutes, but some women required a shorter or longer duration of treatment. Analgesics, including meperidine (Demerol®), nitrous oxide, epidural block (an injection of an anesthetic in the low back that numbs all of the nerves going to the uterus), and hot water bottles were used in both groups as needed for pain. The amount of analgesic medication used was recorded during labour and delivery.

In the group receiving acupuncture, 11% received meperidine during labour, compared with 37% of those who did not receive acupuncture. The percentage of women who required no analgesics at all in the acupuncture and placebo groups was 34% and 18%, respectively. When women who received acupuncture were questioned about whether they would want it if they gave birth again, more than 85% said they would.

The main reason for using analgesic medications during labour is to decrease or eliminate pain associated with uterine contractions. Meperidine is one of the most widely used medications for pain relief during labour but some studies suggest it is not very effective for pain control and may have adverse side effects on babies. An epidural block is effective but is not always appropriate for some stages of labour. Moreover, it is invasive and does not last long, which is problematic for women with prolonged labour. Acupuncture appears to be an effective method of pain control during labour and has no adverse side effects on the mother or baby.

Acupuncture is part of Traditional Chinese Medicine, a system of medicine that has developed over 5,000 years. Other forms of acupuncture have also come from Japan, Korea, and Thailand. The effectiveness of acupuncture for many conditions has been observed over thousands of years and, more recently, in controlled studies. While acupuncture is common in hospitals in China, receiving acupuncture during labour in the United States may be difficult, since acupuncturists are generally restricted from practicing in hospitals. However, some hospitals and birthing centers do allow acupuncture to be performed during the course of labour. For more information, consult a physician or midwife familiar with acupuncture.

THE USE OF ACUPUNCTURE TO TREAT PAIN DURING PREGNANCY

The use of acupuncture to treat pain during pregnancy certainly seems credible

Dr Graham Archard, vice-chair, Royal College of GPs

"Many pregnant women turn to acupuncture to relieve pain, especially pelvic pain.

"It is good because it does not involve any drugs, which women have to be careful about taking during pregnancy."

But he said the medical profession needed to be more consistent in recommending acupuncture as a treatment.

"Some GPs and midwives do refer people on for acupuncture, but some don't. It really does vary from area to area."

Dr Graham Archard, vice-chair of the Royal College of GPs, said 60% of family doctors use alternative therapies.

"The use of acupuncture to treat pain during pregnancy certainly seems credible.

"Pregnant women should be avoiding drugs so acupuncture, which releases the bodies natural painkillers, should be of benefit."

And Sue Macdonald, of the Royal College of Midwives, said: "Women should be offered acupuncture for this type of pain.

Gothenburg (pte/Mar 18, 2005/14:00) - Acupuncture is very effective at relieving pelvic pain during pregnancy, according to a new Swedish study. Pelvic girdle pain is common among pregnant women with one in three affected suffering severe pain. As the BBC http://www.bbc.co.uk reports, researchers found that acupuncture was better at easing the pain than standard and specialised exercising. The team of researchers from Gothenburg's Institute for the Health of Women and Children said that the medical profession should be more open to using acupuncture.

"The study shows that methods other than structured physiotherapy may be effective in treating pelvic girdle pain in pregnancy and that acupuncture represents an effective alternative," said Helen Elden, the report's co-author, who is a midwife at the institute. "A combination of several methods is probably even better," she added.

The Swedish team studied the effect of three six-week treatment programmes on 386 pregnant women suffering from pelvic girdle pain, which is thought to be caused by hormones affecting ligaments and muscles. The scientists gave one group a standard home exercise routine, a second received the exercise routine and acupuncture, while the third group had a specialised exercise regime aimed at improving mobility and strength. Pain levels were recorded every morning and evening and assessments were done by an independent examiner. The women using acupuncture experienced the best results, followed by those who underwent the specialised exercise programme.

According to Daniel Maxwell, a member of the British Acupuncture Council, the regulatory body for acupuncturists, the benefits of acupuncture for pregnant women are well known. "Many pregnant women turn to acupuncture to relieve pain, especially pelvic pain. It is good because it does not involve any drugs, which women have to be careful about taking during pregnancy," he said. "However, the medical profession needs to be more consistent in recommending acupuncture as a treatment. Some GPs and midwives do not refer people on for acupuncture, but some don't. It really does vary from area to area," he added.

Pelvic girdle pain is severe in a third of cases
Acupuncture is effective at relieving pelvic pain during pregnancy, a study says.
Pelvic girdle pain is common among pregnant women with one in three affected suffering severe pain.
Researchers found acupuncture was better at easing the pain than standard and specialised exercising.
The team from Gothenburg's Institute for the Health of Women and Children said the medical profession should be more open to using acupuncture.
Report co-author Helen Elden, a midwife at the institute, said: "The study shows that methods other than structured physiotherapy may be effective in treating pelvic girdle pain in pregnancy and that acupuncture represents an effective alternative." And she added: "A combination of several methods is probably even better."
It [acupuncture] is good because it does not involve any drugs, which women have to be careful about taking during pregnancy
Daniel Maxwell
The team studied the effect of three six-week treatment programmes on 386 pregnant women suffering from pelvic girdle pain, which it is thought is caused by hormones affecting ligaments and muscles.

One group were given a standard home exercise routine, a second received the exercise routine and acupuncture, while the third had a specialised exercise regime aimed at improving mobility and strength.

Pain levels were recorded every morning and evening and assessments were done by an independent examiner.

The women using acupuncture experienced the best results, followed by those who underwent the specialised exercise programme.

Daniel Maxwell, a member of the British Acupuncture Council, the regulatory body for acupuncturists, said the benefits of acupuncture for pregnant women was well known.

ACUPUNCTURE PROMOTES PREGNANCY

This was a story on "Good Morning America" reported by Dr. Nancy Snyderman April 16, 2002

Pairing an ancient Chinese medicine technique with in-vitro fertilization treatments can tip the odds in favor of women waiting to get pregnant, a new German medical study has found.

The study, published in the April edition of the medical journal Fertility and Sterility, found that acupuncture, an important element in the 4,000-year-old tradition of Chinese medicine, increases the chance of pregnancy for women undergoing in-vitro fertilization (IVF.) It does not identify how acupuncture may affect the uterus and reproductive system, but the researchers found the technique enhanced the chances of becoming pregnant for a significant number of the women in their small study population.

Researchers included 160 patients undergoing in-vitro fertilization for the study. The patients, who were all required to have good quality embryos, were evenly and randomly divided into two groups similar in age and diagnosis.

When the patients were examined using ultrasound six weeks after their IVF procedures, the differences in pregnancy rates were notable. In the control group, 21 out of 80 patients became pregnant. Of the patients who had received acupuncture treatments, 34 of 80 became pregnant.

Two Rounds Of Acupuncture

Researchers utilized acupuncture both before and after the embryo transfers of half their patients. According to the principles of traditional Chinese medicine, energy flows through the body along defined pathways, also called "meridians." Acupuncture is a means of influencing this energy to induce a particular affect in the body.

The group receiving acupuncture treatments had one treatment before the embryos were transferred to their uterus, and another treatment after the transfer. The researchers inserted sterile needles into the patients' bodies at very specific points, including along the spleen and the stomach/colon "meridians," in an effort to stimulate blood flow and direct energy to the uterus, and to produce a sedative effect.

Researchers inserted additional needles into the patients' ears, both to influence the uterus and stabilize the endocrine system. Needles were left in place for 25 minutes while the patients rested. The control group also rested, lying still for 25 minutes after embryo transfer, as part of the IVF protocol.

The researchers plan to conduct further studies to try to rule out possible psychological or psychosomatic effects.

TREATING PREGNANCY NAUSEA WITH ACUPUNCTURE

Nausea and vomiting complicate up to 89 percent of pregnancies during the initial 16 weeks. These symptoms may be severe, and medication may be needed in approximately 10 percent of patients. The decision to use medication is complicated by the fear of teratogenicity in early pregnancy. Since 1942, pyridoxine hydrochloride (vitamin [B.sub.6]) has been used to treat the nausea associated with pregnancy, but no controlled trials have been published. Sahakian and colleagues performed a randomized, double-blind, placebo-controlled study to evaluate the efficacy of vitamin [B.sub.6] in the treatment of nausea and vomiting in early pregnancy.

Seventy-four women seen in the obstetric clinic of a university hospital were included in the study. The women were screened to exclude those requiring hospitalization and those with another medical condition that could cause nausea and vomiting. Each patient was examined by ultrasonography to establish gestational age of the fetus and foetal viability. There were no statistical differences in maternal age, gestational age and parity. Of the 59 women who completed the protocol, 31 received pyridoxine (25 mg orally every eight hours for 72 hours) and 28 received placebo. Symptoms were assessed using a 10-point visual analogue scale. The pre-treatment scores of the two groups were not statiscally different.

In the women with mild to moderate nausea and in the group as a whole, no significant improvement occurred in symptoms in the patients receiving pyridoxine, compared with those receiving placebo. However, significant differences were found in patients whose symptoms were initially severe. At the beginning of the study, severe nausea and votiming occurred in 15 of the 31 patients receiving pyridoxine. By the end of the study, severe nausea and vomiting occurred in only eight of these patients. At the beginning of the study, severe nausea and vomiting occurred in 10 of the 28 patients receiving placebo, and by the end of the study, severe nausea and vomiting occurred in 15 of the women

Acupressure for Morning Sickness. *Belluomini, MSN, et al. (1994.)* * Acupressure for Nausea and Vomiting of Pregnancy: A Randomized, Blinded Study. *Obstetrics and Gynecology, 84, 245-47 Aloysio, D. DE, MD, Penacchiloni, P., MD (1992.)* * Morning Sickness Control in Early Pregnancy by Neiguan Point Acupressure. *Obstetrics and Gynecology, 80: 852-4 Bill, K. M., Dundee, J. W. (1988.)* * Acupressure for post-operative nausea and vomiting. *British Journal of Clinical Pharmacy, 26: 225 Dundee, J. W., et al. (1988.)* * P6 Acupressure reduces morning sickness. *The Royal Society of Medicine, 81: 456-7 Mazzotta, P. and Magee, L. A. (2000.)* * A Risk-Benefit Assessment of Pharmacological and Nonpharmacological Treatments for Nausea and Vomiting of Pregnancy. *Drugs, 59(4): 781-800 O'brien, Relyea, and Taerum (1996.)* * Efficacy of P6 acupressure in the treatment of nausea and vomiting during pregnancy. *American Journal of Obstetric Gynecology, 174(2): 708-15.* *Acupressure Wristbands for the Nausea of Pregnancy, *Cheryl L. Stone, M.S.N., R.N., C. Nurse Practitioner, Nov. 1993.*

MOXIBUSTION FOR CORRECTION OF BREECH PRESENTATION A RANDOMISED CONTROLLED TRIAL

Francesco Cardini MD; Huang Weixin, MD

Journal of the American Medical Association, November 11, 1998 - Vol 280, No 18, pp1580-1584.

Context Traditional Chinese medicine uses moxibustion (burning herbs to stimulate acupuncture points) of acupuncture point BL 67 (Zhiyin), located beside the outer corner of the fifth – little - toenail), to promote version of fetuses in breech presentation. Its effect may be through increasing foetal activity. However, no randomised controlled trial has evaluated the efficacy of this therapy.

Objective To evaluate the efficacy and safety of moxibustion on acupoint BL 67 to increase foetal activity and correct breech presentation.

Design Randomised, controlled, open clinical trial.

Setting Outpatient departments of the Women's Hospital of Jiangxi Province, Nanchang, and Jiujiang Women's and Children's Hospital in the People's Republic of China.

Patients Primigravidas in the 33rd week of gestation with normal pregnancy and an ultrasound diagnosis of breech presentation.

Interventions The 130 subjects randomised to the intervention group received stimulation of acupoint BL 67 by moxa (Japanese term for Artemisia vulgaris) rolls for 7 days, with treatment for an additional 7 days if the fetus persisted in the breech position. The 130 subjects randomised to the control group received routine care but no interventions for breech position. Subjects with persistent breech presentation after 2 weeks of treatment could undergo external cephalic version anytime between 35 weeks of gestation and delivery.

Main Outcome Measures Foetal movements counted by the mother during 1 hour each day for 1 week; number of cephalic presentations during the 35th week and at delivery.

Results The intervention group experienced a mean of 48.45 foetal movements vs 35.35 in the control group. (P<.001;95% confidence interval [C1] for difference, 10.56-15.60.) During the 35th week of gestation 98 (75.4%) of 130 fetuses in the interventions group were cephalic vs 62 (47.7%) of 130 fetuses in the control group (P<.001; relative risk (RR), 1.58; 95% CI 1.29-1.94.) Despite the fact that 24 subjects in the control group and one subject in the intervention group underwent external cephalic version, 98 (75.4%) of the 130 fetuses in the intervention group were cephalic at birth vs 81 (62.3%) of the fetuses in the control group (P=.02; RR, 1.21; 95% CI, 1.12-1.43.)

Conclusions Among primigravidas with breech presentation during the 33rd week of gestation, moxibustion for 1 to 2 weeks increased foetal activity during the treatment period and cephalic presentation after the treatment period and at delivery.

BACH FLOWER REMEDIES DURING PREGNANCY & CHILDBIRTH

This article describes a pilot study carried out to determine the effect of Bach Flower Remedies on first-time mothers where birth is delayed. The last phase of pregnancy is often difficult, with exhaustion, breathlessness and panic attacks — the more so when birth is delayed — this can also put stress on couples. *Prior studies in this field* Weisglas (1979) with a double blind placebo test showed that Bach remedies increased confidence and wellbeing. Also a study by Mechthild Scheffer at the Bach Centre in Hamburg (1993), with 700 patients but no control group, demonstrated positive results. An earlier investigation by Rühle (1994) showed that with the use of Bach remedies breathing was more relaxed and women were better able to cope with labour pains. *Fundamental presuppositions for this study* Lewi's description (1967) of the physiological/psychological effects of pregnancy, Read's (1972) and Kuntner's (1991) analysis of anxiety/tension patterns, showing the relation between physiological and psychological stress factors, Bonica's (1976) and Hauffe's (1987) studies showing that use of Bach remedies can reduce stress. *Materials and methodology used* Not a classic placebo double blind, but randomised control group design, with 24 primagravidae, more than 14 days overdue, aged 21 to 35, all married or in a steady relationship, partner in all cases present at the birth. 8 women in the Bach remedy group; another 8 in a group that received psychological counselling; the remaining 8 in a group that was exclusively looked after by gynaecological consultants. *Factors rated* • days to delivery • ease of delivery • use of analgesics • a nxiety • general emotional state. The entire study was conducted at the Bad Urach hospital (Baden-Württemberg, Germany.) Choice of patients was at random. The Bach remedy chiefly used was Rescue Remedy; this however was backed up by the use of other remedies, depending on the needs of the individual patient — eg Mimulus (fear of birth, tools, objects), Aspen (irrational terror, nightmares), Gentian (pessimism, readiness to expect the worst), Honeysuckle (where the mother does not want the pregnancy to end), Wild Rose (apathy, listlessness) and Scleranthus (violent mood swings.) *Effects regarded as desirable* • shorter time till delivery • fewer complications in giving birth • less need for analgesics • more positive state of mind • reduced anxiety. Eight women were excluded from the study for various reasons (irregular period, age, delivery took place too early.) *Results* Bach group needed least medication; also easier delivery (fewer complications.) No evidence however that delivery was speeded up. Assumption was that delivery date depends on the effect and interaction of hormones and stress factors (study by Schmidt and Matthiessen, 1992.) Effect of Bach remedies in retrospect difficult to judge, as too many factors relevant here. The hypothesis that Bach remedies reduce anxiety and improve the general emotional state could not be proved, but again there are many other factors in play. In spite of these caveats, the study shows positive results for Bach remedies. *R ecommendations for future research* • larger groups chosen at random (to balance out possibly contributory social factors) • classic double blind testing • development of a consistent rating scale • better documentation of stress levels.

Department of Psychiatry and Psychotherapy, Albert-Ludwigs-University, Freiburg, Germany.

GBS - Treating Group B Strep: Are Antibiotics Necessary? By Christa Novelli *Issue 121, Nov/Dec 2003*

Most women who have been pregnant in the last few years are familiar with the terms Group B Strep (for Group B Streptococcus), or GBS. The US Centers for Disease Control and Prevention (CDC) and the American College of Obstetricians and Gynecologists (ACOG) recommend that all pregnant women be screened between weeks 35 and 37 of their pregnancies to determine if they are carriers of GBS. This is done by taking a swab of the pregnant woman's vaginal and rectal areas. Studies show that approximately 30 percent of pregnant women are found to be colonized with GBS in one or both areas.1-5

The CDC and ACOG advise all pregnant women who are found to be carriers of GBS to be treated with intravenous antibiotics during labor. Doctors and midwives have such great concern because GBS can be passed from the mother to the infant during delivery and can cause sepsis (a blood infection), pneumonia, and meningitis (an infection of the fluid and lining of the brain) in newborn infants. Therefore, most pregnant women who test positive for GBS choose to follow CDC and ACOG recommendations and attempt to avoid transmitting GBS to their newborns through treatment with IV antibiotics throughout their labors. Given all this, why would any woman choose not to accept IV antibiotics? But no woman can make a truly informed decision about this issue without taking a critical look at any recommendation that a third of all women and their infants be given antibiotics during labor.

GBS is a bacterium that normally lives in the intestinal tracts of many healthy people. A vaginal-rectal area colonized by GBS should not be termed "infected" any more than an intestinal tract colonized by GBS would be. GBS is a problem only when it is present in the genital area of a pregnant woman during labor and delivery. When this happens, there is a small risk that the bacterium will be passed on to the newborn infant, and that she or he will become sick as a result. Approximately 0.5 percent of women found to have GBS bacteria in their genital areas at 35 to 37 weeks into their pregnancies will go on to deliver a baby who becomes ill from GBS. This is 0.5 percent of women who receive no antibiotics during labor and delivery.

We should not take lightly the use of antibiotics for 200 women and their babies to prevent only a single blood infection-however serious that infection might be-especially in this age of increasing resistance to antibiotics. Concerns have arisen in several areas regarding the use of antibiotics for so many laboring women. One dilemma is that colonization of the vaginal area by GBS is, at best, a poor method of predicting whether a newborn will develop a GBS infection. As mentioned, even without any intervention during labor, fewer than 1 percent of infants born to carriers of GBS develop infections.6, 7

Some studies have shown a decrease in GBS infection in newborns whose mothers accepted IV antibiotics during labor, but no decrease in the incidence of death.8, 9 Still other research has found that preventive use of antibiotics is not always effective.10 In fact, one study found no decrease in GBS infection or deaths among newborns whose mothers were given IV antibiotics during labor.11

Perhaps the greatest area of concern to medical researchers, as it should be to us all, is the alarming increase in antibiotic-resistant strains of bacteria. Antibiotic-resistant bacteria can cause infections in newborns that are very difficult to treat. Many large research studies have found not only resistant strains of GBS, but also antibiotic-resistant strains of E. coli and other bacteria caused by the use of antibiotics in laboring women.12-21 Some strains of GBS have been found to be resistant to treatment by all currently used forms of antibiotics.22

While many studies have found that giving antibiotics during labor to women who test positive for GBS decreases the rate of GBS infection among newborns, research is beginning to show that this benefit is being outweighed by increases in other forms of infection. One study, which looked at the rates of blood infection among newborns over a period of six years, found that the use of antibiotics during labor reduced the instance of GBS infection in newborns but increased the incidence of other forms of blood infection.23 The overall effect was that the incidence of newborn blood infection remained unchanged.

The increase in other forms of blood infection among newborns is likely due to bacteria made drug-resistant by the overuse of antibiotics. Evidence exists that increased use of antibiotics frequently leads to increasing bacterial resistance. When a woman is given antibiotics during labor to treat GBS, the antibiotics cross the placenta and enter the amniotic fluid. While the antibiotics may have the desired effect of killing the GBS bacteria, some GBS bacteria can survive and become difficult, if not impossible, to kill with traditionally used antibiotics. Similarly, other bacteria, such as E. coli, that may be present in the mother or infant can become resistant to antibiotic treatment. These bacteria may not have presented a large risk of infection to the newborn until they were exposed to antibiotics and made into "super-bugs."

A study of 43 newborns with blood infections caused by GBS and other bacteria found that, when the mothers of the ill newborns had been given antibiotics during labor, 88 to 91 percent of the infants' infections were resistant to antibiotics. It is unlikely to be a coincidence that the drugs to which the bacteria showed resistance were the same antibiotics that had been administered during labor.24 For the newborns who had developed blood infections without exposure to antibiotics during labor and delivery, only 18 to 20 percent of their infections were resistant to antibiotics.

E. coli, in particular, is becoming an increasing cause of bacterial infection in newborns as the use of antibiotics in labor has increased. One study, which looked at causes of newborn blood infections between 1991 and 1996, found that the incidence of infections caused by GBS decreased during this time, but that the incidence of infection caused by other bacteria, especially E. coli, increased.25 During those years, antibiotic use during labor increased from less than 10 percent to almost 17 percent of the women included in this study. The researchers concluded that increased use of antibiotics during labor was the likely cause of increased newborn blood infections with bacteria other than GBS.

E. coli infection is particularly difficult to treat in premature babies. Unfortunately, the proportion of E. coli bacteria that are resistant to antibiotic treatment has increased astronomically in premature infants in the past few years. In a review of 70 cases of E. coli infection in newborns over a two-year period, researchers found that 29 percent of the E. coli bacteria present in premature babies were resistant to ampicillin in 1998; two years later, 84 percent of the E. coli bacteria present in premature babies were resistant to the same antibiotic.26

Preterm labor (i.e., labor before 37 weeks) is a well-accepted risk factor for transmission of GBS to the infant during labor and delivery. Due to the larger risk of transmitting GBS to a premature baby during delivery, most women who go into early labor will opt to receive IV antibiotics during their labor. However, infants born prematurely are at a greater risk from super-bugs caused by the very antibiotics that are supposed to be reducing their risk of infection. Severe complications for the babies, even deaths, have occurred when women whose waters broke before 37 weeks were given antibiotics to prevent transmission of GBS to their newborns. St. Joseph's Hospital in Denver, Colorado, tracked four cases in which women whose waters broke before 37 weeks were given ampicillin or amoxicillin. Following the administration of antibiotics, infection of the amniotic fluid occurred in all four cases. Two of the infants died as a result of blood infections from resistant bacteria; a third was stillborn, presumably from the same cause.27

Given the frightening results of these studies, what is a woman to do if she tests positive for GBS during her pregnancy? A closer look at the real risks of transmission, a frank talk with her provider of prenatal care, and a consideration of alternatives for eradicating GBS are all good places to start.

How great is the risk of my baby becoming sick from GBS? There are three significant factors that place a woman at increased risk of delivering an infant who becomes ill from GBS: fever during labor, her water breaking 18 hours or more before delivery (prolonged rupture of membranes, or PROM), and/or labor or broken water before 37 weeks gestation.28 Other factors that can contribute to a newborn's risk of contracting GBS infection include age, economic, and medical criteria, such as the following: being born to a mother who is less than 20 years of age,29, 30 being African American,31, 32 the mother having large amounts of GBS bacteria in her vaginal tract,33-37 and being born to a mother who has given birth to a prior sibling with GBS disease.38-40

In the absence of the first three risk factors (fever during labor, PROM, or labor before 37 weeks), the risk of a newborn developing GBS infection is very small. The CDC estimates that, without the use of antibiotics during labor, only one out of every 200 GBS-positive women without these risk factors (0.5 percent) will deliver an infant with GBS disease. Some studies have found even lower rates of transmission. If antibiotics are given to the mother during labor, the CDC estimates that one in 4,000 GBS-positive women with no other risk factors will deliver an infant with GBS infection.

Conservative studies find that the use of antibiotics during labor fails to prevent up to 30 percent of GBS infections, and 10 percent of the deaths from GBS disease or infections.41, 42 Although, by CDC estimations, there is a reduced risk of GBS transmission with the use of antibiotics, one must take into account the risks posed by the use of the antibiotics themselves.

For a woman who has a negative culture for GBS at 35 to 37 weeks, there is a one in 2,000 risk of her newborn developing a GBS infection, and antibiotics are not recommended by the CDC. The CDC does recommend treating all women with risk factors (fever,

PROM, premature labor) with antibiotics if they have not been tested to determine whether they are carriers of GBS.

What are the symptoms of GBS infection in a baby? There are two forms of GBS infection: early and late onset. In early-onset GBS disease, the infant will become ill within seven days of birth. Of those infants who do develop a severe early-onset GBS infection, approximately 6 percent will die from complications of the infection.43 Full-term babies are less likely to die; 2 to 8 percent of them suffer fatal complications.44 Premature infants have mortality rates of 25 to 30 percent.45 Late-onset GBS infection is more complex and has not been convincingly tied to the GBS status of the mother. Late-onset GBS infection in infants occurs between seven days and three months of age.

In newborns, symptoms of early-onset GBS infection can include any of the following: fever or abnormally low body temperature, jaundice (yellowing of the skin and whites of the eyes), poor feeding, vomiting, seizures, difficulty in breathing, swelling of the abdomen, and bloody stools. Of course, any of the above symptoms can also be a sign of a sick newborn who does not have a bacterial infection. Newborns with any of these symptoms should be immediately evaluated by a medical professional.

How great is the risk from antibiotics? The recommended antibiotic for treating GBS during labor is penicillin. Fewer bacteria currently show a resistance to penicillin than to other antibiotics used to treat GBS. The options are fewer for women known to be allergic to penicillin. Up to 29 percent of GBS strains have been shown to be resistant to non-penicillin antibiotics.46 For women not known to be allergic to penicillin, there is a one in ten risk of a mild allergic reaction to penicillin, such as a rash. Even for those women who have no prior experience of a penicillin allergy, there is a one in 10,000 chance of developing anaphylaxis, a life-threatening allergic reaction.

We can compare this to CDC estimates that 0.5 percent of babies born to GBS-positive mothers with no treatment will develop a GBS infection, and that 6 percent of those who develop a GBS infection will die. Six percent of 0.5 percent means that three out of every 10,000 babies born to GBS-positive mothers given no antibiotics during labor will die from GBS infection. If the mother develops anaphylaxis during labor (one in 10,000 will), and it is untreated, it is likely that the infant, too, will die. So, by CDC estimates, we save the lives of two in 10,000 babies-0.02 percent-by administering antibiotics during labor to one third of all laboring women. We should also keep in mind that this figure does not take into account the infants that will die as a result of bacteria made antibiotic-resistant by the use of antibiotics during labor-infants who would not otherwise have become ill. When you take that into account, there may not be any lives saved by using antibiotics during labor.

It should be noted that antibiotics such as penicillin kill GBS as well as other bacteria that might cause a newborn to become ill. Currently, the use of penicillin during labor may be a case in which the benefits outweigh the risks, depending on your individual risk factors for passing GBS on to your baby. However, it was only a few years ago that the same could have been said about other antibiotics. Ampicillin and amoxicillin have been rendered virtually useless for treating GBS by their prior overuse in laboring women in an effort to prevent GBS infection in newborns. How long will it be before penicillin, too, becomes useless in the battle to prevent GBS infections?

More minor risks of the use of antibiotics include an increase in thrush and other yeast infections among newborns. Along with the risks of thrush and allergic reactions, women must take into consideration the risk of creating antibiotic-resistant bacteria in themselves and their newborns. It is possible that exposure to antibiotics during birth could delay establishment of healthy bacteria in the infant's intestinal tract and allow penicillin-resistant bacteria, many of which are harmful, to become established.

Each woman must weigh for herself the likelihood of GBS infection in her newborn, taking into account her individual risk factors as well as the risk of other forms of infection caused by antibiotic-resistant bacteria. This is a good discussion to have with your healthcare provider so that you can be an informed partner in your own health care.

Alternatives to Antibiotics Many women are interested in alternatives to antibiotics that may help get rid of GBS prior to labor. Unfortunately, no scientific studies of alternative treatments have been published. Several researchers have suggested that studies are needed to determine whether alternative approaches to eradicating GBS in pregnant women would be effective. Alternate approaches that have been suggested include vaginal washing and immunotherapy.47 At this point, however, these alternatives remain to be studied, and I am aware of no healthcare providers that use either method.

Some practitioners of natural medicine have suggested supplements for the mother in an effort to eradicate GBS prior to delivery. One suggestion is that, when a woman tests positive for GBS, she should take a course of garlic, vitamin C, echinacea, and/or bee propolis, and then be re-tested to determine if she is still carrying GBS. Any supplements that a pregnant woman considers taking should first be discussed with a homeopathic or naturopathic physician or other knowledgeable practitioner of natural medicine.

Because colonization by GBS is intermittent or transient for 60 percent of carriers, testing positive for GBS once does not indicate that a woman will always be colonized.48 However, most studies indicate that a positive culture at 35 to 37 weeks gestation is a fairly accurate predictor of GBS colonization at delivery. Without an active effort to eradicate the GBS colonization, it is likely that a woman will still be colonized at delivery.

Ultimately, it is the pregnant woman herself who will have to decide what is right for her and her baby. Deciding to follow the recommendations of ACOG and the CDC is not necessarily the wrong choice, as long as a woman is adequately informed of the risks that come with antibiotic use. But none of us should blindly follow recommendations to interfere with the natural birth process without taking a good look at the risks, as well as the benefits, of doing so.

NOTES *1. B. F. Anthony et al., "Epidemiology of Group B Streptococcus: Longitudinal Observations during Pregnancy," Journal of Infectious Disease 137 (1978): 524–530. 2. J. A. Regan et al., "Vaginal Infections and Prematurity Study Group: The Epidemiology of Group B Streptococcal Colonization in Pregnancy," Obstetric Gynecology 77 (1991): 604–610. 3. H. C. Dillon et al., "Anorectal and Vaginal Carriage of Group B Streptococci during Pregnancy," Journal of Infectious Disease 145 (1982): 794–799. 4. K. M. Boyer et al., "Selective Intrapartum Chemoprophylaxis of Neonatal Group B Streptococcal Early-Onset Disease: II. Predictive Value of Prenatal Cultures," Journal of Infectious Disease 148 (1983): 802–809. 5. S. J. Schrag et al., "A Population-Based Comparison of Strategies to Prevent Early-Onset Group B Streptococcal Disease in Neonates," New England Journal of Medicine 347 (2002): 233–239. 6. G. L. Gilbert and S. M. Garland, "Perinatal Group B Streptococcal Infections," Medical Journal of Australia 1 (1983): 566–571. 7. D. Isaacs and J. A. Royle, "Intrapartum Antibiotics and Early Onset Neonatal Sepsis Caused by Group B Streptococcus and by Other Organisms in Australia," Australian Study Group for Neonatal Infections, Pediatric Infectious Disease Journal 18 (1999): 524–528. 8. F. Smaill, "Intrapartum Antibiotics for Group B Streptococcal Colonization," Cochrane Database Syst Rev 2 (2000): CD000115; www.ncbi.nlm.nih.gov/. 9. D. A. Terrone et al., "Neonatal Sepsis and Death Caused by Resistant Escherichia coli: Possible Consequences of Extended Maternal Ampicillin Administration," American Journal of Obstetric Gynecology 180, no. 6, pt. 1 (1999): 1345–1348. 10. D. P. Ascher et al., "Failure of Intrapartum Antibiotics to Prevent Culture-Proved Neonatal Group B Streptococcal Sepsis," Journal of Perinatology 13, no. 3 (1994): 212–216. 11. P. F. Katz et al., "Group B Streptococcus: To Culture or Not to Culture?," Journal of Perinatology 19, no. 5 (1999): 37–42. 12. See Note 9. 13. E. M. Levine et al., "Intrapartum Antibiotic Prophylaxis Increases the Incidence of Gram Negative Neonatal Sepsis," Infectious Disease Obstetric Gynecology 7, no. 4 (1999): 210–213. 14. C. V. Towers and G. G. Briggs, "Antepartum Use of Antibiotics and Early-Onset Neonatal Sepsis: The Next Four Years," American Journal of Obstetric Gynecology 187, no. 2 (2002):*

495-500. 15. C. V. Towers et al., "Potential Consequences of Widespread Antepartal Use of Ampicillin," American Journal of Obstetric Gynecology 179, no. 4 (1998): 879-883. 16. R. S. McDuffie, Jr., et al., "Adverse Perinatal Outcome and Resistant Enterobacteriaceae after Antibiotic Usage for Premature Rupture of Membranes and Group B Streptococcus Carriage," Obstetric Gynecology 82, no. 4, pt. 1 (1993): 487-489. 17. T. B. Hyde et al., "Trends in Incidence and Antimicrobial Resistance of Early-Onset Sepsis: Population-Based Surveillance in San Francisco and Atlanta," Pediatrics 110, no. 4 (2002): 690-695. 18. M. L. Bland et al., "Antibiotic Resistance Patterns of Group B Streptococci in Late Third Trimester Rectovaginal Cultures," American Journal of Obstetric Gynecology 184, no. 6 (2001): 1125-1126. 19. M. Dabrowska-Szponar and J. Galinski, "Drug Resistance of Group B Streptococci," Pol Merkuriusz Lek 10, no. 60 (2001): 442-444. 20. R. K. Edwards et al., "Intrapartum Antibiotic Prophylaxis 2: Positive Predictive Value Antenatal Group B Streptococci Cultures and Antibiotic Susceptibility of Clinical Isolates," Obstetric Gynecology 100, no. 3 (2002): 540-544. 21. S. D. Manning et al., "Correlates of Antibiotic-Resistant Group B Streptococcus Isolated from Pregnant Women," Obstetric Gynecology 101, no. 1 (2003): 74-79. 22. See Note 19. 23. See Note 13. 24. See Note 14. 25. See Note 15. 26. See Note 17. 27. See Note 16. 28. K. M. Boyer and S. P. Gotoff, "Strategies for Chemoprophylaxis of GBS Early-Onset Infections," Antibiotic Chemotherapy 35 (1985): 267-280. 29. A. Schuchat et al., "Population-Based Risk Factors for Neonatal Group B Streptococcal Disease: Results of a Cohort Study in Metropolitan Atlanta," Journal of Infectious Disease 162 (1990): 672-677. 30. A. Schuchat et al., "Multistate Case-Control Study of Maternal Risk Factors for Neonatal Group B Streptococcal Disease," Pediatric Infectious Disease Journal 13 (1994): 623-629. 31. See Note 29. 32. K. M. Zangwill et al., "Group B Streptococcal Disease in the United States, 1990: Report from a Multistate Active Surveillance System," in CDC Surveillance summaries (November 20), MMWR 41, no. SS-6 (1992): 25-32. 33. M. A. Pass et al., "Prospective Studies of Group B Streptococcal Infections in Infants," Journal of Pediatrics 95 (1979): 431-443. 34. E. G. Wood and H. C. Dillon, "A Prospective Study of Group B Streptococcal Bacteriuria in Pregnancy," American Journal of Obstetric Gynecology 140 (1981): 515-520. 35. M. Moller et al.,

Christa Novelli has a master's degree in public health from the University of Northern Colorado and a BA in sociology from the University of California at Berkeley. She currently resides in Northern Colorado with her husband and two daughters, Angelina (5) and Tessa (3). Christa tested positive for Group B Strep with her second pregnancy and opted not to take IV antibiotics during labor. Tessa was born after 15 hours of natural labor with no interventions and did not develop a GBS infection.

OMEGA-3

THE VITAL ROLE OF ESSENTIAL FATTY ACIDS (OMEGA 3) FOR PREGNANT AND NURSING WOMEN

by John Finnegan

Recently it has been discovered that the Omega-3 fats are necessary for the complete development of the human brain during pregnancy and the first two years of life. The Omega-3 fat and its derivative, DHA (docosahexaenoic acid), is so essential to a child's development that if a mother and infant are deficient in it, the child's nervous system and immune system may never fully develop, and it can cause a lifetime of unexplained emotional, learning, and immune system disorders.

Considering the enormous increase in emotional, learning, and immune system disorders in our population today, one cannot help but wonder what effect this widespread nutritional deficiency is having on the breakdown in people's health.

One also wonders whether the prevalence of infant and childhood illnesses like Epstein Barr; Candida albicans overgrowth; sinus allergies; chronic ear, nose, and throat infections; as well as so-called emotional disorders like hyperactivity and autistic behavior, also have their basis in nutritional deficiencies, particularly in the lack of Omega-3 fatty acids.

Further compounding the problem, an estimated 60-70% of all two-month-old babies are bottle-fed, and 75-80% of all four-month-old babies are bottle-fed; none of the powdered baby formulas such as Isomil, Similac, Gerber, and Carnation contain Omega-3 fatty acids.1 To my knowledge, all baby formulas are made with commercially processed oils which contain high levels of poisonous trans fatty acids and other harmful compounds.2

Dr. Donald Rudin, in his excellent book The Omega-3 Phenomenon, states the issue succinctly: There is no comparable substitute for the remarkable mix of nutrients and immunity-boosting factors provided by mother's milk, as long as the mother is eating properly. A well-nourished nursing mother provides her infant with a perfect blend of essential fatty acids and their long-chained derivatives, assuring the fast-growing brain and body tissues a rich supply. Mother's milk also supplies important antibodies not present in cow's milk or in artificial formula. Here is a nutritive comparison:

- Breast milk may have five times more arachidonic acid and two and a half times more EPA (eicosapentaenoic acid) than formula.
- Breast milk may have 30 times more DHA (docosahexaenoic acid) than formula.
- Compared with mother's milk, formulas are also low in selenium and biotin.

Sadly, the breast milk of many mothers in our country reflects the high trans fatty acid and low Omega-3 content in the average diet. American mothers produce milk that often has only one-fifth to one-tenth of the Omega-3 content of the milk that well-nourished, nut-eating Nigerian mothers provide their infants.

This discovery has far-reaching implications. A study in March, 1991 at the Mayo Clinic of 19 'normal' pregnant women consuming normal diets indicated all were deficient in the Omega-3 fats and to a lesser degree, Omega-6 fats.3 Another study of Inuit (Eskimo) women, compared to Canadian women, revealed the same deficiencies in the milk of Canadian nursing mothers.4

Compounding the problem is our nation's pervasive obsession with weight loss programs, which induce women to avoid all fats. The frightening news is that for the past three generations (since the advent of refined oils), the vast majority of the population in North America has not been given adequate nourishment for complete brain development. The part of the brain that Omega-3 affects is the learning ability, anxiety/depression, and auditory and visual perception. The Omega-3 fats also aid in balancing the autoimmune system, and there seem to be a growing number of children with allergies, colic, and skin problems.

There are also indications that Omega-3 fats play an ongoing role in brain function, healthy immune system function, and general growth throughout childhood and adolescence. One study revealed that Omega-3 supplementation induced catch-up growth in a deficient, underdeveloped seven-year-old.5

Since our mental apparatus is developed in the mother's womb and during the first two years of life, one would be wise to heed the advice of the researchers from the Mayo Clinic study.6 They suggest that this important fat be supplemented in every pregnancy, and that refined and hydrogenated fats be avoided during this critical period.

For these conservative researchers to include a message like this in their research paper should make us concerned for our future. I have personal experience with families who have had 'flax' babies. These children (now 3 and 6 years old) are very bright and healthy and have been free from many health problems most young children now experience.

A deficiency of the Omega-3 and Omega-6 fats causes insufficient milk production and breast engorgement. Flax seed oil has been found to substantially increase milk production in women who are not producing enough milk to nurse their infants. It also often clears up breast engorgement. One woman I know was having great difficulty producing enough milk to nurse her newborn child. Within twenty-four hours of taking flax seed oil, her milk production doubled, and one breast that was engorged opened up, allowing the milk to flow freely.

Many authorities recommend that pregnant and nursing women consume fatty fish two to three times weekly and/or add a minimal amount of flax seed oil to their diets to insure adequate intake of Omega-6 and Omega-3 fatty acids.

Another paper worth reading is the report given by Artemis Simopoulos, M.D., a pediatrician and endocrinologist from the International Life Sciences Institute. 7 She takes a comprehensive look at how the Omega-3 deficiency affects many areas, from foetal growth to arthritis and cancer.

A healthy mother's milk is high in essential fatty acids, GLA, and other precursors to prostaglandins. Cow's milk is low in essential fatty acids, and other prostaglandin precursors, and is high in saturated fats. For this reason, cow's milk is not an adequate substitute for mother's milk. Neither is baby formula. At a recent international symposium on Dietary Omega-3 and -6 Fatty acids Dr. Neuringer, an authority on infant milk, stated that the low Omega-3, high Omega-6 content in infant formulas is of great concern because of the imbalance it causes among the resultant prostaglandins. These imbalances could impair the immune system and predispose the infant to cancer and heart trouble later in life. Feeding a nonnursing baby a few drops of flax seed oil will provide the Omega-3 and Omega-6 essential fatty acids.

Note: Since most adults today are deficient in the Omega-3 fatty acids, nursing mothers may not have sufficient amounts to pass along to their infants. It is especially important, therefore, for pregnant and nursing women to supplement their diets…

GENERATIONAL CONSEQUENSES OF DEFICIENCY OF OMEGA-3

There are many serious consequences of generation after generation having diets deficient in an element essential for normal development of the nervous system. Following are a few observations of the effects that inadequate nutrition is having on social and economic conditions today.

- A widespread alienation and pervasive depression in young people, truly alarming to observe in an age group usually known for its boundless enthusiasm and enjoyment of life.
- An increase in suicides and killings among young children, almost unheard of a generation ago.
- The ongoing increase in drug and alcohol abuse.
- An unparalleled growth of immune system disorders like Epstein Barr, Candida, allergies, chronic sinus and ear infections, and digestive disorders.
- A serious decline in the level of scholastic achievement among school children.
- A continued deterioration of the quality of goods produced by American industries. (A nation of people that lives on hamburgers, french fries, milk shakes, cola drinks, TV dinners, and other toxic foods is destined to lose its competitive edge, and will continue to foster drug abuse in the workplace.)

Certainly, there are many social and economic factors contributing to this disturbing state. But there is also a great deal of sound scientific research that clearly demonstrates that, when populations are subjected to serious, continued nutritional deficiencies, the offspring of each successive generation shows an increased deterioration in physical and mental health.8-13 I have spoken with many older doctors who have told me that they find most people in their fifties and sixties to be constitutionally stronger and healthier than those of the next generation, in their thirties and forties.

In his classic work, Nutrition and Physical Degeneration, Dr. Weston Price presents remarkable observations on the diets and health of different cultures around the world. He has extensively documented the degeneration that occurs when healthy peoples, eating traditional diets, convert to modern foods.

Weston Price's time in history was unique. He was able to observe many cultures, living and eating as they had for thousands of years. When these people met the modern age and converted to modern diets, they experienced disastrous consequences to their physical and emotional health.

He studied society after society, from Swiss farmers living in high Alpine valleys to Gaelics on islands of the outer Hebrides, from descendants of ancient civilizations living in Peru to the Maori in New Zealand, the Eskimos in Alaska, Indians in Canada and the United States, Melanesians and Polynesians in the South Pacific, Africans and Malay tribes on islands north of Australia. Again and again, he found the same story repeated. The indigenous peoples had strong, healthy bodies, free from cancer, heart disease, and immune system weakness. And surprisingly, tooth decay and cavities were almost nonexistent, despite the fact that these peoples usually had no dentists or fluoride toothpaste.14-15

He saw, firsthand, how each succeeding generation that converted their diets to modern, refined foods experienced a continued deterioration in health. He also met several doctors who told him that, in several decades of living among native peoples, they never saw a single case of cancer.

This article is an excerpt from The Facts About Fats, by John Finnegan, published by Celestial Arts, 1993.

OMEGA-3 ESSENTIAL COMPONENTS OF CELL MEMBRANES IN INFANCY

There are 2 critical periods for the acquisition of these essential Omega-3 fatty acids: during foetal development and after birth until the biochemical development in the brain and retina is completed.

As already noted, the Omega-3 fatty acid DHA is an important constituent of the cell membrane of these neural structures.

Omega-3 fatty acid deficiency is manifested in both the blood and in tissue biochemistry. Of note is a strikingly low concentration of DHA, which may fall to as much as one-fifth of the normal amount.

In addition, the body attempts to replace the deficient DHA with another highly polyunsaturated fatty acid of the omega-6 series. In rhesus monkeys, Omega-3 fatty acid -- deficient diets fed to pregnant animals and then continued after birth induce profound functional changes such as reduced vision, abnormal electroretinograms, impaired visual evoked potential, more stereotypic behavior (e.g., pacing), and, perhaps, disturbances of cognition.

Some of these findings have been replicated in infants fed formulas deficient in Omega-3 fatty acids. Most studies of premature infants have shown visual impairment and abnormal electroretinograms.

A recent study in full-term infants, in which a standard infant formula was compared with human milk and with formulas enriched with DHA, provided unequivocal evidence of considerable differences in visual evoked potential.

In all of the human studies, the biochemical evidence in plasma, red blood cells, and, occasionally, in tissues from autopsied infants has substantiated the Omega-3 fatty acid deficiency state. The lower concentrations of DHA in plasma and erythrocytes are mirrored by lower concentrations in the brain and retina. Formula-fed infants have lower concentrations of brain DHA than do infants fed human milk. They also have lower intelligence quotients.

During pregnancy, both maternal stores and dietary intake of Omega-3 fatty acids are of importance in insuring that the baby has adequate amounts of Omega-3 fatty acids at the time of birth.
All the polyunsaturated fatty acids, including DHA, are transferred across the placenta into foetal blood. In addition, EPA and DHA in maternal adipose tissue can be mobilized as free fatty acids bound to albumin and be made available to the developing fetus via placenta transport.
Several studies in monkeys have indicated that when the maternal diet is deficient in Omega-3 fatty acids, the infant at birth is likewise deficient as evidenced by low DHA concentrations in their plasma and red blood cells.
In humans, it was shown that the administration of fish oil or sardines to pregnant women led to higher DHA concentrations in both maternal plasma and red blood cells and in cord blood plasma and red blood cells at the time of birth.
Once membrane phospholipids have adequate concentrations of DHA, there is an avid retention of these fatty acids in the brain and the retina, even though the diet may subsequently be deficient. Several studies illustrate clearly the effects of Omega-3 deficiency in both animals and humans.

American Journal of Clinical Nutrition, Vol. 71, No. 1, 171S-175S, January 2000

PREGNANCY AND POSTPARTUM NUTRITION

Eating the right fats and oils can help you and your baby's health.
by Dean Raffelock, D.C., Dipl.Ac. CCN

Underlying a wide range of the postpartum ailments that I often see in my practice-including asthma, allergies, eczema, mood problems, depression, and autoimmune disease-is a single nutritional imbalance: too much of certain fats and not enough of others. You may be accustomed to thinking of fat only in terms of how much of it has collected on certain parts of your body, preventing you from getting into your pre-pregnancy jeans. Or you may only consider it when loading up your shopping cart with low-fat or non-fat foods. If so, its time to change your thinking.

Certain fats are essential for life. Every cell in your body is surrounded by a membrane made from fatty acids, the most basic building blocks of fats. Fats are necessary building blocks for hormones. Prostaglandins, which regulate immune system and reproductive function, inflammation, the constriction and expansion of blood vessels and blood clotting are made exclusively from fats.

BREAST FEEDING AND OMEGA

Your Fat Stores Build Baby's Brain

During pregnancy, your body was literally drained of the fats needed for the building of your baby's brain and nervous system. The human brain is more than 60 percent fat. Research has shown that children who breastfeed score higher on I.Q. tests than those fed formula, because specific fats that are found in mother's milk are important for proper brain development. Those fats continue to flow from your body into the body and brain of your child during breastfeeding. This is another reason breastfeeding for at least a year is one of the best gifts you can give your baby-and why taking special care to maintain fatty acid balance in your own body is so crucial during and after pregnancy.

Research studies have shown that skin problems, asthma, autoimmune disease, unexplained rages, and depression improve when fatty acid balance is restored. Children with learning disability, attention deficit disorder, hyperactivity and autism often improve when given fats that promote this balance.

A hundred years ago, most humans ate a diet containing a ratio somewhere between 1 to 1 and 4 to 1 of two essential types of fats: omega-6 and Omega-3. When we describe a nutrient as essential, we mean that it is needed for survival but can't be made by the body. Today, the omega-6 to Omega-3 ratio is closer to between 20 to 1 and 30 to 1!

The omega-6 fats include linoleic acid (LA), found in sunflower, safflower, sesame and corn oils; gamma-linolenic acid (GLA), found in primrose, borage and blackcurrant oils; and arachidonic acid (AA), found in meat, eggs, dairy products and fish that live in warm waters. The Omega-3 fats are found in far fewer foods: as alpha-linolenic acid (ALA) from flaxseed, walnut, canola and pumpkin seed oils;

eicosapentaenoic acid (EPA) from some cold-water fish and algae; and docosahexaenoic acid (DHA) from other cold-water fish and algae.

The Transformation to Prostaglandins

The form in which you choose to eat your fats-as broiled salmon, margarine, flaxseeds, corn oil, french fries or chicken-fried steak-will have dramatic effects on how you think, feel, learn and remember. Your choice of fats also powerfully influences the formation of prostaglandins, and these hormone-like substances regulate many body systems.

Prostaglandins E1 and E3 are generally anti-inflammatory. Prostaglandin E2 escalates the inflammatory process. If inflammation escalates too far, tissue damage and free radical overload can result. When there's too much PGE-2 and not enough PGE-1 and PGE-3, inflammation can run amok. Allergies, asthma, eczema, joint pain and autoimmune diseases are all manifestations of inflammation that isn't being shut off at the appropriate time.

When you're breastfeeding and giving up PGE-1- and 3-forming fats to your baby, this kind of imbalance can be created in your body. In the worst-case scenario, you aren't even getting enough to give your baby what he or she needs. This could make him or her more vulnerable to allergies, eczema, asthma and even learning disabilities and hyperactivity later in life.

Several enzymes take part in the process that transforms fats into prostaglandins. These enzymes act as gatekeepers, channeling fats into the making of this or that prostaglandin. Like any other enzyme in the body, they require specific nutrient coenzymes to do their jobs. Aspirin and drugs like it work to reduce inflammation by affecting these enzymes, temporarily shutting down the production of both inflammatory and anti-inflammatory prostaglandins. Diet and supplements can be used in a more specific way, enhancing the balance of "good" and "bad" prostaglandins rather than just shutting them all off.

The enzyme delta-6-desaturase acts on linoleic acid (LA, from most vegetable, nut and seed oils) to transform it to gamma-linoleic acid (GLA.) This enzyme also transforms alpha-linolenic acid (ALA) into stearidonic acid (SDA), which then is transformed into eicosapentaenoic acid (EPA), the fat that supports series 3 prostaglandin production and brain cell formation. GLA is used to make the anti-inflammatory series 1 prostaglandins and also supports healthy nervous system function.

The activity of delta-6-desaturase is affected by dietary factors. Transfatty acids (see below) from hydrogenated oils, too much saturated fat (found in meats, fried foods, most junk food and dairy products) in the diet, high stress, too much alcohol or too much sugar or refined flour in the diet all conspire to slow this enzyme down.

The Notorious Trans fatty Acids

Many processed foods contain trans fatty acids. These fats are notorious for slowing down the activity of delta-6-desaturase. They are manufactured from vegetable oils in a process called hydrogenation, which involves the bombardment of liquid oils with hydrogen atoms to make them solid and prevent rancidity. The trans fats have harmful effects on the stability of cell membranes and the structure of nerve and brain cells. They interfere with the formation of antiinflammatory prostaglandins. Trans fats pass readily into your baby's body through your milk supply, and the more of them you eat, the more your baby eats. They show up on food labels as partially hydrogenated vegetable oils, and are present in almost all processed foods.

Large amounts of alpha-linolenic acid (ALA) in your diet can also subdue delta-6-desaturase activity. Some experts say that adding lots of flaxseeds and flaxseed oil to your diet will enhance the production of anti-inflammatory prostaglandins, but we recommend you use flax and other ALA-rich foods with moderation. By suppressing the delta-6-desaturase enzyme, ALA suppresses both "good" and "bad" prostaglandin formation in much the same way as aspirin does. Suppressing all of the prostaglandins doesn't create balance, only a different kind of imbalance.

DGLA (formed from GLA or entering your baby's body in breast milk) can go one of two directions: either into "good" PGE1 or into arachidonic acid (AA.) The activity of the enzyme delta-5-desaturase dictates which way this process goes. Delta-5-desaturase is activated by the hormone insulin and suppressed by the hormone glucagon. Insulin levels rise in the body when you eat lots of sugars and refined carbohydrates; glucagon levels rise when you eat foods that contain balanced amounts of fat and protein.

Eicosapentaenoic acid (EPA), the Omega-3 fat found in fish, also suppresses delta-5-desaturase production. In other words: sugars and refined carbohydrates increase AA and "bad" prostaglandin production, while a diet rich in healthy proteins, fats, and deep-water fish helps to funnel DGLA towards the production of "good" prostaglandins.

Keep in mind that AA is a nonessential fat-the human body can make it from other fats from the age of about six months forward. Your baby gets AA from your milk in her first six months of life. Besides vegetable oils, what do you think is the major source of dietary fat in the typical American diet? Meats, eggs, and dairy products, all of which contain lots of AA. We don't want to make AA into the bad guy here-its an important nutrient, and the cholesterol found in meats, eggs and dairy products is essential to your good health. However, Americans tend to overeat AA-containing foods; we want to encourage you to strive for a more balanced approach.

The bottom line here is that the balance of Omega-3 and omega-6 fats in your cells is directly attributable to your diet and the nutritional supplements you take, and this balance, along with how the other systems in your body are working, influences the balance of inflammatory and anti-inflammatory prostaglandins made in your body. If your family has a history of inflammatory disorders such as asthma, allergy, heart disease, eczema or autoimmune disease, you may have a genetic predisposition to make more of the inflammatory prostaglandins, and you may have to work a little more to hit your balance point.

All of the enzymes that participate in the transformation of fats to prostaglandins require nutrient coenzymes. Vitamins B3, B6, C, E, and A, along with magnesium and zinc, are required in order for delta-6-desaturase to make GLA from LA and EPA from ALA. The transformation of EPA into DHA requires biotin and B6.

The perinatal nutrition of the mother has a profound effect on the development of the fetus and neonate. Over the past five years, the scientific world has recognised the vital and unique role of one particular nutrient in the structure and function of the brain, the retina and the nervous system of the human infant.

This essential nutrient is Docosahexaenoic acid, DHA. DHA is an essential fatty acid (EFA) - 'essential', because very little can be synthesized by our bodies; it has to be obtained from our diet instead. A developing fetus has no capacity to synthesize DHA at all, so it must rely on its mother for an adequate supply. It is important, therefore, that the mother should have an adequate store for both herself and for her child-to-be. In the first few weeks of embryonic development, the mother's blood supplies the fetus with large amounts of DHA, and in the last trimester of pregnancy, the DHA content of the brain's cerebrum and cerebellum - which contains centres for speech and abstract thought - increases threefold.

DHA lacking in modern diet

DHA has been part of the human diet since time began. Described as a long chain polyunsaturated Fatty Acid, or LCP, it is found mainly in fish and shellfish. Significant amounts used to be obtained from some animal meats and products such as eggs, but today, in the industrialised West, these sources often only provide trace amounts, a result of the intensification of agriculture. This, together with the decline in fish consumption, has led to a worrying reduction of DHA in the diet generally, and specifically in the maternal diet. As a result, the DHA content of breast milk has declined by about 35% between 1981 and 1996.

DHA and pre-conception

Essential fatty acids in pregnancy and in early human development are vitally important structural elements of cell membranes and are therefore instrumental in the formation of new tissues. DHA is essential to brain development in the fetus and is enriched throughout the entire brain cortex. The basic building material in the brain is fat: 50% of total fatty acids in the body are concentrated in the retina, adrenal glands and in the brain as DHA. DHA is concentrated in the neurones and synapses of the brain, ensuring optimal function of the brain cell membranes which are essential for the transmission of nerve signals.

BENEFITS OF HIGH LEVELS OF DHA DURING PREGNANCY

Epidemiological studies and nutritional intervention trials have suggested that high dietary levels of DHA are associated with distinct advantages for both the mother and the baby. In Denmark, Scotland, the Faroes, and Canada, for example, babies born in communities eating significant amounts of fish, compared to those born to non-fish-eating mothers, displayed greater birth weight, larger head circumference, longer body length, and greater gestational age. In other trials, fish oil capsules containing DHA have been given as nutritional supplements in the last trimester resulting in significantly increased levels of DHA in the mother and the neonate and heavier babies of greater gestational age at birth.

Similar studies have reported that both fish eating and dietary DHA fish oil supplementation can reduce pregnancy induced hypertension and the incidence of prematurity. Even very high levels (6g per day of fish oil) were tolerated with no adverse effects.

DHA AND LACTATION

The infant brain continues to grow and develop rapidly for the first year after the birth. There is a three-fold increase in brain weight from about 350g to 1100g during this period. Much of this increase in weight is due to nerve cell growth and there is a great demand for DHA during this time, which must be satisfied from breast milk. We know that the neuro-development and the visual acuity of formulated-milk-fed infants is retarded relative to breast feeding infants and that there is a long term consequence of this inducing reduced childhood intelligence. It has also been suggested that postnatal deficiency of DHA may induce a predisposition to adult degenerative diseases.

If the maternal diet is low in DHA, the breast milk will correspondingly be low in this vital nutrient. Breast-milk levels of DHA can be boosted by eating fish regularly, and by the intake of nutritional supplement capsules containing DHA-rich oils, which transfer, in turn into the infant's red blood cells and tissue.

Infants with particular risk of low DHA status at birth include those born to mothers who smoke, consume alcohol, take drugs. Those born to mothers who are diabetic, suffer from PKU, etc. Those born to mothers of poor nutritional status. Those born to mothers who are Vegan. Pre term infants. Twins, multiple birth siblings. Second, third, etc. children (compared to first siblings) ·Those which are small for their gestational age

DHA AND SUPPLEMENTATION

For her own well-being and that of her future child, we always recommend that a woman contemplating pregnancy should begin supplementing her diet with Essential Fatty Acids as early as possible, as it takes time for DHA to become incorporated into human tissue. Many women have low levels or are deficient in DHA, especially in developing countries. Studies indicate that DHA supplementation can be of assistance to the developing child for at least the first 18 months, and longer if a deficiency exists.
Many health practitioners now recommend DHA supplementation for pregnant and nursing mothers as does the World Health Organisation, which has recommended that all infant formulations be DHA enriched.
Zita West, UK Ministry of Agriculture, Fisheries and Food - Report on the review of Additives in Food Specially Prepared for Infants and Young Children. (1991 FDAC – REP 12, London, HMSO) ·*European Society of Paediatric Gasterentology and Nutrition*, Committee on Nutrition. Comment on the content and composition of Lipids in Infant Formulas. Acta Paediatr Scand (1991) 80.887-896 ·*British Nutrition Foundation Task Force on Unsaturated Fatty Acids* - A report of the British Nutrition Foundation (1992) ·*British Nutrition Foundation* - Briefing Paper 10 Groom. 8 and E Ashworth. M (1993) ·*International Society for the study of Fatty Acids and Lipids* - Recommendations for the Essential Fatty Acid requirements of Infant Formula. Newsletter (1994) 1-4. ·*World Health Organisation*

Food and Agriculture Organisation of the United Nations - Fat and Oils in Human Nutrition, Report of a joint expert consultation, Chapter 7, Lipids in Early Development, Food and Nutrition Paper No. 57, SAO Rome, (1994) ·*British Paediatric Association Standing Committee on Nutrition* - Is Breast Feeding Beneficial in the UK? Archives of Disease of Childhood (1994) 71-376-380

OMEGA-3 (DHA)

Developing fetuses cannot make their own Omega-3 fatty acids. So their mothers must meet their nutritional needs. Infants also rely on their paternal supply of DHA for the developing brain (grey matter) and eyes, initially through the placenta and then through breast milk. DHA is the building block of human brain tissue and is particularly abundant in the grey matter of the brain and the retina. DHA is particularly important for fetuses and infants; the DHA content of the infant's brain triples during the first three months of life.

Unfortunately, DHA levels in the breast milk of most women are very low. Therefore, increasing DHA levels should be a primary goal for all pregnant or lactating women.

Low levels of DHA have recently been associated with depression, memory loss, dementia, post-natal depression and visual problems.

Pregnancy and Milk Thistle

Milk Thistle is gentle enough to ensure that there are no adverse effects when taken during pregnancy. It will assist the balanced working of all organs and reduce the side-effects of antibiotics (which it may be necessary to take to fight microbial infection). It helps banish morning sickness as well as motion sickness. It also lessons the likelihood of both varicose veins and haemorrhoids, which are often caused by poor circulation during pregnancy. Historically, Milk Thistle was thought to encourage good milk production in nursing mothers because it brought about a sense of well-being and calm. The latest research seems to support this.

Excerpt taken from: www.herbs-hands-healing.co.uk/singleherbs/milkthistle.html

RELFLEXOLOGY AND PREGNANCY

In a British study in which reflexology was administered throughout the pregnancy labour times were substantially reduced. Results of the study showed, on average, the first stage lasted five hours, the second stage 16 minutes and the third stage seven minutes. This is compared to textbook figures of 16 to 24 hours for the first stage and one to two hours for the second stage.

Reflexology has been known to help women who are overdue (by inducing.) It can also stimulate your body to produce the hormones needed for birth. Reflexology will help you to relax and stay calm so that you can stay focused on what you need to do and be able to cope with the birth experience.

Sorrig, Kirsten, "Easier Births Using Reflexology, "Danish Reflexologists Association, Research Committee Report, Feb., 1995 (Originally published in the Danish daily newspaper "Berlingske Tidende," July 15, 1988)

Dr Gowri Motha, reflexologist, obstetrician and pioneer of water births in London, introduced reflexology 10 years ago into her maternity unit and set-up Friday antenatal clinics where reflexology treatments were given.Dr Motha found that not only did the mothers love receiving reflexology, but also several of the problems they suffered were dramatically reduced. This inspired her to carry out research on the benefits of reflexology during pregnancy. She focused on raised blood pressure and concluded that reflexology not only helped control the blood pressure, but reduced the number of hospital admissions and the length of time women spent in labour.

Thirty-seven of 64 pregnant women, who were offered free reflexology, completed the set course of ten treatments. The effects of reflexology on labour outcomes were perceived as outstanding. Some had labour times of only 2 hours, some 3 hours. The 20 - 25 year olds had an average time of First stage labour of 5 or 6 hours. The 26 - 30 year olds seemed to have the longest labours. In total, the average first stage was 5 hours, second stage 16 minutes, and third stage 7 minutes. This is compared to textbook figures of 16 to 24 hours' first stage, and, 1 to 2 hour's second stage.

"The Effects of Reflexology on Labour Outcome," Dr. Gowri Motha

PREGNANCY STRESS PASSING ONTO THE BABY

The researchers looked at the stress hormone cortisol

Children whose mothers were overly stressed during pregnancy may themselves be more vulnerable to anxiety as a result, research suggests.

High levels of stress hormone may cross the placenta and affect the baby in the womb in a way that carries long-term implications, UK scientists believe.

A Bristol University team found anxiety in late pregnancy was linked to higher cortisol levels in children aged 10.

The work in Biological Psychiatry tallies with earlier animal findings.

Stress effects

Past studies have shown stress in animals during pregnancy affects the body's stress response system - the hypothalamic-pituitary-adrenal (HPA) axis which controls stress hormone levels, including cortisol.

But scientists have not been able to show that it also affects humans in the same way.

US psychologist Dr Thomas O'Connor, from the University of Rochester in New York, working with UK colleagues from Bristol University and Imperial College London, studied 74 children aged 10.

They analysed saliva samples first thing in the morning and three times a day on three consecutive school days to monitor levels of stress hormones.

The children's mothers had completed questionnaires 10 years previously, when they were expecting, about any stress or anxiety they were experiencing during their pregnancy.

Alleviating anxiety

The researchers looked back at this data to compare the results with those of the saliva tests.

The children with high levels of cortisol in their saliva tended to be born to the mothers who reported the most stress during their pregnancy.

Dr O'Connor said: "These results provide the strongest evidence to date that prenatal stress is associated with longer term impact on the HPA axis in children.

Antenatal classes can help allay fears women might have about pregnancy, the birth and the health of the baby

Gillian Fletcher of the National Childbirth Trust
"Several human studies of children and adults suggest that elevated basal levels of cortisol are associated with psychological risk...notably depression and anxiety.
"Our findings point to a possible mechanism by which prenatal stress or anxiety may predict these disturbances in early adolescence, and possibly into adulthood."
However, he said much more work was needed to check that this was the case.
He also pointed out that it was not clear whether high cortisol itself could cause psychological disturbance. Some psychiatric disorders have been linked with low rather than high cortisol levels.
Other factors, such as the personality of the child and the environment they are living in, may play a part in childhood stress too.
Gillian Fletcher of the National Childbirth Trust said: "Its certainly something we need to look at in more detail.
"We don't want to make women who are pregnant more anxious than they already are by saying stress could have long term implications for the growing child."
She said there were many things pregnant women could do to alleviate stress and anxiety.
"Antenatal classes can help allay fears women might have about pregnancy, the birth and the health of the baby.
"They can also teach a women about stress and relaxation and taking life more slowly can help. Its trying to find a balance."

RUPTURED MEMBRANES

Service de Gynecologie-Obstetrique, CHU d'Angers, 49033 Angers Cedex 01.

OBJECTIVE: The aim of our study was to define he best delay for management of spontaneous rupture of the membranes at term. Materials and methods: We conducted a prospective multicentric study in western France defining 3 groups of expectancy (6, 12 and 24 hours) to assess obstetrical, neonatal and maternal outcomes. RESULTS: We included 713 patients. There was no significant difference in neonatal and maternal morbidity between the 3 groups. The rate of Caesarean section was statistically higher in the 6-hour group (12%.) There was no statistical difference between 12 and 24 hours but the rate was lower in the 12-hour group (5.5 versus 7.9%.) CONCLUSION: Based on our findings and a review of the literature, we have decided that in cased of premature rupture of the membranes at term, a 12 hour delay is best. At most two prostaglandin maturations can be performed in unfavorable cervixes.
PMID: 11240504 [PubMed - indexed for MEDLINE]

RESTLESS LEG SYNDROME AND MAGNESIUM

Periodic limb movements during sleep (PLMS), with or without symptoms of a restless legs syndrome (RLS), may cause sleep disturbances. The pharmacologic treatments of choice are dopaminergic drugs. Their use, however, may be limited due to tolerance development or rebound phenomena. Anecdotal observations have shown that oral magnesium therapy may ameliorate symptoms in patients with moderate RLS. We report on an open clinical and polysomnographic study in 10 patients (mean age 57 +/- 9 years; 6 men, 4 women) suffering from insomnia related to PLMS (n = 4) or mild-to-moderate RLS (n = 6.) Magnesium was administered orally at a dose of 12.4 mmol in the evening over a period of 4-6 weeks. Following magnesium treatment, PLMS associated with arousals (PLMS-A) decreased significantly (17 +/- 7 vs 7 +/- 7 events per hour of total sleep time, p < 0.05.) PLMS without arousal were also moderately reduced (PLMS per hour of total sleep time 33 +/- 16 vs 21 +/- 23, p = 0.07.) Sleep efficiency improved from 75 +/- 12% to 85 +/- 8% (p < 0.01.) In the group of patients estimating their

sleep and/or symptoms of RLS as improved after therapy (n = 7), the effects of magnesium on PLMS and PLMS-A were even more pronounced. Our study indicates that magnesium treatment may be a useful alternative therapy in patients with mild or moderate RLS-or PLMS-related insomnia. Further investigations regarding the role of magnesium in the pathophysiology of RLS and placebo-controlled studies need to be performed.
PMID: 9703590 [PubMed - indexed for MEDLINE]

GIVING BIRTH WITH A DOULA

These statistics appear in "A Doula Makes the Difference" by Nugent in Mothering Magazine, March-April 1998. For detailed results from multiple studies, see: http://www.dona.org/positionpapers.html

For more information on the study of the effectiveness of doula support, please see http://maternitywise.org/pdfs/continuous_support.pdf

Women supported by a doula during labour have been shown to have:

- 50% reduction in Caesarean rate
- 25% shorter labour
- 60% reduction in epidural requests
- 30% reduction in analgesic use
- 40% reduction in forceps delivery

Six weeks after birth, mothers who had doulas were:

- Less anxious and depressed
- Had more confidence with baby
- More satisfied with partner (71% vs 30%)
- More likely to be breastfeeding (52% vs. 29%)

For more information on the Community-based Doula Initiative, please see http://www.chicagohealthconnection.org/our_work/doula/

There are a number of search engines available to find doula's listed by locality. For more information on finding a doula see:
http://doulanetwork.com
http://doulasearch.com

http://www.findadoula.com

CHROMIUM AND GESTATIONAL DIABETES

A session of this Summit was focused on the benefits of chromium supplementation seen in women's health. Lois Jovanovic, M.D., of the Sansum Medical Research Center in Santa Barbara, CA, and Patty Trail, R.N.C., C.D.E., of Eastern Virginia Medical School in Norfolk, presented research on gestational diabetes. Michael L. Lydic, M.D., of the State University of New York at Stony Brook, presented research on polycystic ovarian syndrome (PCOS.)

According to Dr. Jovanovic, gestational diabetes is the most common problem complicating pregnancy today. An estimated 135,000 women have gestational diabetes, posing a risk to both the mother and the infant. High levels of blood sugar in the pregnant woman cross the placenta, triggering the beginnings of insulin resistance in utero. The child is then predisposed to overweight. If the child is female, she is more likely to develop gestational diabetes during her own pregnancy as an adult and pass it on to her child. A significant percentage of women with gestational diabetes require insulin to manage blood glucose levels. Pregnancy is a normal state of chromium wasting, so it seems logical that intake should be increased. Most prenatal vitamins, however, contain no chromium. A clinical study was conducted in which 20 gestational diabetic women were given either chromium picolinate supplements or placebo. After eight weeks, those who were given chromium supplements had significantly lower glucose and insulin levels compared with their own baseline levels and with the placebo group.

Dr. Jovanovic concluded her presentation by saying that reduction of the severity of glucose intolerance in pregnancy by chromium supplementation might provide an easy and inexpensive means to reduce the problems related to maternal hyperglycemia and the devastating health effects on both mother and infant.

Patty Trail reported on six case studies in which women were at high risk for developing gestational diabetes and were given chromium picolinate supplementation throughout their pregnancy. The good pregnancy outcome that involved delivery of healthy full term babies observed in these test cases, she said, suggested the possible benefit of chromium supplementation in high-risk patients. Ms. Trail is currently initiating a randomized, placebo-controlled study to assess if dietary supplementation with chromium picolinate during pregnancy can decrease the incidence and severity of glucose intolerance in pregnancies at risk for gestational diabetes.

Both researchers concluded that chromium picolinate supplementation during pregnancy could provide an easy and inexpensive means to reduce the foetal and maternal problems related to hyperglycemia.

THE BEHAVIOURAL EFFECTS OF HORMONES

All the different hormones released by mother and fetus during the first and second stages of labour...have a specific role to play in the mother-newborn interaction. The key hormone involved in birth physiology is undoubtedly oxytocin.... It is after the birth of the baby and before the delivery of the placenta that women have the capacity to reach the highest possible peak of oxytocin. The release of oxytocin is highly dependent on environmental factors. It is easier if the place is very warm (so that the level of hormones of the adrenaline family is as low as possible.) It is also easier if the mother has nothing else to do but look at the baby's eyes and feel contact with the baby's skin, without any distraction....

The high peak of oxytocin is associated with a high level of prolactin, which is also known as the "motherhood hormone." This is the most typical situation for inducing love of babies. Oxytocin and prolactin complement each other. Furthermore, oestrogens activate the oxytocin and prolactin receptors....

The maternal release of morphine-like hormones during labour and delivery is well documented.... The baby also releases it own endorphins in the birth process, and there is no doubt that, for a certain time following birth, both mother and baby are impregnated with opiates. The property of opiates to induce states of dependence is well known, so it is easy to anticipate how the beginning of a "dependency" or "attachment" will likely develop.

Even hormones of the adrenaline family have an obvious role to play in the interaction between mother and baby immediately after birth.... It is advantageous for the mother to have enough energy "and aggressiveness" to protect her newborn baby if need be. Aggressiveness is an aspect of maternal love. It is also well known that the baby has its own survival mechanisms during the last strong expulsive contractions and releases it own hormones of the adrenaline family. A rush of noradrenaline enables the fetus to adapt to the physiological oxygen deprivation specific to this stage of delivery. The visible effect of this hormonal release is that the baby is alert at birth, with eyes wide open and pupils dilated. Human mothers are fascinated and delighted by the gaze of their newborn babies. It is as if the baby was giving a signal, and it certainly seems that this human eye-to-eye contact is an important feature of the beginning of the mother and baby relationship among humans.

~ Michel Odent, MD
Excerpted from "The First Hour following Birth: Don't Wake the Mother!"
"A reduction in the activity of the neocortex is the most important aspect of birth physiology and that the neocortex is that part of the brain that is so highly developed among humans. All inhibitions during the birth process originate in the neocortex. That is why the spectacular development of the neocortex is our specific handicap in childbirth. When the activity of the neocortex is reduced, the labouring woman is as if "on another planet," cutting herself off from our world. She can become almost as instinctive as other mammals. This leads us to understand that the labouring woman needs to be protected against any sort of neocortical stimulation. Language,

which is specifically human, is one of the most powerful stimulants of that part of the brain that is highly developed in our species. Not feeling observed and feeling secure both tend to reduce cortical activity; they are basic needs during the parturition of mammals.

I am amazed by the countless pleas I see for the humanization of childbirth. Today childbirth needs to be "mammalianized."
~ Michel Odent
excerpted from "Preparing the Nest"

The word "obstetrician" is derived from the Greek word for midwife, "obstetrix." It means to "stand in front of," so it is derived from the same root as obstruct, obfuscate, obliterate, etc.
The word itself doesn't have a connotation of right/wrong or good/bad, per se. However, I often think we all need to get out from in front of the birthing woman and turn our backs toward her so we can protect her space while she gives birth perfectly fine. Apparently in elephant communities the older females surround the birthing female with their trunks pointing away from her, and their large gray bums form a protective, encircling wall around her. That elephant mother-to-be has to push out a lot bigger baby than any human mother will ever birth. Their senior matriarchs have complete faith in her ability.
Gloria Lemay
Midwifery today